TOTAL

MARKET

AMERICAN

TOTAL

MARKET

AMERICAN

RACE, DATA, AND ADVERTISING

Marcel Rosa-Salas

DUKE UNIVERSITY PRESS   DURHAM AND LONDON   2025

Project Editors: Michael Trudeau and Livia Tenzer
Designed by Matthew Tauch
Typeset in Alegreya, Canela Text, and Retail
by Copperline Book Services

Library of Congress Cataloging-in-Publication Data
Names: Rosa-Salas, Marcel, author.
Title: Total Market American : race, data, and advertising /
Marcel Rosa-Salas.
Description: Durham : Duke University Press, 2025. |
Includes bibliographical references and index.
Identifiers: LCCN 2024060617 (print)
LCCN 2024060618 (ebook)
ISBN 9781478032540 (paperback)
ISBN 9781478029151 (hardcover)
ISBN 9781478061359 (ebook)
Subjects: LCSH: Advertising—Social aspects—United States. |
Advertising—Moral and ethical aspects—United States. |
Racism—United States. | Marketing—Social aspects—United
States. | Consumer behavior—United States. | African Americans
in advertising—History. | Human behavior.
Classification: LCC HF5813.U6 R56 2025 (print) |
LCC HF5813.U6 (ebook)
LC record available at https://lccn.loc.gov/2024060617
LC ebook record available at https://lccn.loc.gov/2024060618

Cover art: Photo by Ron Lach.

CONTENTS

INTRODUCTION / THE AMERICAN ADVERTISING INDUSTRY'S RACIAL INFORMATION SYSTEM

Just a few months shy of my twenty-first birthday, I began an internship at Dímelo, a Madison Avenue advertising agency specializing in marketing to US Hispanic consumers.[1] On my first day, I got to sit in on a meeting with a European alcohol company that was finalizing the Spanish-language copy for its American grocery store promotional displays. The campaign was targeting a market segment the brand referred to as the "Hispanic consumer of the world." Annie, an account executive I was shadowing for the day, muted the call and elaborated to me that the target market was a "worldly, cosmopolitan type of Hispanic." I jotted down the phrase, intrigued to learn more about the characteristics that made a Hispanic "worldly" and wondered if I might be considered one.

Later that afternoon, I observed a brainstorming session for a Japanese automobile company that wanted to "reposition" or change how Hispanic men in the United States viewed its midsize sedans. The small conference room we sat in was dimly lit by the soft glow of a cloudy gray sky heavy with impending snowfall. As I stared out the floor-to-ceiling windows waiting for the meeting to begin, an offhand comment by the account director sparked the inspiration for this book.

"We know this consumer isn't your typical, white, general market consumer," he said. No one in the room questioned him or asked for clarification; I figured everyone knew this as well. As a college intern hoping to make a good impression on my first day, I didn't ask either. I hurriedly scrawled "White people = general market" in my notebook.

Going into the internship, I knew that advertising's primary goal was to capture attention and influence behavior to drive profits for companies. But at Dímelo, I witnessed firsthand the myriad ways the advertising industry acts as both a reflection and catalyst of entrenched notions about racial difference that circulate in wider American society. The account director's passing comment—"White people = general market"—revealed to me the core premise of an entire business sector known as "multicultural marketing."

Multicultural marketing describes an ecosystem of advertising agencies, brand marketing departments, consumer research firms, data companies, and consultancies dedicated to investigating and influencing the spending patterns, product choices, media preferences, and emotions of people racialized as Hispanic, Asian, and Black in the United States.[2] This industry is premised on the idea that by learning about and appealing to the presumably distinct cultural identities and behaviors of each of these groups, advertisers can better communicate the value of their products and services and foster a positive brand perception that ultimately leads to sales and profit. Multicultural marketing is rooted in an epistemology of race as a natural and stable trait that produces measurable differences believed to directly impact human behavior and cultural practices on a collective level.

Advertisers, agencies, and media companies have historically viewed the American buying public as racially divided into a "multicultural market" and a "general market," which has long presumed a white majority in the US population. However, the US Census Bureau's forecasts of racial demographic change, coupled with technological shifts wrought by the digital advertising boom, are sparking discussions about advertising business practices and terminology.[3] Advertisers in fields from banking to fast food, packaged goods, and the automotive industry are considering racially targeted marketing strategies as the path of the future. Marc Pritchard, the chief brand officer of Procter & Gamble, one of the world's largest consumer packaged goods companies, affirmed that in the United States, "multicultural marketing may be the single biggest source of market growth in our industry now and for the next several years, perhaps even decades" (figure I.1).[4] *Total Market American* explores the US advertising industry's role in the cultural production and commercialization of racial difference in a context of demographic shifts, political change, and digital transformation.

I situate this book at the intersection of scholarship that examines the cultural production of American racial classifications, consumer culture, and the politics of knowledge. Scholars have previously explored the marketing industry's enduring role in producing and promoting notions of American national identity that reflect and refract classed, gendered,

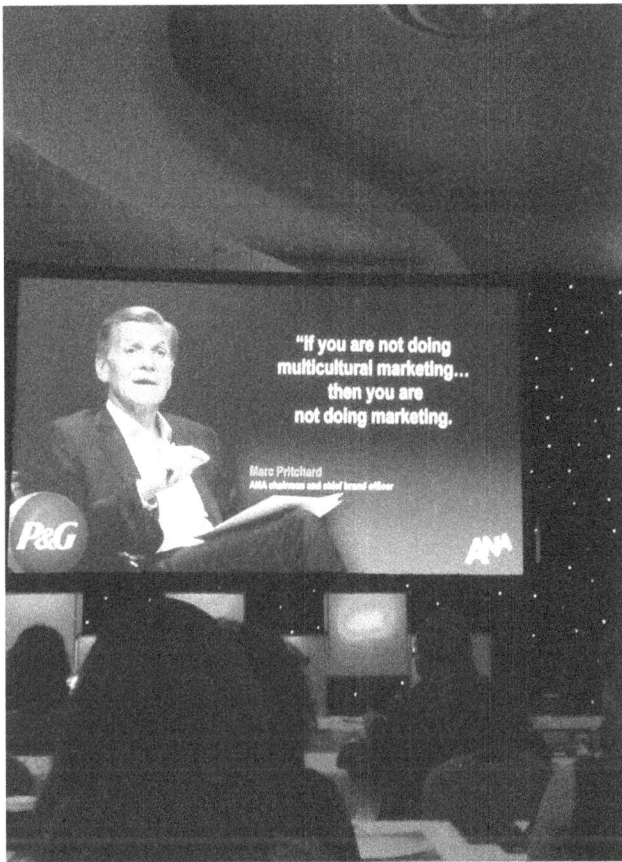

I.1 Marc Pritchard, Procter & Gamble's chief brand officer, speaks at the 2018 Association of National Advertisers (ANA) Multicultural Marketing and Diversity Conference, stating: "If you are not doing multicultural marketing . . . then you are not doing marketing." Miami, Florida. Photo by the author.

and racialized social hierarchies.[5] Communication studies theorists have explored how American consumer culture, retail experiences, and market segmentation practices[6] contribute to the social reproduction of group identities.[7]

Multicultural marketing in the United States is the focus of pivotal works by cultural anthropologists Arlene Dávila and Shalini Shankar who have respectively provided deep ethnographic analyses of the Hispanic and Asian American advertising sectors.[8] Both of their studies document the central place of race in contemporary US advertising practices

and chart how political shifts in immigration policy and census classifications, along with the social and cultural changes they create, have influenced the establishment of US multicultural advertising as a business
sector. Dávila particularly highlights the critical role of market research
and audience measurement in legitimizing Hispanic advertising as a business and in shaping the cultural politics of the Hispanic classification in
the United States more broadly.[9] Shankar explores how multicultural advertising agencies frame Asian Americans as a distinct and desirable consumer group within the broader narrative of diversity as the "new normal"
in a demographically changing nation.[10] *Total Market American* expands on
these and other works by focusing specifically on the American advertising
industry's practices of producing and circulating racial theories of populations and personhood, particularly through the role of advertising strategy
and other modes of knowledge production, which are designed to help advertisers predict and persuade people for profit.

Motivated by the need to understand the "consumer" and maintain demand for products and services in a capitalist economy, the advertising
industry prioritizes specialized expertise that rationalizes and thus "facilitate[s] greater predictability and control" over human beings.[11] Professionals with titles like "brand strategist" and "media planner" play pivotal roles
in this ecosystem. Their approaches combine psychology, anthropology,
statistics, and data analysis to theorize about and anticipate consumer behaviors, equipping their brand clients with information to aid in—as one
ad agency put it at an industry conference presentation—"connect[ing]
Black consumers to ads" (figure I.2). The expertise these professionals generate leads to the classification and objectification of human populations
into consumer segments that are transacted upon within the advertising
industry, branded with designated labels such as "Black millennials" and
the "Hispanic market," whose existence is concretized through practices of
market research, quantification, and measurement.[12]

With this book, I show how the US advertising industry's twin goals
of consumer insight and control lead to the reproduction of ideas that
normalize an understanding of race—not as a political mechanism of
social division rooted in structural racism, but rather as an inherent,
measurable trait inscribed in the body and believed to directly influence
culture, psychology, temperament, and purchasing behavior. As part and
parcel of racism as a system of power, the production of racial knowledge
has been ongoing for centuries, spanning domains such as academia,
government, and large corporations. This process of racial knowledge

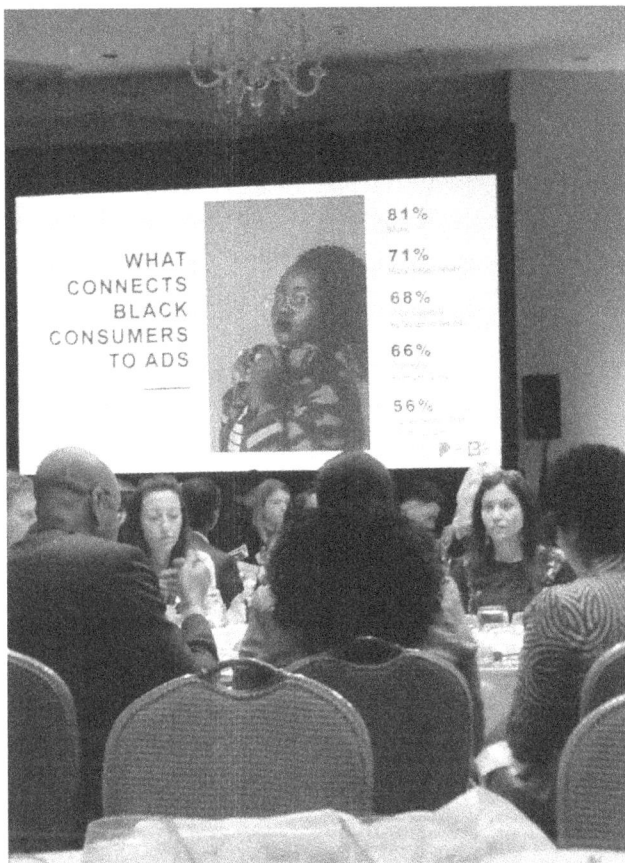

I.2 A slide of racial statistics presented by a multicultural advertising agency making claims about "what connects Black consumers to ads." Presented at the 2018 ANA Multicultural Marketing and Diversity Conference, Miami, Florida. Photo by the author.

production is intrinsically tied to classification systems, which function as a means of exerting power and control over human populations.[13]

Within the American advertising industry, I refer to this phenomenon as its *racial information system*, which encompasses the practices, personnel, technologies, assumptions, and institutions that generate and leverage racial ideas of human difference to tailor and optimize marketing strategies for corporations. Racial information systems of US advertising function at multiple levels, from marketing departments within brands producing race-targeted campaigns to advertising strategists at multicultural agencies analyzing data from consumer research software to come up with branding concepts to pitch to a creative team. This system also entails statistics extrapolated from market research reports and the racialized surveillance involved in targeted digital advertising.

Drawing on ethnographic fieldwork at multicultural advertising agencies in New York City, interviews with nearly one hundred industry professionals, and participant observation at key industry events, *Total Market American* shows how the American advertising industry is engaged not only in promoting products and services but also in the business of race itself.

"LEADING WITH ETHNIC INSIGHTS": US ADVERTISING AND THE COMMERCIALIZATION OF RACIAL THEORIES

On an August afternoon in 2016, I had lunch at a glossy hotel restaurant in the Soho neighborhood of New York City with Sarah, a marketing executive at a global fast-food chain. After learning about Sarah's career trajectory and her decade-long tenure as an African American executive in food marketing, I asked her to describe her current employer's primary consumer base in the United States. "On a national level, our consumers are divided into GM [general market], AACM [African American consumer market], ACM [Asian consumer market], and Hispanic." Sarah noted that the chain hires different advertising agencies to produce tailored campaigns for each racial market. "The GM agency identifies the broad target and the multicultural agencies identify specific differences with multicultural consumers. When we say 'general market,' we are supposed to mean anybody coming into the marketplace, but our actions are to the white consumer," Sarah stated wryly while nodding and taking a sip of her coffee, letting me know that at that moment she was being "unfiltered."

Sarah explained that after developing and launching a new chicken sandwich over the course of a year, the Hispanic marketing consultants she worked with doubted the prospects of the new menu item's success with Spanish-speaking Latinos: "They told us buttermilk doesn't mean anything to the Hispanic consumer." As a reminder that the marketing of products as mundane as chicken sandwiches is shaped by racialized notions of cultural identity packaged as consequential business insight, Sarah explained that the consultants had also warned her that Hispanics wouldn't be able to pronounce the word *buttermilk*.

Sarah's explanation of multicultural marketing industry dynamics matched what I had learned about the largest companies in the space. For example, McDonald's is widely recognized as a brand leader in American multicultural marketing and has been celebrated within industry circles as a pioneer in creating ad campaign strategies and consumer research studies about the tastes, behaviors, and desires of Americans racialized as "multicultural." As early as 1971, the restaurant chain expanded its footprint into Black urban neighborhoods after hiring two Chicago-based marketing companies specializing in reaching Black consumers: Burrell Communications to handle the production of its advertising and the market research company ViewPoint to conduct ethnographic studies, taste tests, and focus groups to develop new menu items intended to attract Black diners.[14] In subsequent decades, McDonald's has expanded its multicultural marketing efforts to include advertising campaigns and product development for Hispanics and Asian Americans as discrete target markets.

"The ethnic consumer tends to set trends, so they help set the tone for how we enter the marketplace," stated Neil Golden, McDonald's former US chief marketing officer in 2010.[15] Golden's assertion was informed by his experience spearheading one of the company's successful Hispanic marketing efforts—the "Fiesta Menu"—which launched at select McDonald's locations in southern California in the year 2000. The offering featured Mexican-inspired cuisine like guacamole and tortas and was a tremendous success not only in Hispanic-dominated neighborhoods but also in majority white locales like Laguna Beach.

"[The Fiesta Menu] over performed in the general market," Golden gushed to reporters.[16] The Fiesta Menu's success inspired McDonald's to formalize "Leading with Ethnic Insights," a marketing strategy that involves the company investing in market research about the behaviors and attitudes of different racial populations, all in efforts to persuade them to eat at McDonald's and ultimately to drive growth in all market segments.[17] "If we're doing nine focus groups," Golden explained at a multicultural marketing conference, "two will be Hispanic, two will be Afro-American, and two will be Asian. It's the best way for us to develop the deepest insight in the products we're offering."[18]

"Ethnic insights" into the coffee preferences of different racial markets prompted McDonald's to launch targeted beverage offerings. The company's research purported that Asian Americans typically prefer "sophisticated" espresso-based drinks while African Americans are drawn to "luxuriant coffee flavor combinations."[19] In 2019, the brand launched its largest Black-targeted marketing campaign in over a decade, titled "Black & Positively Golden" (figure I.3). Described in a press release as "a new campaign movement designed to uplift communities and inspire excellence," the initiative included advertising across media channels, event sponsorships, and the establishment of a scholarship fund.[20] By 2020, amid a noticeable sales decline among younger African Americans, Morgan Flatley, McDonald's chief marketing officer, emphasized in a company memo the importance of racially targeted marketing expertise in the company's branding moving forward. "We need to make sure we are looking through the lens of our operators, our crew, and our people to better connect with African-American youth as we go forward."[21]

McDonald's investment in "ethnic insights" exemplifies how racial theorizing informs the market segmentation strategies of some of the world's biggest corporations. Market segmentation is a commercially oriented practice of human classification that "involves the transformation of social groups, loosely organized around contingent identifying characteristics, into consumer niches, where those characteristics are assumed to be stable, measurable, and powerful in predicting consumer behavior."[22] Multicultural marketing operates on the assumption that race is a definitive human trait that can be used to divide populations into smaller, distinct subgroups: It treats race as a marker indicative of shared group-level cultural behavior, psychology, emotional disposition, media habits, and purchasing patterns—traits that can be observed, measured, analyzed, and strategically leveraged by marketers and brands for economic gain.

From colonization and the transatlantic slave trade to neoliberal narratives that frame diversity as a driver of market growth, capitalism in the United States remains inseparably linked to racism as a system of power[23] and along with it, particular theories about what it means to be a human being.[24] Racial categories were created as frameworks to legitimize economic and social oppression, shaping a racially stratified political order. Racism relies on the production of *racial knowledge*. Philosopher David Theo Goldberg defines this as the making of difference through knowledge production as a means of exerting power. This power operates through the "dual practices of naming and evaluating" populations based on perceived racial distinctions.[25]

Racial knowledge is constructed and sustained through discourse, or the narratives and representations created and circulated by people and across institutions.[26] From academia and the legal system to big business, racial knowledge has been central to American governance—producing

I.3 Advertisement from McDonald's Black & Positively Golden campaign, launched in 2019 and produced by Burrell Communications.

and circulating information about so-called "racial nature . . . about character and culture, history and traditions . . . about the limits of the Other's possibilities."[27] Data collection rituals like the US Census play a critical role in codifying and institutionalizing racial meaning over time, establishing certain classifications while phasing out others. The legal system further reinforces these categories through laws and policies that differentiate and discriminate, particularly in areas like citizenship, legal protections, and resource allocation, often based on perceived racial identities. Meanwhile, media shapes cultural and social perceptions of racialized groups, crafting representations that both reflect and influence attitudes and subjective understandings of race, self, and other.

Racism involves categorizing people "in the name of economic survival or in the name of economic well-being," fed by the epistemological manufacture of racial knowledge.[28] This knowledge is a fundamental mechanism in the social management of life under US capitalism, where racialized personhood is something perceived as natural, universal, and inherent—a fact of life rather than a product of power. Racial knowledge shapes how the state classifies us, how we understand social belonging, and—as this book explores—how corporations construct markets and influence public perception of goods and services.

Theories of racial difference underpin many of the persuasive techniques used in consumer culture. In a competitive marketplace, where companies invest heavily in understanding and predicting consumer behavior, theories of racial difference are both marketing tools and targets, leveraged to feed capitalist growth. US advertising's manufacture and measurement of racial markets underscores the longstanding role that knowledge production has had to play in legitimizing and naturalizing racial difference for economic gain.[29]

In the eighteenth century, the rise of Enlightenment ideals—centered on scientific measurement, objectivity, and classification—gave racial knowledge production significant traction. Influential figures in governments across Europe and North America, along with leading academics, publicly asserted that Africans were inherently inferior and naturally suited for enslavement. These assertions were far from incidental. They served to solidify political hierarchies that became the foundation of the colonies' social and economic systems, colonial violence, and chattel slavery.

Enlightenment thinkers expanded on earlier notions of human differences, theorizing that distinctions based on observable traits such as skin color, hair texture, and other physical features corresponded to inherent psychological and social qualities, which they believed were inscribed in the body and mind and expressed in behavior.[30] Swedish naturalist Carl Linnaeus, often referred to as the father of modern taxonomy, introduced a widely adopted theory of human classification in his popular 1735 work *Systema Naturae*.[31] Like many of his naturalist contemporaries, Linnaeus's perception of human populations around the world were drawn from the writings of travelers, traders, missionaries, and plantation owners who had encountered a diversity of people in the New World.[32] His classification system divided humans into four main varieties that associated physical traits like skin color and hair texture with moral, cultural, and temperamental dispositions.[33] *Homo sapiens europaeus* was described as light-skinned and muscular with flowing blonde hair and blue eyes, characterized as gentle, inventive, and governed by laws. *Homo sapiens asiaticus* was sallow-skinned with dark hair and eyes, characterized as severe, haughty, and governed by opinions. *Homo sapiens americanus* was copper-colored with black, straight hair and wide nostrils and described as stubborn, content, and governed by customs. And *Homo sapiens afer* was described as black-skinned with curly hair and thick lips and characterized as crafty, lazy, and governed by caprice. Linnaean typologies, considered a beacon of scientific expertise, laid the groundwork for the belief that racial classifications reflect an inherent essence—an underlying sameness presumed to be shared by all members of a given racial category.[34]

Such theories linking perceived racial appearance to an essential and deeper biological and cultural behavior have been reinforced over time with lasting impact. Nineteenth-century proponents of scientific racism, like physician Samuel Morton, popularized craniometry (the measurement of skulls) to claim that not only were there racial differences in skull size but that these differences correlated with intelligence and moral characteristics. Morton, who was a believer in polygenism (or the idea that racial groups evolved separately and did not share a common ancestor) argued that the "Caucasian race" had the largest brains and were therefore intellectually superior while the "Ethiopian race" had smaller skulls but were "joyous, flexible, and indolent."[35] These racially typological notions of personhood gained wide acceptance, influencing academic and political spheres, and were institutionalized in the epistemologies of American governance through US Census enumeration practices and segregation policies.

At the turn of the twentieth century, a parallel statistical paradigm emerged focused on the reification of supposed racial types through quantitative measurement.[36] The rise of the US eugenics movement saw statistical knowledge produced and used to legitimize racist theories of intelligence, health, and criminality.[37] Anthropology, a discipline deeply intertwined with the European and American colonial enterprise, faced internal debates and contradictions regarding racial theories.[38]

The mid-twentieth century witnessed a partial retreat from scientific racism, driven by the global denunciation of Nazi Germany, and then later, the progress of the civil rights movement, and the momentum of decolonial struggles. Advancements in genetics have since shown that racialized populations are neither genetically homogeneous nor distinct. [39] As political constructs shaped by history and context, racial categories are inherently fluid, making race an unreliable scientific basis for establishing rigid boundaries between groups.[40]

Yet the belief that one's race determines moral, spiritual, intellectual, and behavioral traits remains deeply embedded in US society.[41] This assumption manifests across various domains: from popular journalism attributing Black athleticism to genetics to the pharmaceutical industry's pursuit of race-based medicines, to the media's reliance on political polling that treats racial categories as fixed predictors of shared behaviors and beliefs—reinforced by concepts like "the Black vote" or "the Hispanic vote."[42] Scientific racism is also experiencing a twenty-first-century resurgence, now rebranded under the moniker "human biodiversity" and gaining traction in academic journals, research networks, and foundations.[43] The revival of racial essentialist knowledge production aligns with rising global anxieties over demographic shifts and the proliferation of anti-immigrant policies in the United States and beyond.[44]

Indeed, the cultural practices that are often perceived as "racial" are, in reality, products of history and policy. They reflect how a US society shaped by racism often dictates where we live—through residential and school segregation—how we are classified, and who we interact with. These political factors contribute to the development of shared sociocultural practices at the population level. Furthermore, racialized cultural traits are not static and are always contextually specific, informed by geography, class, migration patterns, and historical inequalities, resulting in significant diversity within racialized groups. This diversity challenges essentialist understandings of race and culture, and shows that racialized cultural traits are shaped by social and political structures rather than biological determinism.

However, as historians Evelynn Hammonds and Rebecca Herzig observe, persistent "differentiation, segmentation, and segregation of bodies along racial lines" are "acquiring novel forms of social and financial investment."[45] Advertising is one of the institutions that contributes to imbuing racial categories with meaning and salience. Brands like McDonald's, noting declining interest among Hispanic consumers, launched music-oriented marketing campaigns that celebrated the "optimism *inherent* in Latino culture," as mentioned in the company's 2021 global diversity, equity, and inclusion report.[46] In 2024, PepsiCo's market research division published a report, which, among other racial theories about Hispanics, presented an infographic for the "Circle of Joy," the "virtuous cycle" of Hispanic "togetherness" that "fuels the large family gatherings . . . [and] fuel[s] a life of laughter, warmth and belonging," which ultimately "drives and sustains growth in food & beverage" industries (figure I.4).[47] Market research firm Kantar advertises itself to brands as "helping clients grow via inclusion," selling syndicated survey research on "topics of cultural importance to Hispanics and other high-growth populations" (figure I.5). This type of commercial racial expertise is regularly purchased and used by advertisers and agencies to inform market predictions, shape sales strategies, and guide product development. Commercial motivations for racial theorizing are embedded within American advertising's racial information system, serving both as "active creators of categories as well as simulators of existing" racial categories.[48] These marketing research notions, which echo eighteenth-century Linnaean typologies, claim that race correlates with group-level temperament and disposition, suggesting measurable markers of difference between groups.

Advertising industry knowledge-production practices—such as audience research, media planning, and advertising strategy—are embedded within a broader, historically entrenched system of racial knowledge production that spans academic, legal, and state institutions, all operating in an American society still deeply structured by racism. The advertising industry's production and use of racial knowledge is not isolated; it is part of this long-standing epistemological ecosystem that shapes and sustains racialized understandings of humanity, linking those ideas of difference to notions of economic value, American citizenship, and national belonging.

THE RISE OF AMERICAN RACIALLY TARGETED ADVERTISING

Since its very beginnings, US consumer culture has been a site of racial knowledge production and meaning making.[49] During the colonial period, advertisements in newspapers and other public forums promoted the sale, capture, and return of enslaved African laborers, reflecting and reinforcing racialized power dynamics.[50] As modern advertising developed in the

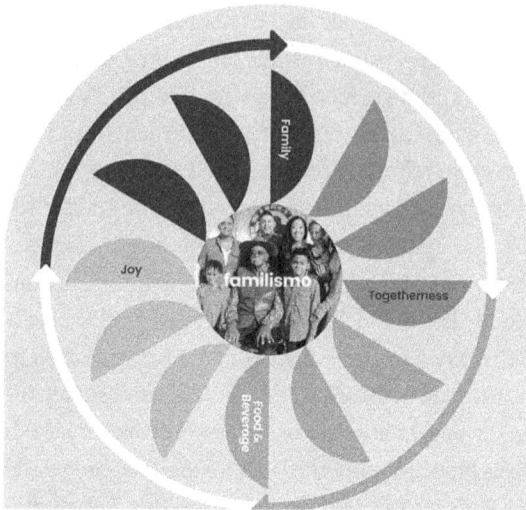

I.4 A data visualization from PepsiCo's 2024 report, published by its Data and Insight division, illustrating the "Circle of Joy"—a racial theory of Hispanic family dynamics. From Pepviz, *Circle of Joy.*

I.5 Market research company Kantar professes to help advertisers "grow via inclusion." Kantar, 2023.

late eighteenth and nineteenth centuries, racism became a visual tool for promoting consumer goods on a national scale.[51] Evidenced by the massive and long-standing popularity of brands like Aunt Jemima, a key element of these early marketing strategies was a type of "commodity racism,"[52] or what bell hooks once referred to as "eating the other"—the exploitation of non-white racial and ethnic representations to attract white consumer attention and evoke pleasure.[53]

The racial segregation policies codified by the 1896 *Plessy v. Ferguson* decision were pivotal in shaping the US advertising and media industry's business structure, division of labor, and ways of envisioning the nation as a marketplace.[54] For much of the twentieth century, advertising in mass media predominantly catered to white consumers, often using demeaning imagery of non-whites in marketing messages. However, as millions of Black Americans migrated from the rural South to urban centers seeking economic opportunities and refuge from racial violence, companies started to recognize the potential of the "Negro market."[55] By the period between World War II and through the 1960s, advertising agencies began to hire Black employees in "special markets" divisions to focus on Black consumers. The advertising agency J. Walter Thompson's Seven-Up ads reflected this segregated organization of American society and its effect on the business structure and practices of mid-century advertising and media industries. Assuming that replacing white models with Black ones would suffice in attracting Black consumers, Seven-Up placed these advertisements in the Black-oriented publication *Ebony* magazine, as opposed to a mass-market title like the *Saturday Evening Post*, where the ad featuring exclusively white models was placed (figures I.6 and I.7).

Yet, in the wake of social movements of the 1960s, the enterprise of racially targeted advertising expanded. On college campuses across the United States, student activists representing Black liberation, Chicano nationalism, Asian American Yellow Power, and Indigenous sovereignty repudiated civil rights–era liberal emphases on reform and integration, in favor of a politics of multiculturalism that decentered white hegemony and emphasized representation, recognition, and the virtue of cultural distinctiveness as a basis for activism and political solidarity.[56] Such "assertions of minority difference," as Roderick Ferguson puts it, were soon absorbed by institutions such as universities, philanthropies, and corporations, with the federal government using multiculturalism as a racial discourse to serve its own agendas, particularly in the upholding of US capitalist imperialism.[57]

Boys like girls who make Seven-Up "Floats"

What every young girl should know is this: *Nobody* can resist a 7-Up "Float"! Want to see? Put a scoop of *his* favorite ice cream or sherbet in a tall glass. Tilt the glass, and pour chilled, sparkling 7-Up gently down the side. The fresh, clean taste of 7-Up works a special magic with ice cream. And don't forget a 7-Up "Float" for yourself! P.S. Boys like 7-Up—girls like 7-Up—for regular thirst-quenching, too. Take home a case of 7-Up so you'll have plenty on hand. You like it . . . it likes you!

Copyright 1960 by The Seven-Up Company

This advertisement appears in:
EBONY . . . . JUNE, 1960

I.6 and I.7 Two Seven-Up advertisements from 1960 reveal the racial segregation prevalent in mid-century American advertising. Both ads feature identical creative elements, including the tagline "Boys like girls who make Seven-Up 'Floats,'" but are produced in separate versions: one featuring white models, the other Black models. Ads created by J. Walter Thompson Company. Source: David M. Rubenstein Rare Book & Manuscript Library, Duke University.

Boys like girls who make Seven-Up "Floats"

What every young girl should know is this: *Nobody* can resist a 7-Up "Float"! Want to see? Put a scoop
of *his* favorite ice cream or sherbet in a tall glass. Tilt the glass, and pour chilled, sparkling 7-Up gently down the side.
The fresh, clean taste of 7-Up works a special magic with ice cream. And don't forget a 7-Up "Float"
for yourself! P.S. Boys like 7-Up—girls like 7-Up—for regular thirst-quenching, too. Take home a case
of 7-Up so you'll have plenty on hand. You like it . . . it likes you!

Copyright 1960 by The Seven-Up Company

4734

A parallel changing tide in the U.S. advertising industry at this time saw leaders embracing the antiestablishment ethos of youth-led student movements, which inspired a "creative revolution" in corporate management philosophy.[58] This new vanguard of ad industry leaders wanted to distance themselves from the staid mid-century values of mass society conformity and instead embraced a renegade spirit of flexibility and individuality. In the post-Fordist era, capitalism began telling a different story to the public, drawing on symbols and the multicultural politics of difference from student movements, suggesting that consumers could "participat[e] in revolutions that did not antagonize capital but presumed it."[59]

As the economy transitioned from Keynesian economics to a hyper-segmented, neoliberal one characterized by market deregulation, privatization, and globalization, consumerism became further ideologically engrained as a path to self-fulfillment and social belonging. Technological advancements in media distribution, including the rise of cable television, along with the use of computers, enabled companies to gather and cluster increasing amounts of consumer data into a seemingly endless combination of niche market segments.[60] The advertising industry's objective to integrate their clients' brands into personal identities while capitalizing on societal trends became evident through the adoption of multicultural discourse in American consumer culture. By the 1990s, this shift, spurred by changes in immigration policies that led to an influx of people from Latin America and Asia, gave rise to the multicultural advertising industry. Distinct racial marketing agencies emerged, where different racial populations were treated as market niches outside of the mainstream. This shift gave rise to a racial information system of agencies, practices, personnel, technologies, assumptions, and institutions that construct and leverage racial concepts of human difference to optimize marketing strategies. Indigenous American people have largely been excluded from this system, as their perceived market size and lower incomes are deemed insufficient to warrant inclusion in the broader racial biopolitics of consumer segmentation by national advertisers.

Multicultural marketing has long served as an entry point for non-white professionals to establish themselves in the predominantly white and elite American advertising industry. Paradoxically, while capitalism has historically exploited racial differences for profit, the sustained commodification of racial expertise in US advertising is neither guaranteed nor easily secured. Multicultural marketers must continually advocate for the recognition of their specialized knowledge and the economic potential of the populations they represent. Although incorporating racialized "diverse" populations into consumer culture may seem like an economically rational choice, the marginalization of multicultural marketing expertise highlights the enduring power of racial ideologies that devalue people of color—even when such inclusion could drive financial success. The racial reckoning of 2020—sparked by George Floyd's murder and the global protests that followed—compelled corporations to pledge billions toward racial justice initiatives. This period also saw a surge in commitments to multicultural marketing, only to be swiftly curtailed following Donald Trump's second election to the presidency.[61]

Total Market American sheds light on US advertising's pivotal role in the ever-shifting, ambivalent, and politically charged production of racial knowledge about what it means to be human and American.

OVERVIEW OF CHAPTERS

This book shares my ethnographic insights across five chapters. Chapter 1, "The 'General Market': On the Commercial Construction of American Whiteness," explores the "general market" category in US advertising discourse and its role in establishing and maintaining a consumerism-centered definition of American whiteness as the standard national identity. Although seemingly race neutral, this industry term operates as a racial construct within American advertising's racial information system, reflecting and reinforcing ideologies of white normativity that imply white people of economic means are the default standard against which all other racial groups are measured as valuable consumers. The distinction between the "general market" and "multicultural market" in industry discourse reveals a racial dichotomy at the core of American advertising's business model, driving market segmentation strategies, shaping media buying, and influencing the division of labor.

Chapter 2, "Multicultural Strategy and the Production of Racial Expertise," focuses on the role of industry professionals known as *multicultural strategists* in US advertising and media agencies and the tools, technologies, and practices they use to produce marketable depictions of racialized populations for clients and colleagues. Strategists—along with the software platforms, corporate vernacular, ideologies, and other tangible and intangible elements from which they produce and analyze data on the purported behavioral traits of people of color—provide a key lens for understanding the advertising industry's *racial information system*. I focus closely on how strategists produce and utilize proprietary survey research platforms to demonstrate that, as in-house race consultants, their primary work is to (re)produce race ideology as data and expertise. While the immediate objective of this racial knowledge is to drive consumption and generate profit for advertisers and agencies, many professionals in the multicultural advertising industry see their work as more than a profit-driven exercise: they also consider it a vital tool for creating positive, socially beneficial, nonstereotypical media representations of non-white populations within American society.

The lax regulations surrounding the commercialization of the internet in the United States have enabled the rapid expansion of various surveillance methods to support consumer data collection and targeted advertising. Using a range of algorithmic decision-making and measurement techniques, marketers and media platforms now focus on transforming populations into audience data to facilitate prediction and economic extraction. As marketing budgets increasingly shift toward online platforms, the future of multicultural marketing hinges on its ability to align racial identity with the technological frameworks of online advertising. A key aspect of this adaptation is how effectively machine learning can deduce consumers' race and ethnicity based on algorithmic analyses of their online behavior.

Chapter 3, "Reaching 'Verified Hispanics': The Racial Science of Digital Advertising," delves into the impact of digital advertising on the multicultural marketing industry and the racial theories underlying how data companies and digital advertising professionals target and sell to "Hispanics" online. Multicultural advertising industry leaders argue that "multicultural" consumers are underrepresented in these audience datasets, which they claim hinders brands' ability to effectively engage with these consumer groups in the digital age. The chapter highlights that by participating in and advocating for the marketplace of racial audience data generated by algorithmic technologies, advertising professionals are repackaging centuries-old racial science theories that aim to quantify and predict racial traits. This practice subjects non-white racialized groups to heightened corporate and state surveillance, further exposing them to harm, criminalization, and exploitation.

US Census racial data are a foundational element of American advertising's racial information system, shaping the way multicultural marketing is presented to corporate America by emphasizing racial demographics as central to consumer culture trends. Chapter 4, "The Total Market Turn: US Census Projections and Making the New Mainstream Consumer," looks at discussions within the US advertising industry about the rise of a majority non-white "total market" closely linked to long-standing debates over the definition of "mainstream" American identity and the perception of racial differences as either a unifying or divisive force in nation-building. These conversations also highlight political and economic struggles within the US advertising industry over who has the authority to be considered an expert in the American "mainstream" as whiteness is no longer assumed to be the default. In the ongoing effort to gain recognition and access to the marketing budgets they believe they deserve, multicultural advertising professionals have variously embraced, critiqued, and redefined the "total market" concept.

The conclusion, "Intersectionality, Inc.: Anti-Racism as Consumer Fantasy," examines US advertising's "racial reckoning" and explores how the American advertising industry's racial information system proposes that racial justice can be achieved through market-driven strategies, such as increasing the visibility and representation of people of color in advertisements, and aiming to make them "feel seen," validated, and respected by corporations. This shift aligns with what scholars Felice Blake and Paula Ioanide describe as "anti-racist incorporation," a discourse that acknowledges the issues of racism and racial justice but neutralizes their transformative potential. Unlike color-blind or diversity discourses that downplay systemic racism, anti-racist incorporation openly names these issues while maintaining the status quo. The growing use of intersectionality as a marketing strategy and calls for greater racial diversity in advertising might seem like progress. However, this evolution of anti-racism rhetoric within consumer culture reveals the false promises, contradictions, and ambivalence inherent in US capitalist culture, where a push for racially inclusive advertising exists alongside ongoing racialized violence, systemic oppression, and exclusion.

METHODS AND PREMISES

This book is the culmination of ethnographic fieldwork in the multicultural advertising industry in the United States between 2014 and 2020. My desire to understand the processes and political economy of racial knowledge production in the US advertising industry led me to following people and their ideas across a variety of settings, including inside agency meetings and trade conventions, invitation-only industry events, trade press articles, and even the social media platform LinkedIn. Having interned at a Hispanic ad agency in college, I knew that the best way for me to embed myself in multicultural advertising epistemologies and practices was, to some degree, to do the work myself.

My fieldwork included two three-month internships at two different agencies: a Hispanic creative agency that I will refer to with the pseudonym "Soar" and a media agency that I will call "Vista." I chose to base my fieldwork in New York City because of its enduring status as the advertising mecca of the world. The agencies offered me exposure to distinct yet interconnected industry functions of advertising creation and placement. My agreement to use pseudonyms for the agencies I interned with and people I interviewed in any writing I produced from my research also afforded me extended access to meetings and more candid insights from research interlocutors.

I was able to present myself at both Soar and Vista as an anthropologist and an unpaid intern who, in exchange for participant observation opportunities, would be available to assist them on assignments on an ad hoc basis. These requests were generally kept at a minimum, but I was asked periodically to help with research and writing needs. Both agencies took great interest in and saw significant value in my being a cultural anthropologist who had prior professional experience in the marketing industry at respected global brands, as humanities and social science have been incorporated into consumer research methods at least since the 1950s.[62] Furthermore, I believe that my self-presentation as a twenty-something, light-skinned, educated, cisgendered woman of Puerto Rican ancestry aided my foray into the multicultural advertising world. Arlene Dávila refers to this as the "Latin Look," which in her view also facilitated her acceptance as a researcher by Hispanic advertising professionals by presenting "no threat to their normative ideal of Latinidad."[63]

At the Hispanic creative agency Soar, I was an intern in the strategy department. As will be explained in further detail in chapter 2, strategists are responsible for gathering and analyzing information about consumers and applying their analyses to unearthing the campaign's target consumer and core premise. Soar's strategy team was small and led by Vince—a longtime Hispanic advertising executive—along with a senior strategist, two junior level strategists, and a summer intern. All the strategists self-identified as Hispanic except for one, who was a Black male. The agency was the multicultural advertising subsidiary of a general market advertising shop that I will refer to as "Blue." As I will explain further in chapter 1, *general market* is a term that industry professionals use to refer to advertising agencies not explicitly marked by race or ethnicity but simultaneously indexes non-Hispanic whiteness as the American consumer norm.

Both Soar and Blue were owned by the same global advertising holding company. For the most part, Soar functioned entirely separate from Blue and pitched for its own clients, sometimes even competing with Blue for the same accounts. Soar and Blue's respective strategy departments were situated on opposite ends of the same floor of a large open-concept office space in Manhattan, separated by a long hallway and automatically locking glass-paned doors that one needed an agency ID card to open.

One important affordance of this segmented corporate structure for my research was the access that I had to the general market side of the advertising agency business, which scholars have previously remarked as being difficult to achieve.[64] Soar's and Blue's strategists attended several agency-wide meetings and trainings together. These gatherings served as important sites for me to become acquainted with strategists and executive leadership at Blue and subsequently conduct interviews and observe meetings with them. While I was primarily situated on a day-to-day basis with Soar's strategy team, I also had purview into their relationship with Blue agency staff and the dynamics that informed their interactions and business dealings.

My internship at Soar provided me a context for understanding the epistemological practices that shape how multicultural advertising strategists produce racial knowledge. However, I knew that if I wanted to understand the impact that digital advertising is having on how companies and industry professionals conceptualize and sell race, I would have to spend some time at a media agency. Media agencies are the companies that brands contract with to determine which media channels to place the ads that their creative agency makes for them. Vista, a successful independent media agency based in downtown Manhattan, also had an in-house multicultural brand strategy department. The team was staffed by seven self-identified Latinas and one woman who described herself as mixed race. Vista's multicultural brand strategy department was subdivided into two main functions. I spent most of my internship with a team of three Latina women who worked primarily on fulfilling consultative requests from their colleagues who worked on general market accounts. These requests were usually for audience research about Hispanic consumers, along with recommendations for the television networks, radio, and digital media platforms that advertisers should expend their media budgets on when targeting them.

The other half of Vista's multicultural brand strategy team was solely dedicated to planning the media placements for two wireless carrier clients who had dedicated internal Hispanic marketing departments and media targeting budgets. Their desks were situated far away, on the other end of the open-plan office, where they sat with the accounts' general market teams. As an intern, I was granted access to join and observe most meetings and agency events that the multicultural brand strategy department attended. By attending those meetings, I also became acquainted with other Vista employees, including members of the agency's digital advertising team, who were responsible for devising strategies for targeting US Hispanic online users across the web with their wireless carrier client's ads. In addition to my participant observation with the multicultural brand strategy team, I also was able to attend a weekly Hispanic digital advertising client conference call and interview the digital advertising professionals responsible for devising racially targeted digital ad campaigns.

I supplemented my agency internships with periodic trips to Miami, Los Angeles, and San Francisco to attend key industry events, including the Association of National Advertisers Multicultural Marketing and Diversity Conference, the Culture Marketing Council Conference, Hispanicize, the Interactive Advertising Bureau's Cross-Cultural Marketing Conference, and Google's Culture Marketing Conference, among several others. These convenings enriched my internship experiences by offering me insight into the social relationships that comprise the multicultural advertising industry along with how professional discourse about race takes shape. These events were also key sites for me to reconnect with research interlocutors and make contacts with new ones. I documented these events with audio recordings of panels and presentations as well as with photographs.

In addition to my participant observation fieldwork, I conducted ninety-eight semi-structured interviews with multicultural advertising industry professionals from across the United States. Most were people in strategy positions at multicultural creative and media agencies, although I spoke with general market agency strategists and executives along with multicultural marketers at several brands. While I did speak to African American and Asian American advertising professionals, the majority of those I interfaced with would likely consider themselves Hispanic advertising specialists. In many instances, the term *multicultural marketing* is now synonymous with *Hispanic advertising*, as the non-white Hispanic demographic represents, according to US Census data, the largest non-white population in the United States, and its population growth is among the most significant.[65]

To conclude, I want to clarify my use of terminology. Throughout this book, I use the terms *race* and *racial* rather than *ethnoracial* or *ethnic* when discussing American advertising practices, including Hispanic marketing. The classification of Hispanics by the US Census has shifted over time, evolving from the 1930 Census, when "Mexican" was listed as a racial category, to the introduction of "Hispanic" as a pan-ethnic category in the 1980 Census. Yet, in practice, the ethnicity attributed to the Hispanic category is often treated as equivalent to a racial category. In demographic surveys, government reporting, public policy analyses, and market research, Hispanics are frequently grouped together—regardless of intracategory racial differences—and compared to other official US racial populations. The racialization of people of Latin American ancestry as a distinct non-white group, with many identifying with the "some other race" category on the census, is also well documented.[66] As a testament to the ever-shifting politics of classification, the 2030 US Census will list "Hispanic or Latino" among other racial groups. In this book, I use the terms *racial* and *racial information system* to reflect how I observed American advertising professionals construct and deploy racial knowledge to shape understandings of human difference.

1   THE "GENERAL MARKET" / ON THE COMMERCIAL CONSTRUCTION OF AMERICAN WHITENESS

"There is no 'Caucasian market,'" stated Mark Turner, chief strategy officer of the advertising agency Saatchi & Saatchi in a 2017 comment to the *New York Times*.[1] In the American advertising industry, there has been a prevailing belief that white consumers do not constitute a distinct market segment and, therefore, are not racially targeted by advertisers. However, the notion that white people of elevated economic standing represent the prototypical American consumers has been central to US marketing strategies since the industry's inception and continue to influence how industry professionals conceptualize the national consumer marketplace, even as shifting racial demographics challenge this assumption.

This chapter examines the "general market" category in US advertising discourse and its role in defining and perpetuating a consumerist-centric definition of American whiteness as the standard form of national culture and identity. While ostensibly race-neutral, the "general market" is a racial construct within American advertising's racial information system. It operates as a silent catalyst in marketing practices, reinforcing white normativity by positioning economically privileged white consumers as the default standard against which the value of all other racial groups is assessed and measured. The distinction made between the "general market" and "multicultural market" in US advertising industry discourse reveals the racial binary at the core of American advertising's business model and division of labor. This chapter explores how the "general market" category reflects a pervasive notion of whiteness in the United States as a cultural norm—one that is both deeply influential yet deliberately ambiguous.

MAKING THE MASS MARKET WHITE

The term *general market* is American advertising industry jargon used by professionals to talk about the nation as a marketplace across different business sectors, including brand marketing, advertising firms, media agencies, content platforms, and consumer research companies. It provides industry professionals a common reference point and category for planning and executing marketing campaigns and media plans, and facilitates efficient communication about American consumers within the advertising field.

But in this function, the term *general market* is also a racial construct that reflects and reproduces particular racialized and classed notions about the prototypical American subject. A senior-level executive from a multicultural advertising agency shared with me that the *general market* is a term used by advertisers in instances when a marketing message is not intended to be targeted to a specific demographic group: "If it's ethnically targeted or somehow segmented based on mindset, that is 'targeted.' That's not 'general market.'" After saying this, he paused for so long that I checked to see if our call had dropped. He continued: "For other clients, general market is another term for 'white people,' which I don't necessarily agree with because all Black people aren't the same, and all white people aren't the same, so you can't use the term 'general market' as a catch-all for 'white.' But some people do that."[2]

Krista, a multicultural media planner at a Manhattan media agency, described that the general market implicitly refers to white consumers, a notion she explained is widely accepted by many people she works with without explicit acknowledgment in routine business operations. She noted that this assumption becomes especially evident during discussions she has with clients about the allocation of media budgets: "It just becomes the *thing*," she emphasized while shaking her head in discontent. "You go 'Oh, that's the general market budget. That's the Hispanic budget.' Then you realize, 'That's the budget to target everybody—mostly the whites. And this is the budget to target the Hispanic market.' It's implied."[3] I was told that this habitual equation of the white population with the general market reflects a discomfort among professionals from both multicultural and general market agencies to explicitly refer to white people as part of a racial group. This reluctance was encapsulated by a consumer research professional I spoke to who observed, "It's kind of weird but in our industry, 'general market' is a politically correct way to say 'white people.'"[4]

A former Hispanic marketing manager at a consumer packaged-goods company shared with me that in his career, media planning activities like placing TV advertisements targeted at demographic segments like "women aged 18–34" typically has meant targeting "white women" because people racialized as white have historically constituted the majority of the US population, according to the racial statistics that marketing and media agency employees attain from the US Census Bureau. A junior-level strategist I spoke with from a creative agency in Chicago confirmed this common industry practice: "An assumption across brands is that [advertisers] will always talk to the 'general market,' because 'general market' has always been synonymous with the majority market and that is the Caucasian market."[5]

Other advertising industry professionals relayed to me that the term *general market* is used not just as shorthand for white consumers but also to refer to the American public as a market. A managing director at a New York City advertising agency indicated that this blending of meanings is central to the industry's longstanding interpretation of the category: "We develop communications that we feel are based on values that everyone can resonate with. But when it's time to execute, 'white' is still considered generic enough to say, 'OK, great, this is for everybody.'"[6] Just as someone could refer to a consumer good in a store that lacks a widely recognized brand name as a "generic" product, the term *general market* is a cultural commodity transacted upon within the advertising industry that on its face refers to a broad and demographically unspecific consumer base. In the context of US racial discourse, however, the advertising industry's "general market" often implicitly equates whiteness with both the normative standard and the essence of American nationhood.

Whiteness is a political construct rooted in the legacy of Euro-American colonialism.[7] It functions not simply as a racialized attribute, but as a material reality of economic and political power and a symbolic formation linked to concepts of civilization, citizenship, and humanity itself.[8] Historians trace the conceptual development of the white racial category in the United States to the late seventeenth century, where it was invented by the colonial ruling elite to combat growing political solidarity between

European, Indigenous, and African laborers rebelling against their shared experiences of economic subjugation.[9] Within the United States' "racial contract," white racial identity has evolved into the nation's political, cultural, and legal somatic norm, where it represents the "neutral or standard category of human beings."[10] This phenomenon, termed "white normativity" by scholars, refers to a system of knowledge in which institutions from the legal system, education, and media participate in imbuing whiteness with the authority to "speak for the commonality of humanity."[11]

White normativity has been central to US governance since its inception, with the 1790 Naturalization Act establishing a legal framework that required white racial identity (and maleness) for full civic participation and protection of the law. Throughout the twentieth century, US Supreme Court rulings adjudicated the boundaries of American whiteness based on shifting criteria and confirmed its status as a protected form of social and political property.[12] White normativity is a way of knowing that remains powerful in American racial discourse, legitimizing dominance without seeming explicit.[13]

White normativity ideology manifests not only through legal and political mechanisms but also through cultural customs and symbolic expressions. At the end of the nineteenth century, as the country grappled with the aftermath of the Civil War and the legal abolition of slavery, the rise of mass advertising became a tableau for negotiating the relationships between Blackness and whiteness, helping to establish a postwar national identity that reanimated racial tensions and dynamics. The advertising trade card was an influential form of media at the time that "occupie[d] an integral place not only in the history of US advertising but also in the imagistic development of the United States as a specifically white, consumer nation," explains scholar Marilyn Maness Mehaffy.[14] Trade cards issued by American companies as marketing material depicted a consumerist ideal of white, middle-class female domesticity, characterized by visual depictions of such white women's differentiation from and dominance over Black working-class women, as exhibited in the image used in the American Wringer Company's 1885 trade card for its Universal Wringer (figure 1.1).[15]

In 1889, Aunt Jemima pancake mix, one of the first nationally marketed convenience foods, introduced a new category of ready-made products to American consumers by exemplifying this racial narrative. Intertwining images of white consumer leisure with the nostalgic fantasy of a genteel Southern plantation lifestyle, the brand promoted a vision where

1.1 An 1885 advertising trade card from the American Wringer Company, selling its Universal Wringer machine, depicts a Black woman domestic worker and her white female employer. Source: Library Company of Philadelphia.

modern, upwardly mobile white American consumerism was linked to a romanticized longing for slavery and the unequal power dynamics it entailed. Aunt Jemima's marketing reinforced the idea that continued Black subjugation was an essential part of the American consumer experience.[16]

Throughout the twentieth century, the advertising industry disseminated imagery and ideas that celebrated consumption as central to a modernizing national identity.[17] Advertising executives of the age commonly framed the United States through the metaphor of a "market democracy," where brands sought approval from "consumer citizens" through the concept of "one dollar, one vote," linking spending with patriotism and participation in the nation's social fabric.[18] N. W. Ayer, an advertising executive who founded one of the first US advertising agencies, encapsulated the sentiment that advertising bolstered "the common welfare of the common people," proposing that the surge in the economics of mass consumption was a democratizing force.[19] William Armistead, another advertising pioneer from the early twentieth century, once proclaimed that "mass advertising played its part in making this country a united nation."[20]

As marketers professed to be unifying the nation through consumption and advertising, anxieties were emerging over changes in the boundaries of American whiteness, fueled by the massive influx of immigrants from Southern and Eastern Europe. Although these immigrants were classified as racially white by the state, there were delineations with regards to what historian Matthew Frye Jacobson calls "variegated whiteness," in which some European ethnic groups were deemed "suboptimal" by the prevailing Anglo-Saxon majority.[21] Over time, these groups were able to achieve "whiteness," but the process was uneven and partly facilitated by consumer culture.

Turn-of-the-twentieth-century advertising navigated the shifting boundaries of American whiteness through varying strategies and approaches. Some brands appealed directly to European ethnic differences as a market segmentation strategy.[22] Crisco vegetable shortening targeted Jewish Americans' kosher dietary needs, complementing its marketing with a Yiddish cookbook (figure 1.2).[23] Maxwell House also cultivated appeal with recent European immigrants by obtaining kosher certification and confirming its coffee's appropriateness for Passover. During the Great Depression, Maxwell House offered with every purchase a free branded Haggadah—a book containing prayers, statements, and commentary on the Passover story—a move specifically targeting American Jews of Eastern European origin.[24]

Amid exclusionary immigration quotas and Progressive Era thinkers' nativist concerns about the direction of national culture, the advertising industry proclaimed itself as "the great Americanizer," promoting consumption as a means of cultural assimilation.[25] Brands like Quaker Oats, Heinz, and Coca-Cola targeted Eastern European immigrants in foreign-language media, presenting American products as pathways to health, modernity, and integration into US society.[26] A prominent advertising executive from the time highlighted the industry's aim to forge "a homogenous people out of a nation of immigrants,"[27] suggesting that advertising be used to bridge the cultural divides of diverse European immigrants, thus expanding the boundaries of American whiteness.[28] By positioning itself as an assimilative force, advertising became part of enculturating a "systematic push toward the cultural homogenization of whites" in and through consumer capitalism.[29]

1.2 Crisco vegetable shortening's booklet *Crisco Recipes for the Jewish Housewife*, put out by Procter & Gamble in 1935. Source: Dorot Jewish Division, New York Public Library.

In this context of nativist concerns over changes in national character, the advertising industry's growing fascination with decoding the desires and spending habits of the "typical" American consumer was also influenced by the rise of research and measurement techniques such as statistical sampling, opinion polling, as well as the application of social science to business. These tools enabled marketers to analyze and interpret trends on a mass scale. One of the landmark social-science-turned-market-research studies to influence twentieth-century mass advertising was *Middletown: A Study in American Culture*, published by sociologists Helen and Robert Lynd in 1929. Commissioned by the Rockefeller Foundation to gain insight into the preservation of American Protestant traditions within the shifting tides of industrialization, the study focused on everyday life in the "ordinary" American town of Muncie, Indiana, which the researchers called "Middletown." For business leaders, *Middletown* was valuable as a treasure trove of insight into the typical American's consumer lifestyle. Advertising sales representatives from the monthly women's publication *McCall's* journeyed to Muncie to investigate how its "average American" residents shopped, and the publication *Business Week* called the study "a godsend."[30]

However, the qualities characterizing the "sameness" of the typical American consumer of the early twentieth century were not objective reflections of the national populace but were selective interpretations crafted by the advertising elite.[31] As historian Roland Marchand points out, rather than representing the true diversity of the American population, these idealized norms were shaped by the experiences and ideals of advertising professionals, emphasizing white, middle-class aspirations of consumerism as modernity.[32] The bucolic small-town life depicted in *Middletown* as representative of American cultural authenticity was in fact a reflection from a distorted mirror that enhanced certain narratives while obliterating others.[33]

The Lynds did not include the entire Muncie community in their study but intentionally excluded Black members of the population from their research, which they justified on grounds that their study concerned only "civilized, white Americans."[34] Rather than regarding them as constitutive parts of the community, the Lynds relegated Black Midwesterners to the status of deviant racial others, framing them as "complicating factors" whose presence would disrupt the validity and generalizability of the study's findings.[35] Robert Lynd's decision to conduct the study in Muncie, Indiana, in the first place was due to "his belief that the hope for social progress lay uniquely in the spirit and vision of the 'substantial type' of American, the native-born Protestant of the Middle West."[36] The advertising industry's embrace of "Middletown" residents as representative of the "average American" consumer reflects the enduring romanticization and racialization of the Midwestern "heartland" as a cornerstone of American national identity.[37]

The "typical" American consumer, as conceptualized by marketing professionals in trade journals and industry discussions, was a racialized and classed social construct. In this framework, the term *mass audience* typically referred not to the majority of the American population but rather to a smaller, more affluent subset.[38] Trade journals and media companies explicitly excluded groups like tenant farmers, Black Americans, and non-English speakers from market research.[39] The Curtis Publishing Company, which pioneered one of the first market research divisions in modern American business, excluded Black people from all their market studies, relaying to advertising clients that "its readers were not 'Negroes' or members of other 'subnormal' consumer groups."[40] Companies like Johnson & Johnson, targeting "young, white, upwardly mobile middle-class Americans and the millions who wanted to be like them," relied on survey research that intentionally excluded Black communities from its population count.[41] Early twentieth-century marketing discourse presented the mass market as "an aspirational ideal masquerading as quantified empirical fact"—an idealized composite of the nation constructed through the politicized lens of normative whiteness and economic purchasing power.[42]

During the Great Depression of the 1930s, consumer demand plummeted, prompting companies like Cadillac to reconsider its racially exclusive marketing strategies. Although Cadillac had previously refused to sell vehicles to African Americans, it began targeting the Black upper-middle class to offset declining profits.[43] In the wake of the economic crisis, New Deal reforms, designed to provide economic relief, further institutionalized racial segregation.[44]

The public-private partnership that perpetuated racial segregation continued into the post–World War II economic boom. Bolstered by policies such as the GI Bill—which sought to sustain consumer demand and high employment levels—the program enabled millions of working-class veterans to become first-time homebuyers through government-subsidized home loans. Suburban developments became the backbone of the postwar economy, driving mass consumption and fostering a new middle class with significant discretionary income. However, the policies of this period also promoted a racially discriminatory "consumer's republic."[45] Suburban communities, supported by the Federal Housing Administration and the US Department of Veterans Affairs, were intentionally segregated and designed to be predominantly white. Restrictive covenants and loan agreements ensured that homes could not be sold to Black families, effectively barring them from these neighborhoods. As a result, white racial identity became a key determinant of socioeconomic mobility and consumer citizenship in mid-twentieth-century America. The consumer-oriented image of the prototypical American as a white, middle-class suburban resident also downplayed the significance of ethnic distinctions among whites while amplifying racial disparities between a consolidated and expanded notion of American whiteness and all other racial groups.[46]

A 1952 General Electric advertisement in the *Saturday Evening Post* encapsulated the racially segregated version of the American Dream being sold to the public. Advertising during this era predominantly depicted a white customer base enjoying a high standard of living (figure 1.3). The strategy behind this approach, as advertising specialist Arthur Dix noted in 1957, was seemingly rational enough: Advertising should target the primary buying demographic, which was overwhelmingly white.[47] Together,

1.3 A General Electric advertisement published in 1952 in the *Saturday Evening Post* showcases the white, middle-class suburban family that mid-century advertisers and their agencies imagined represented the typical American consumer.

postwar economic policies and marketing strategies positioned American whiteness and middle-class economic standing as mutually reinforcing social positions.

While early to mid-twentieth-century advertising primarily targeted an idealized white middle-class market, largely ignoring non-white people, in the 1960s, marketers recognized the economic limitations of this approach and began exploring market segmentation based on diverse demographics. Concurrently, the civil rights movement, anti–Vietnam War protests, and student movements of 1968 heightened social consciousness about group identities and rights. These political and social forces pressured brands and advertising agencies to reform hiring practices and to represent a broader spectrum of racial groups in their campaigns. Additionally, post-1965 immigration policy changes led to greater diversity in the United States, prompting businesses to consider targeting new consumer segments amid economic shifts and the rise of neoliberalism.

A cohort of advertising firms, media companies, and consultancies soon emerged, grounded in a framework that saw moral, political, and economic value in the representation of non-white populations in the media as an indicator of social progress, coupled with the theory that race and ethnicity were defining, group-level traits that could be used as the basis from which to create new markets and predict consumer behavior. African American ad agencies had their golden age on the heels of the civil rights movement.[48] "Hispanic" ad agencies came to the fore during the 1960s when Puerto Rican and Cuban immigration to urban centers created new opportunities for Latin American elites to reestablish advertising careers in the United States and target a growing market of Spanish speakers with in-language marketing messages.[49] Advertising agencies targeting Asian consumers in the United States emerged by the 1990s, driven by changes in immigration patterns, as well as by a telecom industry keen on cashing in on the long-distance phone call market.[50] The arrival and adoption of cable television transformed the nation's media infrastructure by offering significantly more channels for brands to send out messages to specific slices of the population. A business sector that became known as "multicultural marketing" was well suited to thrive in this identity-oriented commercial culture.

As the foundation of its business proposition, the multicultural marketing industry had to establish and enhance the value of its distinctiveness from the white-dominated mainstream advertising business. In a 1964 opinion piece in the industry trade magazine *Advertising Age*, John H. Johnson, the publisher of *Ebony* and *Jet* magazines (the first national publications targeted to a Black middle-class audience and a trailblazer of African American market research), articulated the fundamental nature of this racialized market separation when he said, "The Negro market . . . is not a special market *within* the white market—it is, on the contrary, *a general market* defined, precisely, by its exclusion from the white market."[51]

Similar efforts to emphasize racial differences to create markets were exhibited in the rise of the Hispanic marketing industry. Sociologist G. Cristina Mora documents that between the 1960s and 1980s, executives at the Mexican media company Spanish International Network (SIN)—an early pioneer in the US Spanish-language media and marketing industries, later renamed Univision—had to sell national advertisers on the idea that its Spanish-speaking audience was sizable, profitable, and distinct from the white "general market," toward which the majority of ad dollars was expended.[52] The SIN executives did so in part through producing market research to change advertisers' preconceived notion that Latin American immigrants would—like Europeans at the turn of the twentieth century—eventually assimilate to be "Americanized and would thus prefer English language programming" over SIN's Spanish-language content.[53] Rather, SIN executives depicted the US Hispanic market as a distinctly non-white and upwardly mobile, nationally dispersed population of Spanish speakers who shared cultural proclivities like religiosity, hard work, and brand loyalty.[54]

A strategy director at a multicultural ad agency reflected on this history, explaining that early multicultural advertising reinforced the existing racial divide between the presumed white "mainstream market" and the racialized "multicultural market" to validate its expertise as valuable to national advertisers. "They needed an 'other' to compare against. And in the early running for these folks, their reason for being was to establish that these communities were *so* different. Everything was about the fundamentals of how different we were, that we spoke these different languages, and so on," he recalled.[55] The multicultural marketing industry is premised on an epistemology of white normativity, where professionals racialized as "multicultural" can only speak for their respective racial or ethnic markets. In contrast, white professionals are not confined to any specific racialized identity and are considered capable of marketing to everyone, representing the entire nation.

Throughout the late twentieth century, as media outlets and marketing firms arose to address African American, and then later Hispanic and Asian populations as distinct consumer markets separate from the general market, the advertising industry, with the addition of racialized multicultural agencies, left the presumption of white normativity intact. Marketing executives Ola Mobolade and David Burgos remark that "once multicultural marketing was an established cottage industry, a new term was needed for marketing geared toward everyone else. Hence the 'general market = White' code in effect today."[56]

The concept of the "general market" in the American marketing industry's racial information system reflects long-standing Western epistemologies of the human as white. This racialized framing of the universal standard human can be seen in the nineteenth-century statistical concept of the "average man," which Belgian statistician Adolphe Quetelet based exclusively on data from Scottish men.[57] This statistical concept fed into the Eurocentric *Homo economicus* model in neoclassical economics, which depicts humans as rational, self-interested actors within capitalism.[58] Philosopher Sylvia Wynter critiques the Western bourgeois notions of "Man" as overrepresenting the Western male as the standard of humanity, marginalizing non-white and non-Western peoples, and thus perpetuating systems of racial and economic exploitation.[59] The general market, in keeping with this ideological tradition of racial knowledge, functions as the marketing industry's imagined "invisible center," a racial representation of American identity that "claims universality without ever defining itself."[60]

At its core, the *general market* category reflects the American advertising industry's white-dominated power structure. In the words of a multicultural marketing executive I interviewed, "The general market is classically the lead agency and gets—in terms of structure, in terms of power—the boatload of the dollars, and the multicultural agency gets the scraps. The multicultural agency may not necessarily be at the table at the beginning of the conversation (with an advertiser) and be forced to come in later and still deliver within the same timeline."[61] Another longtime multicultural advertising executive likened the economic structure of the multicultural/general market paradigm to "sharecropping," characterizing it in a 2023 article in *Fast Company* as an "incredibly oppressive and discriminatory system [that] is responsible for the majority of income at many minority agencies."[62] Racial disparities in ownership and leadership within the American advertising industry highlight persistent inequalities. Industry reports indicate that in 2023, 90 percent of US-based advertising agencies were led by white executives.[63]

"NHW"

In American advertising's racial information system, the term *general market* implicitly defines whiteness as the standard, linking it to capitalism and consumer culture as a fundamental way of being. The category is often presented as a universal identity, serving as the default against which other market segments are defined. By remaining unmarked and blending into the background, the general market's normalized whiteness is perpetuated by institutional practices that obscure its racial particularity and politically constructed nature. "White normativity derives great advantage from its ability to operate without drawing attention to itself. It is racialized thought masquerading as objectivity. It plays out subconsciously in what we fail to consider," writes legal scholar Michael Morris.[64] When I asked a Black male marketer with experience at several top companies how he learned that "general market" was synonymous with white consumers, he seemed annoyed that I would even pose a question about something so seemingly obvious. "You just *know*," he replied brusquely. "You don't need to talk about it. What is there to talk about?"[65]

I noticed that industry professionals I interacted with frequently described the *general market* by defining it in contrast to what it supposedly is not, reinforcing the notion of whiteness as "non-raced," "non-diverse," "non-multicultural," or "non-cultural." "The word 'general market' *should* be everyone," said a multicultural brand strategist from a media agency, "but because it's a white-dominated society, it usually means non-Hispanics, the non-multicultural market."[66] A senior level multicultural media agency executive echoed this understanding to me, stating flatly that "general market is just white; it is anyone who is *not* a color."[67] In a conversation I had while walking to a presentation at a marketing conference in Miami, a consumer researcher at a major financial institution stated matter-of-factly that "general market is anyone who is *not* a minority."[68] Moments later, both of us attended a presentation by a Nielsen representative who shared quantitative data measuring alcohol purchase trends in the United States by comparing the consumption patterns of "multiculturals and their *non*-multicultural counterparts" (figure 1.4).

The use of the prefix *non* in terms like *non-diverse, non-multicultural, non-cultural*, or *non-minority* signifies the absence or negation of the concept it precedes. These terms, when employed in the place of *general market*, highlight the reproduction of whiteness as the normative American consumer identity in advertising discourse, defined through its negation and exclusion of "multicultural" people. Evidently, cultural is what the general market is not; race is what it lacks.

American advertising's consumer categories are deeply infused with racialized views of culture that have historically functioned as "the essential tool for making other" in academic anthropology and many realms outside of it.[69] This racialized interpretation of culture confines people to hermetically sealed groups, where "both whiteness and nonwhiteness are reified, made into objects rather than processes, and robbed of historical context and human agency."[70] In this framework, the general market is perceived as the "unmarked or neutral category," implicitly setting the standard, while other groups are distinctly labeled and categorized based on the distinctiveness of cultural characteristics.[71]

When I asked a strategist from a multicultural agency to explain her use of the term, she referred to the general market as representing a reference population whose behaviors are not influenced by "cultural" factors: "General market is just the initial lens that we use that doesn't have a cultural

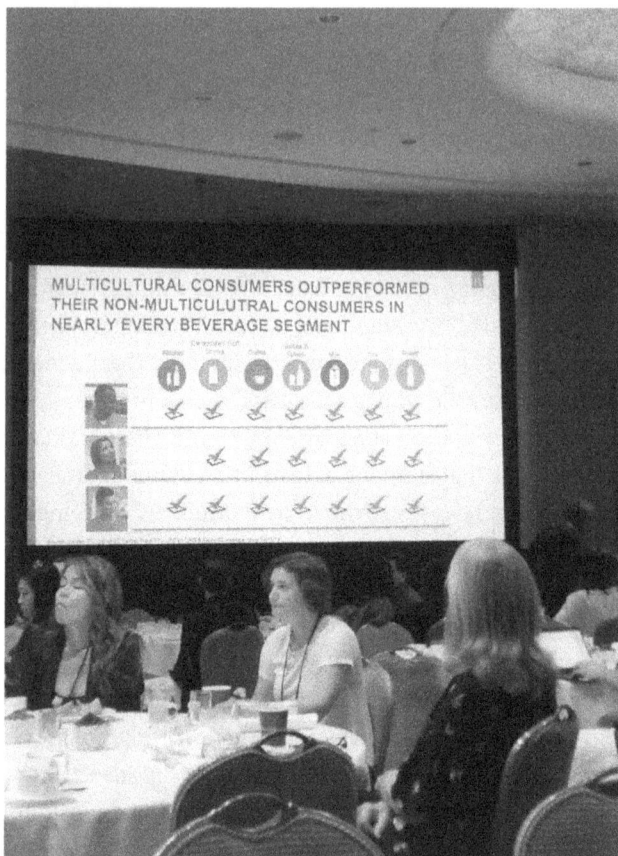

1.4 A slide from a presentation by a Nielsen representative at the 2018 ANA Multicultural Marketing and Diversity Conference, sharing data about racial differences in beverage preferences, with the claim that "Multicultural consumers outperformed their non-multiculutral [*sic*] consumers in nearly every beverage segment." Miami, Florida. Photo by the author.

layer. It's just people without the cultural layer."[72] In her analysis, a *cultural layer* refers to a racialized distinction that sets multicultural groups apart from what is considered the normalized or default whiteness, which is not explicitly marked by racial distinction. This concept was further emphasized by a senior strategy executive at the creative agency Blue, whose comparison between media networks was a clear example of advertising's racial politics of culture: "General market just means everybody—everybody that's not labeled under a cultural label. NBC is general market. Telemundo is not."[73]

In US advertising's racial information system, *culture* euphemistically refers to racialized "multicultural" people, whose lifestyles and perspectives become a reservoir of inspiration and raw material that is mined to generate value for brands.[74] When marked racially within the advertising industry's information system, culture is a commodity up for incorporation and appropriation, integrated into the mechanisms of capital and the propaganda that sustains it. I asked a longtime Hispanic marketer who is now an account manager at a general market creative agency if he had ever heard whites spoken about in cultural terms over the course of his career:

> In my experience, no. If you look at those who are influencing culture, those who are leading culture, frankly I've never heard of a white person's name being stated as "this is the one leading culture." When we use inspiration and we start putting stuff on the wall . . . if it's music—it's hip-hop. If it's fashion—it's the Black community. If it's food—it's ethnic food. So, it's very difficult to say that . . . I really can't think of one time where honestly a white person, or white culture, has influenced this or that. It's very difficult.[75]

However, in certain instances, the whiteness of the general market is more explicitly racially marked. In a PowerPoint presentation that the Hispanic ad agency Soar prepared for a pharmaceutical company client, the agency evaluated the potential profits that racially targeted advertising could bring to the company. They presented all manner of quantitative data demonstrating patterns in Hispanic and Black populations' consumer preferences for a variety of over-the-counter medicine brands, along with their sentiments on health and wellness, and even their respective somatic experiences with disease and pain. Nearly every data point they presented measured Hispanic and Black consumer sentiments in comparison to the term *non-Hispanic white* (NHW), or the category that the US Census Bureau defines as "whites who are not of Hispanic origin."

One of the slides stated that Hispanics and African Americans were more likely than NHWs to report using one of the pharmaceutical company's cough suppressants. Another claimed that Hispanics and African American consumers were a viable market for one of the brand's pain relief medicines because they experienced more bodily pain in comparison to non-Hispanic whites. "Body pains are common in multiculturals," read the top of one slide, which was accompanied by a bevy of statistics from a market research company that claimed Hispanics and African Americans experience twice as much back pain as NHWs. Throughout the presentation, NHW was the conceptual anchor from which the multicultural advertising agency produced racial data integral to its business offerings. Indeed, NHW was the pivot point from which the agency was measuring multicultural consumers, "a statistical artifact that distinguishes a certain population from others."[76]

At another presentation I attended, hosted by the industry trade group Hispanic Marketing Council, NHW was used in the context of survey data claiming that "most NHW like diverse shows simply because 'they are good.'" This data point was used to emphasize the appeal of media that is personally relatable to younger audiences, reflecting a shift in entertainment preferences: White people now seek media and advertising that include various racial and ethnic groups, moving away from the traditionally white-dominated media landscape assumed by past generations (figure 1.5).

I noticed that the multicultural advertising professionals I observed demonstrated a degree of ambivalence toward the general market category, reflecting a blend of competition with and dependency on its implied white normativity. On the one hand, the general market signifies the dominant power structure within the advertising industry that multicultural advertisers must strategically compete against. At the same time, multicultural advertising exists in direct relation to the general market's normative whiteness, which frames racial difference as a cultural commodity to justify its industry's role and the demand for its expertise within the marketing landscape. When Tom Burrell founded his eponymous African American ad agency in Chicago in 1971, the logic of racial differentiation from whiteness became his guiding business principle—and a signature idea he became widely known for. As he put it, "I had to convince clients to understand that *Black people are not dark-skinned white people.*"[77]

1.5 A slide from a market research presentation hosted by the Hispanic Marketing Council in 2018 in New York City discusses media preferences of "NHW" (non-Hispanic whites). Photo by the author.

A strategy executive I interviewed at a multicultural agency explained that his job hinged on justifying racially targeted advertising by framing it in contrast to an assumed white identity standard. "The *general market* is kind of understood as what equals 'normal.' So often, we find ourselves in a situation where we're not trying to explain what's 'Black' about something as much as we're trying to explain what's *not white* about something. And that's a very hard place to be."[78]

Although the general market category figures prominently in the US multicultural advertising lexicon, in my conversations with professionals at "creative agencies" or advertising firms that are not explicitly marked by multicultural racial difference, the concept was largely disavowed and discredited. "I don't think I've ever said 'the general market.' It's never been something that I have thought about because it's such a false term," said one of Blue's high-level strategy directors.[79] Another white male executive at the vice-president level rebuffed my question: "We don't use that term at all. The only place I hear that name is when I talk to a US Hispanic shop. If you talk to an agency person you will not hear the term. You'll hear 'consumer.' You'll hear segment names because we're not thinking of a 'general market.'"[80] With his use of the term *agency person* to distinguish himself and his colleagues from multicultural agencies, this executive also establishes a clear racialized barrier in expertise between what their respective industry roles are and the differences in their perceptions of the American consumer public.

When questioned about the general market category, I observed a consistent pattern among employees at mainstream agencies, embodying what the late philosopher Charles Mills termed "white ignorance."[81] Positioned in dominant roles, they embraced a strategic form of not-knowing, adopting a color-blind stance that upholds and perpetuates white normativity. Another white executive at Blue claimed that he had never encountered the term *general market* in his career: "I've never heard the term 'general market.' I feel like it's an invented word. I don't think people are walking around the US going 'I'm a general market person' and 'I'm a Hispanic person' or whatever. I would hope they would say 'I'm an American.'"[82] As a structure of power, whiteness functions through discursive distancing, where the principles of color-blindness reinforce an "illusion of race neutrality," concealing the racial dynamics at play.[83]

The organizing assumption of the *general market*, whether it is explicitly acknowledged or not, sets the limit and determines what sort of discourse is possible. White normativity is the organizing frame because it is not directly present but evident in how markets and value are delineated. In these same contexts, white racial identity is rarely discussed as an essential or cultural trait that is consequential to consumer behavior. Anthropologist Helena Hansen highlights how white normativity influenced the pharmaceutical industry's marketing of opioids in the United States, noting that a strategy of targeting prescribers in white suburban and rural communities was an "unrecognized form of ethnic marketing that, because it targets white people, works by *not* marking itself as racial."[84]

"There's definitely no talk of the 'Caucasian market.' Ever. They're never called out," said Sean, a white male strategist based in Los Angeles when I asked him if he ever experienced whites targeted as a racial market segment.[85] His colleague Sam agreed: "It's very rare that anybody would actually say 'we're targeting white people,' which is so weird."[86] In the discourse of "agency people," whiteness is an unspoken norm—never explicitly stated, yet always implicitly understood.

But this does not mean white people are never targeted as white by advertisers. Rather than make direct references to white racial identity, I noticed that employees who worked at agencies used a host of other euphemisms instead. A white Australian strategist at Blue shared with me that he cynically used the phrase "pale, male, stale, and Yale" to refer to the high-net-worth white male consumer that was the target audience for a banking services client.[87] For a Los Angeles–based strategist, white consumers were never explicitly a distinct racial market in his campaign work for the automobile company that was his main client. Other terms were used instead. "It's not discussed as 'targeting the whites'; It's always a discussion about the 'conservative mindset.' We also have to consider that there's the middle of America and there's also this conservative mindset that may not like two dudes getting married in our spot."[88] *Conservative* and *middle America* were euphemisms invoked to refer to an imagined white American consumer base without explicitly racializing them. A digital strategist at a media agency recalled, "One campaign asked me to target heavily conservative people. . . . You know, it's not like they specifically said 'target white Americans,' but, in that category, a lot of it ends up being white Americans."[89]

US Census projections about the impending demographic minority status of non-Hispanic whites have become the linchpin of ongoing furor about the continuing evolution of national culture and American whiteness as a social category. Anger and anxieties over shifting political dominance, driven by discourse about projected demographic changes, are fueling the resurgence of a white American identity politics as a distinctly racialized cultural identity.

The advertising industry is taking notice. In the wake of Donald Trump's first presidential win in 2016, the *Washington Post* reported that "advertisers are reflecting on whether they are out of touch with the same people—rural, economically frustrated, elite-distrusting, anti-globalization voters—who propelled the businessman into the White House."[90] Several agencies have begun to view sectors of the white population in the Midwest and rural parts of county in terms historically used by multicultural agencies, referring to them as an "underserved" and "misunderstood" market waiting to be perceived as valuable by brands. Harris Diamond, CEO of the ad agency McCann Worldgroup, critiqued the focus of US advertising on an urban and cosmopolitan audience typically presumed to be the mainstream: "Marketing needs to reflect less of New York and Los Angeles culture, and more of Des Moines and Scranton."[91] The resurgence of advertising interest in decoding the white American "heartland" hearkens back to the Lynds' early twentieth-century *Middletown* study, while also signifying an emergent shift in the racialization of white people in American advertising as both a marked and culturally distinct market segment. Rob Schwartz, former chief executive of the advertising agency TBWA\Chiat\Day New York, emphasized the importance of getting more intensive consumer research on white people in middle America: "There's going to be scrutiny on data and a big demand from clients saying, 'Yes, there's data, and what do we really know? Who's been to Kansas to understand what they're consuming in Kansas, and is it the same in Nebraska? And don't just Google it.'"[92]

This shift in white American racial formation can be seen in the rise of new media networks that specifically cater to white people as a media audience and consumer demographic. Rated Red, a Nashville-based digital media company founded in 2017 for a right-leaning American "Heartland youth culture," targets a predominantly Caucasian audience (74 percent), ages eighteen to thirty-four, with interests in sports, gaming, outdoor activities, cars, and the military (figure 1.6). On a slide called "Rated Red Archetypes" in its media kit for advertisers, the company delineates five consumer profiles within its "heartland millennial" market demographic— from the varsity-jacket-wearing "hometown hero," described as "the captain of the football team, who will proudly enter the family business and still goes to church with his family every Sunday," to the horn-rimmed glasses, flannel shirt–donning "heartland hipster" who "embraces some aspects of Northern culture, but is more interested in making the Heartland progressive than leaving it" (figure 1.7). Rated Red's depiction of its audience, rather than labeling it as the normalized general market, constructs its American heartland whiteness as a distinct cultural demographic that is in need of preserving and marketing to.

Throughout history, the advertising industry's racial information system has reinforced the notion that higher-income white Americans represent the normative standard, upheld through the "general market" category. These practices have played a key role in the discursive production and commodification of American whiteness within consumer culture. As demographic shifts challenge the assumption of white population dominance, the future of the general market's white normativity is in flux. Ad-

THE RATED RED AUDIENCE

AGE:
18-34

PASSIONS:
Culture, Sports, Gaming, Outdoor, Rides, Military

ETHNICITY:
74% Caucasian, 16% HA, 8% AA, 2% Asian

TOP MARKETS:
Austin, Dallas, Nashville, Charleston

Source: Google Analytics 2017

1.6   The audience profile from Nashville, Tennessee – based digital media company Rated Red's 2017 media kit for advertisers details the key traits of its target audience.

RATED RED ARCHETYPES

HOMETOWN HERO
The captain of the football team, who will proudly enter the family business and still goes to church with his family every Sunday. An all around stand up guy who married his high school sweetheart. He's a young parent or soon to be.

TRANSPLANT
Ex-pat of the heartland who has since moved to a city like Chicago, LA or NY for her career but maintains an affinity for the lifestyle she grew up with. For her, Rated Red is like a plane ticket home.

HEARTLAND HIPSTER
Heartland guy who embraces some aspects of Northern culture, but is more interested in making the Heartland progressive than leaving it. He is also a trendy influencer, who loves the Nashville and Austin music scenes.

POST-GRAD BRO
SEC or Big TEN alum, who you'll find at the sports bar or day-drinking/tailgating. Loves social media. Very into web culture and what's trending. Gamer, pick-up truck enthusiast; talks about first-life daily. He's also aspirational and seeks the approval of others.

OUTDOORSMAN
Rugged yet refined outdoorsman, he loves Hunting & Fishing and has the means to buy the best gear out there. A weekend warrior. Military background. Plays *Call of Duty* when not at the shooting range.

1.7   Rated Red's "archetypes" from its 2017 media kit reflect how representations of American whiteness figure into the construction and sale of the media company's target audience to advertisers.

vertising industry discourse provides a crucial lens for understanding the evolving, unstable construction of American whiteness and its meanings.

In chapter 2, I explore the role of multicultural strategists in creative and media agencies—professionals tasked with generating expertise for brand clients on racial differences in consumer behavior. Their knowledge production and data analysis in advertising continue to shape and renegotiate racial theories of humanity.

MULTICULTURAL STRATEGY AND THE PRODUCTION OF RACIAL EXPERTISE

One winter day, I met with May, a multicultural consumer strategist at a shopper marketing agency.[1] Over a cup of tea at her office in midtown Manhattan, we spoke about a campaign she had just completed to launch a European wine and spirits brand in the United States. Our conversation occurred just a month after the release of the blockbuster Marvel movie *Black Panther*, which was celebrated not only as a milestone for media representation with non-white actors in leading Hollywood roles but also as a testament to the profit potential of a superhero franchise featuring an all-Black cast and a Black director.[2]

"We recommended that the brand focus on African Americans to unlock the opportunity," May explained to me in a glass-walled conference room. When the project started, marketers at the alcohol company briefed May and her team about its goals and the core philosophy that the brand sought to communicate with American consumers, which was centered on the concept of "reinventing tradition." May's job was to unearth and synthesize information on current consumer trends in the product category and figure out how to position it in the wine and spirits market by creating opportunities for positive emotional perceptions between the company's brand and "African Americans in three US cities in a very authentic way," she said.[3]

May's research led her to develop a marketing strategy based on a conceptual connection she observed between the client's intended brand image and her observation of the influential role African Americans have played in shaping American popular culture: "Who is reinventing things today?" May asked rhetorically. Quick to answer her own question, she replied, "African Americans, for sure—if you think about *Black Panther* as an exercise in reinventing what a superhero can look like. So, we told the brand: 'You should put this group as a center focus and let them spread out the news about the brand.'"

May opened her laptop to show me the presentation she had prepared for the client. "We recommended African Americans as the opportunity because of who is at the center of creating culture today and the type of culture that [the brand] is aiming for."[4] Over several slides, May shared research she had compiled and analyzed from data sources like the audience measurement firm Nielsen, the US Census Bureau, and the Pew Research Center think tank to detail what she envisioned as the defining traits of the Black consumers who could be marshaled to support the liquor company's success in the United States, in particular, those who were millennials living in Atlanta, Georgia, with upper-middle-class incomes.

May paused on a slide that featured images of several young and stylish Black social media influencers: a chef, a fashion stylist, and a beauty salon owner. Accompanying each influencer's headshot was a bullet-pointed list detailing their respective interests, along with data on their social media followings and screenshots of their most highly engaged Instagram posts. May explained that she was showing me the result of hours spent using a market research software called InfoScout, a "social listening platform" that gathers data from public social media profiles, enabling marketers to aggregate and analyze mentions and conversations in real time.[5] InfoScout is just one of the many tools available for advertising strategists to monitor and analyze consumer behavior, often turning internet users into unwitting participants in the creation of marketing campaigns.

"All the photos that you see here, they're basically like our 'alpha consumers,'" May said with a buzz of excitement in her voice. "They're *actual* people in Atlanta, Georgia, who are millennials, who are hip and cool, and who are out there drinking wine on a regular basis. All that you see here are photos from their actual social media."

I asked May about the specific role that multicultural strategists like herself play in the marketing process and her reason for joining the profession. "I came to this discipline because I'm very passionate about representation and social justice. My work is about bringing the *outside* into the conversation. It can be research and qualitative and quantitative data but also trends and what people actually talk about. Anything from intersectionality to politics, it is my job to bring it into the conversation and onto the radar of our clients." As a consumer analyst, May offers advertisers expertise about how the "outside" lives. The "outside," in this instance, are consumers who have been racialized as "multicultural" in the American advertising industry's racial information system, and who have been historically relegated to the periphery of the industry's assumed and entrenched white "general market" norm.

Motivated by the desire to predict and influence attitudes for business purposes, the advertising industry relies on rationalization techniques grounded in "bureaucratic organization, an increased emphasis on calculation, and the generation and utilization of specialized knowledge" about human beings in their roles as consumers.[6] In this chapter, I examine how multicultural strategy functions as a commercialized form of racial theorizing, positioning the American advertising industry within a broader system of knowledge production that defines human difference through the lens of race. I explain how multicultural strategists primarily focus on generating data-driven depictions of racial differences in consumer behavior, which they refer to as nuance. *Nuance* is a term used to emphasize the perceived distinctiveness of racial markets from one another and from the general market—insider insights into racialized emotions, meaning-making, and cultural specificities that advertisers can exploit for economic gain. Nuance is a concept born from the advertising industry's racial information system—the amalgamation of institutions, individuals, processes, and artifacts that create, sustain, and commodify racial knowledge for commercial purposes.

Many of the multicultural advertising strategists I interviewed and observed expressed a commitment to "humanizing" consumers racialized as "multicultural" through their research and data analysis, aiming to challenge racial stereotypes in advertising. However, their efforts to add nuance are often constrained by the corporate cultural industry's focus on rationalization—prioritizing predictability, measurability, and objectification over complexity and ambiguity. As a result, strategists may unintentionally reinforce the very racial archetypes they seek to dismantle.

ADVERTISING STRATEGY AND THE PURSUIT OF NUANCE

During my final year of undergraduate studies, I interned in the strategy department of Dímelo, a Hispanic advertising agency in New York City. As a social sciences student with a growing interest in the political economy of media—and having been affectionately nicknamed "fashion plate" by my parents due to my childhood obsessions with Folgers commercials and Old Navy clothing—I was eager to gain an insider's perspective on the advertising industry and understand the processes that shaped its power to influence how I felt about brands and, in turn, how I viewed myself.

During my internship, Dímelo was pursuing new business with a company in the technology sector, and I was tasked with identifying a subset of the US Hispanic population that could be presented as a potential target market for one of its products. My assignment was to develop a "consumer profile": a form of market research knowledge that provides detailed information about a specific demographic's habits, feelings, predispositions, and motivations toward a brand, product, or service. After perusing the technology company's website, I decided to create a consumer profile for prospective Hispanic users of a pocket-sized projector.

My work culminated in a PowerPoint presentation to the agency in which I pitched the promising profit potential of a market segment I called the "Hispanic Artrepreneur." I described this group as "English-dominant, bicultural Hispanic young adults (ages 18–35) who are part of a thriving community of DIY trendsetters" and positioned them as an influential target market for the pocket projector (figure 2.1). I assembled my portrait of the Hispanic Artrepreneur from a constellation of data sources that I had observed other employees at Dímelo draw on during my internship: audience research statistics from Univision (the Spanish-language media company), the Pew Research Center, and a slew of market research reports published by advertising industry trade publications. In my presentation, I cited racial statistics from an *Adweek* study that described Hispanics as "family-oriented" and "keen on using mobile devices to stay connected to loved ones in Latin America." One of my slides claimed that "Young Hispanic Americans are more likely than any other racial or ethnic group to embrace cutting-edge mobile and social networking technologies." I also made sure to highlight the projector's potential appeal to a broader market of Hispanics, stating in my pitch: "Whether *Hijo* is using the projector to show off his new music video to a prospective investor in his indie music career, or *Mamá* wants to project her Skype conversation with *Abuelita* in Colombia on the living room wall, the projector can be a great piece of shared family technology as well." I followed this description with a smattering of quantitative figures purporting to demonstrate that Hispanics were more likely than non-Hispanic whites to be early adopters of the latest technology.

While the creation of the Hispanic Artrepreneur might have suggested a process of discovery, my experience creating it revealed to me that this

who they are

- 18–35 yrs
- Bicultural male and female
- "Tech Wizards"
- Creative Digital Age Entrepreneurs

2.1 This slide describes the "Hispanic Artrepreneur," a consumer profile created by the author during a 2013 internship at Dímelo, a Hispanic advertising agency in New York City. Slide by the author.

racial market was more manufactured than found—a selective abstraction largely reflecting aspects of my personal identity as a Nuyorican millennial college student who identified with the arts, technology, and entrepreneurial ethos I was pitching as a trendsetting demographic. Also reflected in the profile was my own racial epistemology, shaped by my American upbringing, which uncritically accepted a dehistoricized and naturalized notion of "Hispanic" identity as an essential, inherent trait inscribed in the body as if it determined specific cultural behaviors and perceptions.

I consciously tailored certain aspects of my presentation to align with what I believed Dímelo—and, ultimately, the client—would find appealing about Hispanics as consumers. For instance, I peppered in some Spanish words (even though I do not speak the language) because I understood its symbolic importance as a crucial marker in legitimizing Hispanic marketing as a specialized field.[7] "Without market research, there can be no markets," writes communication studies theorist Katherine Sender.[8] Indeed, in my role as a multicultural advertising strategist intern, I participated in the discursive construction of the Hispanic Artrepreneur who was

mediated—"made and made up"—through various forms of datafied racial representation and interpretation.[9]

My experience also revealed something unexpectedly empowering for me
as a twenty-one-year-old college intern: My identity as a Nuyorican young
woman and consumer could be leveraged as a form of expertise within
corporate America. My initial engagement with multicultural advertising
strategy, which I later came to understand as a form of "identity entrepreneurship," appeared to open up career prospects for me in the American advertising sector that I had not previously envisioned.[10] I began to recognize
that my standpoint could be used to shape widely seen marketing campaigns
and, as I optimistically believed at the time, influence less negatively stereotypical notions of people like myself in media and corporate settings.

Yet my realization was accompanied by a growing sense of ambivalence.
I became increasingly aware of—and uneasy about—the ways in which racialized populations were commodified by advertisers as a site of corporate
accumulation and the potential for exploitation. After all, multicultural
strategy's provision of racial expertise and data storytelling to companies
is ultimately about control—using racial knowledge production to influence how people racialized as Hispanic think, behave, and act in ways that
serve advertisers' economic interests.

Strategists play a crucial role in shaping advertising content, reinforcing its fundamental purpose as a persuasive tool of capitalist propaganda.
Through systematic research and analysis of consumer trends, strategists
are often considered the "voice of the consumer" within an agency, providing the creative team and client with information to ensure that campaigns
capture the attention of and evoke positive emotions within the target
market.[11] "My job is to understand what is at stake in our society by studying social trends: what people think about and why," explained Andrea, a
strategist from the general market agency Blue. Andrea elaborated that her
role as the strategist is to research relevant and pertinent "problems" in human lives that corporations can redress with their products and services: "I
try to find the key insights to bring attention to what's happening in the society or in the consumer's life that is a problem that we can solve."[12] Advertising strategists like Andrea are cultural workers whose job it is produce
knowledge about people in the service of companies' interests to "create
desires [and] to bring into being wants that previously did not exist."[13]

At the time of our interview, Andrea was working on the launch of a new
fragrance brand. The client, a US retail outlet, came to Blue with a prelimi-
nary sense of the product's target consumer: "Women, 18 to 34, who are a

little bit interested in natural things, but not in a granola, crunchy way," she explained. After consulting a variety of data sources—from paid subscription consumer research platforms like Mintel to publicly available articles in the news media and on Google Scholar, Andrea further refined the client's proposed concept of its target consumer to be "more detailed and accurate and realistic. It's learning about what the consumer says, what they do online, what they think, what their life values are. What's their priority in life? Is it being happy? Is it earning money? Or is it self-fulfillment? We try to get to know life through this person," she said.[14]

Sandee, a high-level strategy executive at a New York City agency, emphasized to me the importance of strategists' expertise in the advertising production process, highlighting how their understanding of the complexity of human subjectivities and life contexts is key to making advertising persuasive and attention-grabbing. "My job as a strategist is to represent the consumer. I have to understand what's going on in the consumer's life, as well as their cultural context, while keeping in mind the business imperatives. This helps us develop an overall strategy that drives our messaging. Without that insight about the consumer, commercials wouldn't really have any impact," she said.[15]

Advertising strategy is a modern extension of the twentieth-century "motivational research" field, often linked to public relations pioneer Edward Bernays (Sigmund Freud's nephew). Bernays believed that experts could help businesses manipulate human behavior to their advantage by tapping into the subconscious minds of the masses.[16] In the 1940s and 1950s, Austrian American psychologist Ernest Dichter expanded the use of Freudian psychoanalytic theories in market research. Through in-depth interviews and focus groups, he and his colleagues investigated the "hidden motivations" behind consumer decisions. Today's advertising strategists are the successors to the "depth men" described by Vance Packard in *The Hidden Persuaders* (1957)—market researchers who analyzed desires, fears, and impulses to influence consumer behavior.

Advertising strategy, also known as *account planning*, emerged as a formal industry profession in the mid-to-late 1960s at British agencies J. Walter Thompson (JWT) and Boase Massimi Pollitt (BMP) amid shifts in advertiser-agency relationships.[17] Previously, advertising agencies served as primary market researchers for their clients. Yet, as competition intensified and the scale of consumer data increased, advertisers began to develop in-house consumer strategy departments. Concerned that account managers had too much power in developing creative concepts for campaigns without sufficient grounding in research, Stanley Pollitt of the agency BMP championed the formalization of the "account planner" position, responsible for leading knowledge production to inform and enhance creative development. The role evolved into a special position responsible for "using consumer research to clarify the issues and enrich the advertising process."[18]

Although the advertising strategists I spoke with from both general market and multicultural advertising agencies described the nature of their jobs in substantially similar terms, I noticed that strategists who worked at multicultural advertising agencies described their work as involving an "extra layer" of expertise that was not readily available at general market firms. Ben, a strategist at a Hispanic ad agency in Miami, claimed that multicultural advertising strategy is more labor-intensive than strategy at general market agencies because it involves "defending, specifying, and understanding the core nuances that would make [an ad campaign] relevant or relatable to a very specific subculture."

Ben explained that general market strategy typically focuses on identifying macrolevel cultural trends that are broad and widely applicable. In contrast, multicultural strategy requires additional labor and a specialized skill set, like identifying distinct microlevel details about the lived experiences of people racialized as "multicultural" and translating that information into a compelling narrative. This process is not just about gathering and analyzing data—it is also about persuading clients that multicultural advertising is both meaningful and strategically sound.

The word *nuance* frequently surfaced in my conversations with multicultural strategists as they described the specific genre of racial knowledge they specialized in producing for advertiser clients. I learned that *nuance* is a euphemism used to name the seemingly subtle yet significant differences in the psychologies, emotions, behaviors, and cultures of Hispanic, African American, and Asian populations as markets. These racial distinctions are believed to have a measurable impact on how these groups engage with the marketplace and consumer culture more broadly, including their reception of an advertisement's persuasiveness. "Nuances might be that an ethnic group consumes a product in a different way. Nuances could be found in how they use the product. Another nuance could be the price point they're looking for. What we need to do is understand those nuances," explained a high-level executive at a multicultural media agency.[19] Nuances are forms of racial knowledge that are used to shape advertising strategies, content, and representations and to justify a company's investment in multicultural advertising. Through research and measurement, multicultural strategists play a crucial role in "bolster[ing] a kind of consciousness that" aims to make nonwhite consumers "rush towards the dispossession of racial capitalism."[20]

Multicultural strategists convey their expertise in nuance through intentionally pithy and conclusive statements about racial markets that are presented to the creative team and advertising clients as truisms, also referred to as "consumer insights." Examples include phrases like "US Hispanics are mobile first" or "US Hispanics are tastemakers for their family," as a multicultural digital strategist based in Miami explained to me, elaborating that, "for instance, if a [Hispanic] mother buys Bounty, her children are likely to buy Bounty as well because she is considered a tastemaker. Another example is 'US Hispanics rely on their family for advice,' which is a cultural nuance that brands use to shape their messaging."[21]

Multicultural strategists emphasize *nuance* not only to differentiate racial markets but also to position themselves as indispensable experts, enhancing multicultural marketing's value proposition within the competitive creative services industry. American data marketing company Resonate promotes its Hispanic marketing services to advertisers by emphasizing nuance, asserting that their "consumer intelligence dives deep into the *nuances* of individuals to help brands and agencies segment, plan, and strategize around cultural differences and sensitivities."[22] Monique Nelson, the CEO of Uniworld, a long-standing multicultural advertising agency in New York, noted, "Our agency views the world through a lens made sharper by our expertise in identifying the forces that bring consumers together, while specializing in the cultural *nuances* that make them distinct."[23] Mining for nuance, or information about racial differences in consumer behavior and sentiment, has a cash value for multicultural advertising that is reflected in multimillion dollar agency fees and new client prospects.

The commodification of nuance in multicultural advertising strategy reflects US capitalism's continued role in reinforcing race as a tool of social division and economic extraction, legitimized through data and measurement. In particular, US marketing's systematic research on racial differences can be traced to the creation of the "Negro market," and specifically to the Great Migration, a period in the early to mid-twentieth century when millions of African Americans migrated from the rural South to Northern cities, fleeing racially motivated terrorism and seeking economic opportunity. As large Black populations concentrated in urban locales, "some white businesses ... sensed the growing practicality and profitability of wooing

African American shoppers, [and] sought insights into reaching this heretofore little-known segment of the American buying public. To assist those white businesses interested in courting blacks, business periodicals began to feature an increasing number of articles related to the 'Negro market,'" explains historian Robert E. Weems.[24] One of the first of these articles, published in 1930 in the trade publication *Advertising and Selling*, aimed to refute commonly held stereotypes about Black consumers as poor and uneducated, relaying "that Northern Blacks were literate, [had] good-paying jobs and [were] receptive to advertising."[25] Racial statistics sourced from government entities like the Department of Commerce and the US Census served as foundational datasets for a marketing industry assessing the scale, characteristics, and economic value of the "Negro" market.[26]

Between the 1920s and 1940s, sales representatives from Black newspapers and radio stations played a pivotal role in circulating market research piloted to legitimize the existence of a viable Black consumer audience to national advertisers. These inaugural consumer studies gained momentum during the Great Depression as companies looked for untapped markets that could "compensate for reduced spending among their traditional" (white) consumer base.[27] As African Americans emerged from World War II with relatively higher incomes due to their participation in war industries, several major advertisers, including Pepsi and Coca-Cola, hired "Negro market specialists" and sales representatives to promote their beverages in Black communities with targeted marketing, product placement, and events.[28] During the 1940s, an African American market researcher named David J. Sullivan emerged as the country's leading "Negro market expert," pioneering a genre of influential "how-to" articles in the marketing trade press with statistical profiles on Black spending patterns, product preferences, and other key demographic insights with the aim of "dispel[ing] the notion that the black consumer market was peripheral and irrelevant."[29]

By the 1950s, even more companies aimed to follow Pepsi's lead in boosting sales among Black consumers, which led to a notable increase in Negro market experts across agencies and brands within corporate America. The mainstream New York advertising agency BBDO (Batten, Barton, Durstine, and Osborn) hired its first African American sales representative, Clarence L. Holte, in 1952 to lead its Ethnic Markets division, the first department and executive level position of its kind for a Black person in the American advertising industry. "Beyond demographic statistics and facts pertaining to the consumption behaviors of the black consumer market, Holte also provided industry executives with compelling interpretations

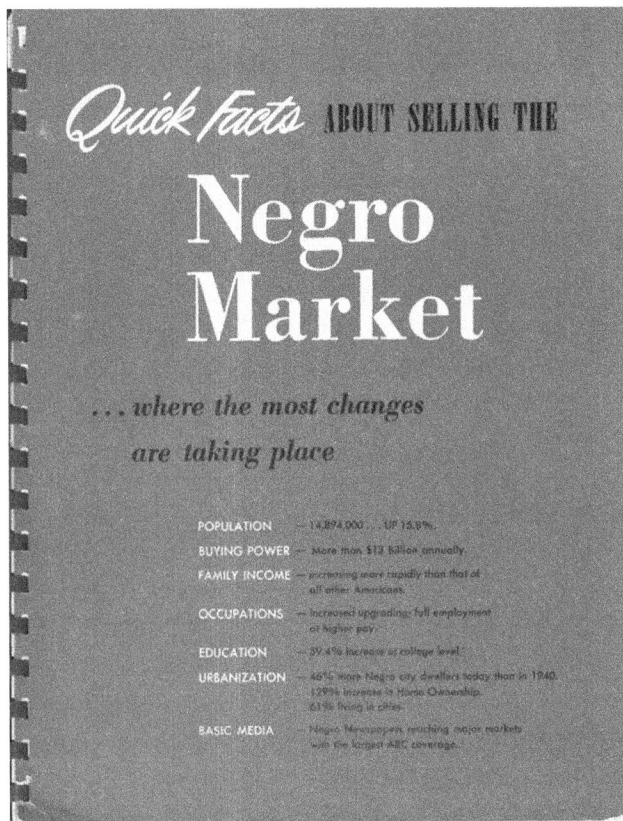

2.2 Cover of *Quick Facts About Selling the Negro Market* (Associated Publishers, 1952), a marketing brochure with racial statistics about African Americans made for advertisers. Source: John W. Hartman Center for Sales, Advertising, and Marketing History, Duke University Libraries.

of perceptions, attitudes and motivations of black consumers as they related to various marketing efforts," explains marketing historian Judy Foster Davis.[30] The same year, the Associated Negro Press, the nation's first Black newswire service, published its marketing how-to guide for advertisers, titled *Quick Facts About Selling the Negro Market*, which contained data on population size, household income statistics, education levels, media use, and more (figure 2.2).

When discussing BBDO's decision to create the Ethnic Markets division with reporters from the advertising trade publication *Tide*, research director Lyle Purcell stressed that the move was not driven by civil rights concerns but was purely an economic decision: "I'm not a crusader. . . . This is a cold, calculated move on my part for the dollar sign only."[31] As Purcell and other advertising executives saw it, there was profit to be extracted from Black consumers, and Negro market specialists offered the expertise necessary to inform their efforts.

Two years after BBDO launched its Ethnic Markets division, John H. Johnson, the African America media mogul and publisher of the magazines *Ebony* and *Jet*, released *The Secret of Selling the Negro*, the first market research documentary of its kind to focus on painting a data-oriented portrait of the Negro market for corporate America.[32] Produced in the format of a newsreel, the twenty-minute film was hosted by the staid, three-piece-suited white journalist Bob Trout, who spoke with authority and urgency about the rise of a flourishing Black middle-class market composed of avid consumers readily available for advertisers to reap economic benefits from. Drawing on data from the US Department of Commerce about the Black populations' rising incomes in the postwar economy, the "secret" shared in Johnson's market research film sought not only "to convince White advertisers to spend money in Black/Johnson-owned media spaces" but also "to convince both Black and White America that such myth promulgation," or in other words, targeted advertising, "would be the requisite solution to increasing material inequality," writes communications studies theorist Jared Ball.[33]

Throughout the 1960s, as the civil rights movement reshaped social norms and legal desegregation advanced, a wave of trade articles offering guidance to corporations on targeting the Black consumer market gained more prominence. John H. Johnson became the era's leading consultant, solidifying his influence with the publication of *The Negro Handbook* in 1966, which "subtly assured U.S. corporations that seeking more black customers was both profitable and socially responsible."[34]

By the height of the social justice movements and anti-colonial struggles of the 1970s, big business did not openly resist calls for social change. Instead, it appropriated and leveraged symbols and discourse, such as the notion of multiculturalism, in order to project an image of hipness and social progress to youth while maintaining capitalist economic power. The advertising industry, in particular, capitalized on shifting racial discourse that centered on identity, pride, and cultural distinctiveness, aligning brands with the symbols and affective sentiments of insurgent social movements as signifiers of youthful cool.[35]

Big Tobacco, for one, invested heavily in racial expertise. Companies like Philip Morris and R. J. Reynolds hired researchers and advertising agencies to conduct what historian Keith Wailoo calls "corporate race work"—using focus groups, billboard analyses, and other research methods to frame menthol cigarettes as an inherently "cool" cultural staple in Black inner-city communities.[36] By the 1990s, advertisers like Sprite and Nike made inroads with hip-hop-influenced youth culture, targeting the so-called Black urban consumer. Nike, in particular, has hired marketing consultants and multicultural strategists to conduct ethnographic research at basketball courts, sneaker stores, and barbershops across major US cities, gathering insights, seeding products, and feeding racial knowledge back into product development and advertising.[37]

Hispanic advertising has also been shaped by a quest for corporate racial expertise that could support the industry's institutionalization and legitimacy with brand managers. Arlene Dávila's interviews with first-generation Hispanic ad industry executives detail their experiences of having to supplement the initial dearth of market research budgets with stereotypical "performance[s] of Latinness" as fun-loving and boisterous, particularly at business development dinners and meetings. These interpersonal sales encounters essentially served as a proxy for more detailed and quantitative research about the Hispanic market. As one of Dávila's interlocutors put rather bluntly, "The less quantifiable your value is, the better wine you need to buy at dinner."[38] By the time the US Census released the first official government dataset about the newly codified panethnic "Hispanic" population in 1980, commissioned marketing expertise about this broad group exploded, led particularly by the nascent US Spanish-language media industry, which released the first national Hispanic market studies in 1981 and then in 1984.[39] This recourse to and valorization of formalized racial expertise has since become a staple of Hispanic advertising. Every year, the leading industry trade organization, the Hispanic Marketing Council, hosts its Strategic Excellence Awards, "the only award of its kind that honors Hispanic and multicultural strategic thinking and cultural competence in marketing."[40]

Today's multicultural strategists carry forward a nearly century-long legacy of commercial racial theorizing within the American marketing industry. Through the elicitation of nuance, these experts play a key role in broader social and discursive processes of racialization, producing knowledge that attaches both cultural meaning and economic value to supposed racial groups.

"I help large corporations understand Black people. I do it through research and insights and workshops," stated Mary, a multicultural consumer strategist who specializes in the African American market, in a phone conversation we had in 2018. Mary explained that her approach as a multicultural strategist is foregrounded by her subjectivity as a Black woman and her expertise in the impact that historical legacies and contemporary manifestations of racism have on African American consumer behavior on a collective level. "I basically always start with Blacks in context and understanding that we have a different beginning, a different history, a different lens, different treatment, and different behavior. US-born Black people tend to have this one characteristic that is different from others, and that's the psychological baggage of slavery, post-slavery, and discrimination."[41] Mary foregrounds her expertise to advertisers in the forces of structural racism that shape Black Americans' lives and marketplace interactions.

At the time of our conversation, Mary had recently pitched her strategy consulting services to a performing arts center in a major American city that expressed interest in increasing ticket purchases by African American concertgoers. After learning that the venue had been marketing tickets for its events quite early in advance of performance dates, Mary advised the venue to promote its programming closer to the show's date. Central to her suggestion was her theory that African Americans inherently experience the passage of time differently: "Because Black people tend to live day to day and in the moment, that tracks back to our history. That is important to understand as a marketer and connects to how you are selling tickets to an event and how you plan your marketing."

Mary elaborated on her racial theory that African Americans possess a collective relationship to time informed by historical legacies of, and ongoing experiences with, structural racism. This racialized temporality, she argued, is characterized by a sense of precarity linked to state violence and systemic marginalization wherein African Americans are denied the privilege of stability and, as a result, struggle to plan for a future that often feels uncertain or unattainable. When applied to selling concert tickets, Mary's racial theory could inform a tailored go-to-market strategy for the performance venue. She believed that her theories were not only beneficial to businesses but also served a broader purpose. "I'm a thought leader, a researcher, and an activist," she told me. Her expertise in translating knowledge about Black life for advertisers was, in her view, a means of contributing to the elevation of African Americans' social standing.

"My role is to add value to the Black consumer market," Mary explained. "Homogenizing ethnic culture, particularly Black culture, results in a loss of value. . . . If marketers and the business community can embrace Black value, they can also embrace the value of LGBTQ, Latino, Asian, and other diverse groups." For Mary, her expertise in multicultural nuance lay in understanding the cultural specificity of racialized consumer decision-making —insights rich with economic value for brands seeking to connect with consumers through persuasive advertising appeals. In a stridently anti-Black US society, Mary posited that if advertisers could view Black consumers as an appealing market, it could generate a "halo effect," whereby other historically marginalized groups could also be recognized as valuable consumers worthy of targeted advertising investment. By applying commercial racial expertise to marketing, Mary believed the marketplace could be a space where issues of marginalization and social devaluation could, at least partially, be addressed.

Many of the multicultural strategists I spoke with and observed did not view their expertise in nuance merely as a tool for brand capitalization; they also perceived their knowledge as a necessary political intervention for racial justice that could challenge the predominantly white advertising elite's limited and often stereotypical understanding of non-white racialized populations. In this context, *nuance* means using data to confront and amend racial stereotyping, as well as ascribing social value to non-white people through market-oriented priorities. Ben, a strategist from a multicultural advertising agency in Miami, expressed his frustration with brand clients seeking "insights" about Hispanic consumers that only served to corroborate their already held stereotypes, such as the belief that all Mexicans are soccer fanatics, emotionally passionate, or have big tight-knit families. He saw his role as showing the client Hispanic consumers' "lived realities," giving the client a window into their worlds and lives. "What I try to do, at least, is humanize these consumers," he explained, by offering "nuanced" consumer insights that add complexity, depth, and dignity to their portrayal in advertising.

Market segmentation is a commercial form of social classification that is grounded in three core assumptions—homogeneity, separation, and essence—as communication studies scholar Katherine Sender observes. With the "assumption of homogeneity," industry professionals presume that a consumer segment shares one defining characteristic, rendering all other differences within the group unimportant.[42] In multicultural advertising strategy, race and ethnicity are seen as the primary traits shaping, on a collective and totalizing level, how Hispanic, African American, and Asian American people think, act, and shop. The second assumption is "separation." Sender explains that "in order to efficiently separate desirable from undesirable consumers, marketers must assume that there is a stable, identifiable, and discrete characteristic that identifies people in the target group."[43] Advertisers and media companies tailor their campaigns to specific populations under the belief that the approach is the most financially expedient and psychologically effective for eliciting desired behaviors and sentiments for a brand. The third assumption is "essence," which is closely tied to homogeneity. In multicultural marketing, this assumption posits that each racial market shares intrinsic characteristics that meaningfully correlate with their cultural behaviors, purchases, and media consumption patterns. As a result, each market is assumed to have a racial essence that defines and predicts consumer behavior.

By crafting racial theories that emphasize the purchasing power and cultural influence of racialized multicultural markets, multicultural strategists seek to demonstrate to advertisers that targeting these groups is not only a social responsibility but also a financial opportunity. However, as part of the processes of rationalizing human identity that underpins market segmentation, multicultural strategy reproduces the idea that race is an inherent trait with predictive power. This assumption remains central to the American advertising industry's racial information system.

THE "HISPANIC POSITIVE PAIN FIGHTER"

When I arrived at my internship at the Hispanic ad agency Soar one spring morning, Vince, a longtime Hispanic marketing executive and the agency's head of strategy, appeared to be in good spirits. One of Soar's clients, a pain reliever brand, had provisionally approved a creative concept the agency had developed for a new advertising campaign targeted to Hispanic consumers. After I congratulated him, I noticed Vince started rapping his pen on the desk. His formerly relaxed, assured face flashed with a glint of worry: "Now it's just about refining the ideas and getting them to testing." With ad testing, companies collect feedback on the effectiveness of advertising campaign concepts from a sample of the target audience, soliciting their reactions on everything from how much the ad stands out to how entertaining they find it. The pain reliever brand was organizing a focus group to test Soar's concept and sought Vince's advice on screening criteria to ensure participants accurately reflected the campaign's target audience. In windowless conference rooms across the United States, and increasingly from their mobile devices, people are recruited for and paid by market research firms to offer their opinions on everything from new product development to political party positions.[44]

It seemed like Vince was glad to be involved in the focus group recruitment efforts. If Soar's creative concept got "killed" because it did not test well with the focus group, it would potentially be detrimental for the agency's relationship with the client and, by extension, their billings and business. I joined Vince in a conference room along with a young Black male junior strategist named Kyle and the campaign's account director, a Hispanic woman in her thirties named Lisa, to discuss the recommendations they planned to share with the client. On a large wall-mounted television screen, Lisa projected an email from the client detailing the initial recruitment criteria they had come up with for the types of Hispanics they believed would be the best suited for the focus group. Vince narrowed his eyes at the screen, scrutinizing the email.

"Respondents must be articulate in language, outgoing, and enthusiastic about sharing their opinions," he read aloud. The company specified the breakdown of Hispanic nationalities they surmised should be represented in the group: a "majority" who named the Caribbean and Central and South America as their "country of origin" and the remaining from Mexico. They also proposed that half of the focus group consist of "unacculturated" Hispanics and the other half of "bicultural" Hispanics. Advertising agencies and media networks often use the term *bicultural* to describe a younger segment of US-born Hispanic consumers who, as NBC Universal's Telemundo network describes, are "bilingual, and flawlessly jump between cultures . . . a valuable asset to companies who need to reach out to more diverse audiences every day."[45]

Vince had a pained expression on his face when he said the word *unacculturated* out loud. "Unacculturated? It hurts my eyes," he grimaced.

In a previous conversation we had, Vince expressed his vehement dislike of the continued use of acculturation as a framework for classifying and theorizing about Hispanic consumers in multicultural advertising. As Arlene Dávila points out, the "unacculturated" have long served as a trope of Hispanic racial authenticity within multicultural marketing—Spanish-speaking consumers who "renew" the market.[46]

"Correct the client every time. Don't ever respond with acculturation terms," Vince emphasized to the account director, demonstrating his aim to challenge the clients' perceptions of Hispanics as existing outside dominant US culture but also to disrupt the notion that cultural change is linear and predictable. However, Vince's apparent disappointment with how the client characterized its Hispanic consumers also seemed to make him even more excited to advise them on the appropriate demographic criteria for the ad test focus group.

His next steps involved using a subscription-based market research software called Simmons OneView to reshape a consumer profile of the campaign's target market. With this tool, Vince explained that he would be able to glean any revisions that needed to be made to the client's proposed respondent criteria. Vince ended the meeting with a spirited call to action for those of us in the room: "Don't be subjective about this shit." Lisa, the account director, sighed deeply, closing her laptop while nodding her head in agreement. "Right, we need numbers." Her passing commentary affirmed the symbolic value of quantitative data within the advertising industry's racial information system "as ritualistic assurance" of decision-making and risk mitigation.[47]

Vince gathered his things, and I followed him and Kyle into another conference room to observe his re-creation of a consumer profile on the Simmons software (now known as MRI-Simmons). "Simmons delivers the mindset of the American consumer," professed one of the company's sales presentations. Accessing the company's National Consumer Study (NCS), a quarterly survey consisting of a sample of twenty-five thousand US adults, strategists use the platform to create custom reports and analyze hundreds of demographic and psychographic variables "on product and brand usage, spending behavior, media usage/habits, and more."[48]

The Simmons platform is also considered the gold-standard research tool for Hispanic advertising because of its annual National Hispanic Consumer Study (NHCS). According to company press materials, the NHCS is "the only national, multi-media syndicated research instrument targeting the Hispanic market."[49] The NHCS is conducted annually with approximately seventy-five hundred Hispanic adults who are recruited from high-density Hispanic zip codes via a telephone interview.[50] Selected respondents are then mailed a survey booklet to complete in the language of their choice (Spanish or English). Simmons surveys contain questions on "Hispanic cultural identification" that the company then uses to measure survey respondents' attitudes and opinions on a range of subject matter, from "heritage" to "language use" to those who "have a personal appearance that reflects Hispanic/Latino."[51]

While Vince logged on to the Simmons software, Kyle, the junior strategist on the account, tacked onto a bright-orange corkboard wall several pages from a segmentation study that the pain reliever brand had previously commissioned from a multicultural market research firm. Brands typically commission segmentation studies to investigate ways to divide a broader target market into smaller subgroups based on shared demographics, behaviors, or dispositions. The data are used with the end goal of developing strategies and tactics for different market segments. According to the documents Kyle pinned up on the wall, the pain reliever brand had paid a multicultural market research firm to conduct a survey with nearly one thousand US Hispanics to help identify opportunities to cultivate more "nuanced emotional connections to Hispanic consumers," read the report.

The research company pinpointed the "Hispanic Positive Pain Fighter" as the consumer segment that presented the biggest growth opportunity for the pain reliever brand. The firm described the positive pain fighters as a relatively young population with an average age hovering in the mid-thirties, educated, and economically stable, with most of them earning $75,000 annually. "Positive pain fighters" were depicted as strong believers in the power of positivity in one's life and health outcomes, coupled with having a "traditionally Hispanic" relationship to pain, which was described by the company as a fondness for using health products from Latin America and using exclusively Spanish to get information about new medications. Most strikingly, the research company claimed that being "stoic in the face of pain" was an affective trait inherent to Hispanics. Indeed, the racial stereotype that people classified as Hispanic have a higher pain tolerance pervades American medical settings as well, leading to Hispanics being less likely than non-Hispanic whites to be given pain relief medication in emergency rooms.[52]

"What did the brand define as the positive pain fighters?" Vince asked Kyle, who was pensively studying the collage of pages pinned onto the wall. Kyle focused his attention on a page that featured an image of an attractive, brown-haired, olive-skinned woman in her twenties who was smiling while wearing a trendy motorcycle jacket. A speech bubble placed above her head attested that "Hispanics are not going to let pain take away from their happiness. It might put them down from time to time, but they are not ones to easily give up. They can control pain by staying positive and by managing their symptoms when they are severe."

Kyle glanced back at Vince. "We are looking for a positive disposition. They're saying that Hispanics have generally a positive attitude to life, and they have an indifference to pain."

"OK, so they must be Hispanic and open to pain relievers," Vince sighed, as his fingers moved rapidly across his keyboard. "Now, I'm going to try to find attitudes." He clicked on a drop-down menu called "the optimism metric," selected the phrase "I am an optimist," and dragged it into an area at a lower corner of the Simmons software interface.

"Should we put an age range on it?" Vince asked. Before Kyle could answer, Vince replied, "Let's go with twenty-five to forty-nine," and clicked his cursor. Vince dragged, dropped, and stacked up the Hispanic Positive Pain Fighter's attributes like one would items in an online shopping cart. Once Vince collected all the variables, he clicked an icon to "run" the data and after a few seconds the Simmons software produced an Excel spreadsheet.

"Here are our positive pain fighters!" Vince exclaimed proudly after downloading the file. The consumer profile he had created contained numerous rows of data about the Hispanic Positive Pain Fighter segment's median household income, age, marital status, education level, and countries of origin. What to me looked like a dizzying array of numbers and percentages was for Vince an anthropomorphized conjuring of an existing population of Hispanics, brought to life in the agency's conference room with the help of the Simmons research platform.

Vince laid out why the consumer profile he had made was such a marvel: "With that re-created group, I can query the living daylights out of it—their insights on health, wellness, and life. I can tell you about their overall mindset." Vince reputed the Excel spreadsheet as one would a vaunted totem, capable of transparently representing the Hispanic Positive Pain Fighter population with truth and accuracy. Yet, as sociologist Michael Rodríguez-Muñiz observes, "Data does not convey bare truth. . . . Rather, they are like a ventriloquist dummy; they must be made to speak."[53] In this case, Vince could use the Simmons software and data export to say what he wanted to hear—namely, that his initial reservations about the client's screening criteria for the focus group were well founded, thus reinforcing the validity and value of Soar's multicultural strategy expertise.

Vince's process of reproducing the Hispanic Positive Pain Fighter segment with Simmons illustrates the role of market research software in making racial markets and highlights a key practice within advertising's racial information system. The Hispanic Positive Pain Fighter, represented in an Excel table reflective of human attributes, echoes media scholar Ien

Ang's analysis of how television ratings statistics create "fictive pictures of the audience."[54] Ang explains that such representations are not false but fabricated—abstractions constructed from data rather than in direct interaction with actual viewers. Similarly, the Hispanic Positive Pain Fighter is a commercial racial typology generated by the advertiser, strategists, market research companies, and segmentation software; it is an ideal racial type, "which can only be known and encountered in and through discursive representations such as . . . the statistical figure."[55] Multicultural strategists like Vince invent racial markets with data and software that claim merely to discover them.

Amid multicultural strategists' desires to produce nuanced, nonstereotypical portrayals of multicultural consumers, their embeddedness in advertising's audience rationalization procedures can lead to the reproduction of limiting conventions they often chafe against. Cultural theorist Anamik Saha observes that capitalist logics of rationalization within the culture industries—such as the emphasis on specialized labor, formatting, measurement, and control—lead to the creation of products designed primarily to ensure economic returns. This process often reinforces racialization by emphasizing historical forms of difference as a means of market segmentation and commodification.[56] Market segments, as cultural commodities, "have racial logics structured into them that ensure race is made in a consistent, reductive, and homogeneous fashion."[57] When racial categories are treated as fixed traits that directly shape behavior and identity, multicultural strategy's *nuance* obscures the unstable, political nature of racial meaning-making—how subjectivity is shaped by social and political structures rather than racial essence.[58]

The Hispanic Positive Pain Fighter market is a racial formation produced "as an instrumental convenience in the circulation of goods,"[59] predicated on theories that envision race as an essential trait that impels behaviors and psychological dispositions.[60] To be sure, the production and circulation of this type of commercial racial knowledge does not necessarily mean that nodes in advertising's racial information system, including strategists, audience measurement, and market research firms, are not self-aware of the limitations of these frameworks. In the methodology section of a 2019 report titled *La Oportunidad Latinx* (figure 2.3), Nielsen, the storied audience measurement and market research firm, admits the following: "The profiles of Latinx households featured in this report were gathered using an independent online survey, which was voluntarily completed by households. The responses are the personal opinions of re-

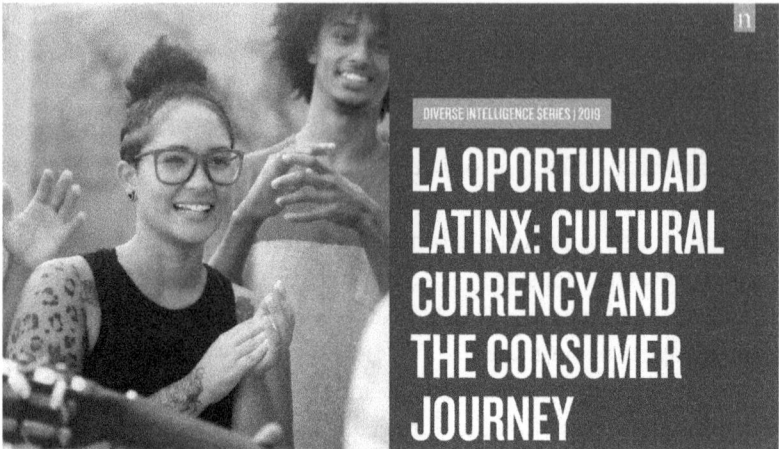

2.3 The first page of audience measurement firm Nielsen's 2019 report *La Oportunidad Latinx: Cultural Currency and the Consumer Journey*, which offers research on the Latinx audience/market segment.

spondents and should not be interpreted as a scientific analysis of Latinx consumer sentiment as a whole. Rather, the responses contained in household profiles can be read as a contextual background to the Nielsen data in the report."[61]

Despite the disclaimer, during my fieldwork, I frequently observed advertising industry professionals use Nielsen and other quantitative-data sources like Simmons OneView as reliably generalizable. These sources are taken for granted as providing objective social facts used to justify the respective business goals for which the data are being invoked.

Advertising strategy's penchant for quantitative data is meant to offer advertisers "a sense of control and foster the illusion that the multiplicity of experience can be contained."[62] This approach strives to mitigate the risks and unpredictability inherent in advertising production and reception. Despite Vince's "trust in numbers" to convey nuanced insights about Hispanic consumers, he also approached the process with cynicism and self-aware ambivalence. He recognized that his racial expertise depended not just on uncovering "truths" about Hispanic consumers but on using data to craft a compelling narrative that sold his agency's proficiencies and ideas to the client. Indeed, as Vince pointed out to me, advertising's racial research and measurement often serves to validate decisions already in progress. Strategists like Vince, while aware of these limitations, find themselves contending with and working within the rationalizing assumptions of the industry's racial information system. "In marketing, you have to mitigate risk, to prove that what you are doing will succeed," Vince explained as he prepared for his lunch break. "Marketers use research like drunk people use street poles: for support."

As advertising becomes more digitized and hypertargeted, the question of what it means to be included in American commercial representation has gained new urgency within multicultural advertising. In the twenty-first century, representation in large-scale audience datasets—now in the form of aggregated clicks, site visits, and social media behaviors—has become crucial for multicultural marketing. However, if racialized consumer segmentation only matters in predicting behavior, what role do race and ethnicity play in digital advertising, where tech platforms, data brokers, and e-commerce sites already know what users buy, when, and how? In the digital advertising economy, audience data are the primary site of racial representation, and the future of multicultural marketing depends on navigating this landscape. Chapter 3 explores how multicultural advertising professionals are working to integrate themselves into the surveillance apparatus of online behavioral advertising and the new racial science at its core.

3 REACHING "VERIFIED HISPANICS" / THE RACIAL SCIENCE OF DIGITAL ADVERTISING

One morning at Vista, the New York City–based media agency where I was interning, I was invited to attend a weekly "digital reporting call" with a mobile phone carrier client. Media agencies are the companies that advertisers hire to strategize where to place their promotional content so that the intended audiences will see it. That day, I sat with about ten Vista staff who were gathered around a conference table to review the performance of an ongoing digital advertising campaign targeting a US-based audience identified as "Hispanics in-market for phones and phone plans." Everyone had the same Excel spreadsheet open on their laptops, which provided detailed information of the campaign's results from the previous week, including metrics like the number of "impressions" (the frequency with which the brand's ad is displayed on user screens), total number of times the ad had been clicked (click through rate), and the cost per click incurred by the brand.

One of Vista's digital advertising specialists—a young white woman in her early twenties with sandy-brown hair—tightly clutched a mug of tea as she stretched her neck in the direction of the phone at the center of the conference table. She relayed to the client, who was on speakerphone, the digital advertising campaign strategies that had been "working well so far." The wireless phone company was spending a considerable portion of its budget targeting "bilingual Spanish speakers" across the internet, and the tactic was proving successful in generating new sales prospects while keeping advertising costs reasonably low. But the surefire winning tactic was "Hispanic audience retargeting," a technique that displays advertisements to internet users who had been identified as Hispanic and who had also previously visited the mobile phone carrier's website or social media pages. The intricacy and meticulousness involved in prompting people to perform such seemingly mundane actions as clicking or tapping on a banner advertisement were striking, bordering on obsessive. However, my curiosity was directed more toward how both Vista's digital advertising team and the client were confident in the "Hispanic" identity of the consumers whose attention they sought after on the internet, and the methods being used to conduct this form of online racial profiling.

Advertisers in the United States now expend the majority of their annual marketing budgets—to the tune of over $260 billion—on data-driven targeting tactics.[1] This phenomenon, known as online behavioral advertising, entails "the practice of monitoring people's online behavior and using the collected information to show people individually targeted advertisements."[2] Such personal data—which includes everything from web browsing, articles read, search histories, location, language settings, app usage, purchases, social media activity, and more—is algorithmically analyzed and used to infer identity and place people into audience categories that marketers can target with tailored online advertisements. From Google and Meta to retailers like Amazon, mobile apps, and lesser-known third-party companies, the sweeping scale of the commercial surveillance and data collection apparatus exceeds many internet users' full awareness yet impacts us all; it is the fuel in the roaring engine of the US internet economy, providing funding for nearly all commercial websites in the United States.[3] Whether labeled by data companies as "Connected Bohemians," "Heavy Spenders," or "Hispanics in the Market for an iPhone," internet users are subject to surveillance and algorithmic segmentation and commercialization, underscoring the role that digital media and marketing companies wield in shaping the contemporary practices and politics of human classification.[4]

Advertising technology companies have promised brands that audience data are the key to the long-awaited marketing holy grail: the ability to reach the right consumer, with the right message, at the right time, and for the most efficient price. Data-driven behavioral advertising, these companies boast, enables advertisers to "crack identity" by leveraging predictive analytics technologies.[5] This shift has emboldened some marketers to declare that "demographics are dead" when it comes to market segmentation, leading them to instead concentrate on seemingly more precise categories that reflect consumers' actual online behaviors and interests.[6]

As marketing budgets increasingly shift toward digital platforms, multicultural marketing's present and future relevance to advertisers hinges on its ability to integrate with the technological frameworks of online behavioral advertising and data collection. A central aspect of this evolution involves how effectively machine learning can be used to infer consumers' racial and ethnic identities from internet behavior and other digital traces.

In this chapter, I examine how the American advertising industry's racial information system is adapting to the rising dominance of online behavioral advertising. Rather than relying on the hallmark visual markers of racial identification like skin color and facial features, in the digital advertising landscape racial identities are increasingly assigned to users through algorithmic analysis—often without the user's full awareness of how they are being classified. This shift redefines racial categorization not just as a political and sociocultural practice but also as a technological process, with marketing companies using digitized behavioral data—like site visits, app downloads, and language preferences—to predict and classify a user's race. For data companies selling race-based audience data to advertisers, their business models draw on a centuries-old legacy of racial science, leveraging the authority of technology and measurement to reinforce the legitimacy of racial categories as predictive mechanisms for extraction and control. Relying on surveillance, these companies sell the capacity to infer race from online behavior and proprietary identification formulas, further embedding racial classification into systems of economic and social regulation.

However, for multicultural marketers striving to maintain relevance in the digitized platform economy, many argue that there is insufficient data to conduct racially targeted digital marketing effectively at scale. In response, an advocacy movement within the multicultural marketing industry has emerged, calling on data companies to improve the accuracy, availability, and representation of race-based "multicultural" audiences in the data market. Although framed in the language of social justice and representation, this push for more plentiful and precise racial marketing data primarily serves business interests. It overlooks the broader harms associated with increased commercial surveillance of racialized people in American society, reinforcing systems of data extraction and control.

When I met Tom, an Asian American digital advertising strategist at Vista, he was involved in planning a digital ad campaign strategy for an automotive company aiming to reach Hispanic consumers on the West Coast of the United States. I asked Tom how he was sure that the users seeing his client's ads were indeed "Hispanic." Tom explained, "There are various triggers we use. For instance, it could be the language setting on your device or operating system. For example, we can often target users based on whether they're browsing content in English or Spanish. But it's not just about language settings. It can also involve behavioral data, such as users who have visited Hispanic sites previously. Essentially, we look at past behaviors to categorize users into specific buckets."[7] He proceeded to explain an aspect of the campaign aimed at targeting a Hispanic audience on a popular sports website: "We have reached out to data providers that have Hispanic data, and they can see if a user has a Hispanic affinity or Hispanic behavior, or if they've been on Spanish sites or whatever." Tom's casual reference to the audience data company's capabilities framed "Hispanic behavior" as an object—something that could digitally ascertained, predicted, and sold.

Multicultural marketing's relevance in the digital age is reliant on the transformation of race and ethnic classification into audience data, which is then sold and used to deliver targeted advertisements across the internet. "The specialization in Hispanic advertising now occurs on the back end, rather than the front end," remarked the CEO of a Los Angeles-based multicultural market research company in a trade press article.[8] Data companies build audience segment models using historical data and statistical analysis to predict the "typical" behaviors and characteristics of specific groups. For instance, users might be grouped into a segment like "Hispanics in the market for an iPhone" based on their online activity. Behaviors such as searching for iPhone models on a search engine, visiting tech-related sites in Spanish, physically visiting stores in Hispanic-majority areas, or interacting with iPhone-specific ads are continuously tracked. Algorithms then assign users a "fit" score based on how closely their actions match the predefined segment model of a "Hispanic in the market for an iPhone." Once a user is classified into an audience segment, they are targeted with ads that are believed to most likely resonate with that segment. This process is dynamic, as a user's classification can change over time with new behaviors, interactions, and modifications of models.

Online behavioral advertising represents a new form of capitalist accumulation and extraction, as business historian Shoshana Zuboff observes, where value is generated not from material goods but from monitoring, measuring, and monetizing predictions about human behavior as intangible data.[9] In this system, people's future actions become a commodity, with companies competing to control and sell these predictions with the aim of manipulating behavior for profit. Oscar Gandy Jr. describes this as a form of information-based surveillance that "defines life in the modern capitalist economy," functioning as a "discriminatory technology" that sorts people into groups based on their presumed economic value to companies.[10]

A 2021 Facebook market research study claimed that "online advertising featuring diversity tends to have higher ad recall," meaning that consumers consider such ads more memorable and enjoyable.[11] Marketers tend to present racially targeted online behavioral advertising as a consumer-driven desire that is also a business imperative for a nation undergoing demographic change. "[Consumers] want brands to recognize them not just as a demographic statistic but as individuals with specific desires and motivations," writes multicultural market researcher Sylvia Vidal in a Hispanic marketing blog. "Inclusion, in this sense, becomes a form of personalization, where marketing efforts are tailored to fit the unique identity of each consumer."[12]

Companies specializing in the manufacture and sale of Hispanic audience data promise exactly this level of targeted personalization. Data company Retargetly describes the Hispanic audience data business in its marketing materials as the "holy grail" for media planning and buying.[13] Retargetly and other companies like it monitor internet users by embedding tracking technology like cookies or pixels on partnered websites and mobile apps, which allow the company to classify users' devices into audience segments, determined by proprietary algorithms. Lotame, an advertising technology company and audience data provider, offers advertisers audience data categorized into various Hispanic subgroups, including Hispanics of specific genders, age demographics, income levels, countries of origin, purchase intentions, inferred "cultural interests," and "acculturation levels."[14]

Data broker giant Acxiom markets to advertisers its proprietary methods for identifying Hispanic consumers through computational analyses of user data collected from various sources, including government voting records and third-party services. The company's Personicx suite, which provides "segmentation solutions," offers Personicx Hispanic: "the most advanced and powerful classification [of Hispanic consumers] in the market." This tool claims to classify each Hispanic consumer in the United States into "55 clusters, based on factors such as age, income, net worth, marital status, presence and age of children, generations in the household and Hispanic assimilation," the last being the degree to which a consumer has adopted English and the culture of the United States. Acxiom assures marketers of the economic value of its algorithmic technology when applied to multicultural marketing, stating that "to fully realize the potential of the Hispanic market, and to maximize the effectiveness of [Hispanic marketing] campaigns, marketers need segments that are statistically derived, meaningful, [and] stable."[15]

At their core, the processes by which marketing and data companies manufacture Hispanics as audience data are conducted through *racializing surveillance*, which sociologist Simone Browne defines as a form of social control where surveillance practices reinforce "boundaries, borders, and bodies along racial lines, and where the outcome is often discriminatory treatment of those who are negatively racialized."[16] In *Dark Matters: On the Surveillance of Blackness*, Browne explores how surveillance practices, employed by both governments and private companies, are used to maintain and exploit racist power structures and the social divisions they create.[17] She links modern data surveillance practices to the transatlantic slave trade, where surveillance was crucial for the creation of "Blackness as a saleable commodity in the Western Hemisphere."[18] Slaveholders used various surveillance methods, such as descriptive advertisements to track down those who escaped, mutilating enslaved peoples' bodies with insignias that branded them as marketable property, and implementing laws like slave codes and lantern laws to restrict their movement and ensure control.

Browne argues that historical racialized surveillance techniques, such as those used during slavery, have paved the way for modern technologies like biometric monitoring, facial recognition, location tracking, and predictive policing—tools employed by governments, law enforcement, and private companies to "forecast" crime, suppress racial justice movements, and overpolice marginalized communities.[19] She highlights how the algorithms at the basis of these tracking technologies transform "parts, pieces, and . . . performances of the body" into searchable, commodifiable data, facilitating the dehumanization and racialization of individuals by marking them as "other" and suspect.[20] This process extends to the "cybernetic border" described by Iván Chaar López as the increasing integration of digital technologies and automation in the governance and control of international borders that disproportionately targets groups like Mexicans, Arabs, and Muslims, reinforcing their status as perpetual foreigners.[21]

While the technologies and mediums implicated in the boom of online behavioral advertising are relatively new, the imposition of surveillance as a form of racialized disciplinary power is not, especially for populations such as "immigrants, minorities, and workers, both within and outside the United States," writes cultural anthropologist Sareeta Amrute.[22] Scholars have argued that digital technologies and algorithms, especially within the commercialized internet landscape of the United States, contribute to a fragmented society and reproduce racial discrimination.[23] Latanya Sweeney's research revealed that Google AdSense advertising algorithms disproportionately associate names commonly racialized as Black with criminal background checks, regardless of an individual's actual history.[24] Safiya Noble highlights that Google and other search engines, driven by advertising revenue, prioritize content that generates clicks and profits over accuracy, resulting in algorithms amplifying racial and gender stereotypes, as seen in searches for terms like *Black girls* or *Latina women*, which yield hypersexualized or harmful content. Noble argues that these corporate-driven priorities perpetuate intersecting oppressions of racism and sexism, a form of "technological redlining" that "reinforce[s] oppressive social relationships."[25]

In the digital advertising realm, user data collection and analytics are geared toward optimizing marketing efforts that directly address the intended consumer wherever they are on the internet. "Addressability is about discrimination and exclusion/inclusion. It is a technical means of delimiting the population of message recipients, sometimes at the level of individuals or individual devices," observes communications theorist Lee McGuigan.[26] This is where racializing surveillance comes into play—by companies' deployment of machine learning techniques to assign racial significance to digitized performances of the body—such as clicks, video views, and app downloads, which have only recently become measurable and commodifiable. Much like any other product, racial audience data are branded, marketed, and sold through demand-side platforms (DSPs), software systems used to automate the purchase of digital ad inventory. DSPs integrate with third-party data providers, who license audience segments to advertisers for a fee, sometimes through DSP-operated audience marketplaces. Digital advertising's racializing surveillance classifies based on "a vision of social organization in which users are what they do."[27]

During a digital advertising professional development training I attended while interning at Vista, I observed how media agency employees, acting on behalf of their clients, utilized software platforms to access racially categorized audience segments. One of the agency's digital advertising specialists demonstrated this to me by typing "Hispanic" into the DSP's audience marketplace search bar, which generated a list of data broker companies offering a variety of "Hispanics" labeled with the respective brand names such as "Hispanic Culture Extreme," "US Hispanic Fashion and Beauty," "Hispanic Culture: Strong Affinity," and "Hispanic Premium." The specialist explained the significance of these labels to me: "'Strong affinity' means that you might be researching Spanish music. So, it shows that you have sentiments towards the Hispanic culture. With 'culture extreme,' I'm assuming that you consume mostly just Spanish media. For 'premium,' I think it's just branding."[28] DSPs present racial populations as marketable data commodities, offering them for selection and sale from a menu like any other product.[29]

Sales pitches from Hispanic audience data purveyors were a regular occurrence during my internship at Vista. One afternoon, the agency's multicultural brand strategy team held a meeting with a sales representative from a company I will refer to as Hispanitech, an audience data provider and digital advertising network.[30] Hispanitech purchases US-based online advertising inventory—such as web banners and display ads embedded within website content—from various Latin American and Spanish publishers, both within and outside the United States. They then resell this inventory, as well as access to decoupled audience data, to advertisers planning digital campaigns targeting US Hispanic consumers.

As Andy, the affable Hispanitech sales representative, got his laptop set up to project a PowerPoint presentation, he queried the Vista multicultural brand team about the advertisers that were still "active" in the United States' Hispanic digital advertising space. Daphne, one of Vista's multicultural brand strategists, furrowed her brows as she recounted with frustration that a fast-food restaurant chain had recently stopped its US Hispanic digital advertising and explained her ongoing efforts to encourage her colleagues at the agency to present multicultural audience targeting as a viable and valuable component of their media budgets. "We're constantly educating our internal teams on the value of reaching the multicultural segments separately, reaching them in a culturally relevant way," she declared. Andy nodded in agreement. "Your messaging *has* to differentiate."

As we ate the salads provided by Hispanitech, Andy began his sales presentation, highlighting the company's extensive access to US Hispanic audience data. He explained that Hispanitech had partnerships with various websites focused on Latin American and Hispanic cultural content, allowing them to install tracking technologies such as pixels and cookies on these sites. These tools monitor visitor activity, collecting detailed data at both the page and browser levels, along with comprehensive behavioral insights such as browsing history, time spent on pages, and clicked links. Through these methods, Hispanitech makes "Hispanics" by "using everything it can measure."[31]

During Andy's sales pitch, I asked if he could use me as a hypothetical user in Hispanitech's audience database to clarify how their technology worked. Based on a quick assessment of my appearance, his knowledge of my occupation as a researcher, my admitted lack of Spanish-language skills, and my Nuyorican heritage, which I shared during small talk, Andy speculated that Hispanitech would classify me similarly to himself—as part of the "acculturated" audience segment. He characterized this group as having a higher level of cultural adaptation to American life, such as primarily using English-language web browser settings and visiting websites *not* specifically labeled as "Hispanic" (that is, Spanish-language news and entertainment sites from the Dominican Republic and other Latin American countries). Andy contrasted me with the "less acculturated" audience segment, which he discussed by invoking a hypothetical "45-year-old man in the Bronx," whom he described as a type of "Hispanic" who is frequently consuming content on Spanish-language websites hosted by Latin American publishers.

Hispanitech's classification of "acculturated" versus "unacculturated" Hispanic audience data reflects "epistemologically fabricated" digital archetypes—categories that are constructed within US racialized frameworks of personhood, emphasizing specific identity boundaries that are then reproduced through marketing segmentation algorithms.[32] The concept of "acculturation," which Hispanitech's segmentation relies on, has its roots in early twentieth-century American anthropology and sociology, positing that immigrants would gradually align their cultural practices with an American national "mainstream," often characterized as "largely white, Protestant, and Anglo-Saxon."[33]

Although the acculturation framework is debated and even discredited in some marketing circles, multicultural marketers like those at Hispanitech use it to inform the modeling of audiences for digital marketing.[34] A key part of this process involves training machine learning models to analyze user data and classify individuals as "acculturated" or "unacculturated" Hispanics. This is achieved during the feature selection phase of model training, where data scientists, marketers, and other business stakeholders collaborate to identify the most relevant data points they believe to be strong indicators of Hispanic identity —such as visiting Spanish-language websites, device language preferences, and engaging with Hispanic-themed cultural content. An algorithm is then trained on labeled data representing these preselected features to recognize patterns and relationships between them and the target outcome—"Hispanic" identity. Once trained, the machine learning model infers whether new users' data fit into modeled Hispanic identity, enabling marketers to tailor advertising campaigns accordingly. Hispanitech places particular emphasis on Spanish language as a defining feature of "unacculturated" Hispanic identity, reflecting a long-standing trend in multicultural marketing that positions Spanish as the "authentic" marker of the Hispanic market. As Arlene Dávila argues, this dichotomy between Hispanic and American cultures reinforces a cultural hierarchy, treating these categories as naturalized, rigid, distinct entities rather than recognizing their fluidity and overlap.[35]

Hispanitech markets its "Hispanic" audience segments based on the implicit assumption that users identified as such will, with a reliable degree of probability, self-identify as Hispanic on the other side of their screen. Rampant fraud in the digital advertising ecosystem has impelled audience data companies to sell their wares through discourses that assure their clients—advertisers—of the veracity of their audience data, first as representing real human beings (and not bots) and then as members of certain consumer segments. External third-party verification is a quintessential part of the processes by which such companies validate the objects of its gaze.[36] Hispanitech capitalizes on this by positioning itself as a leader in "verified U.S. Hispanic reach." As Andy noted during the meeting in the Vista conference room, "Our biggest competitive differentiator is verified reach—some players may have larger reach, but you are more likely to reach a verified U.S. Hispanic with us."

Hispanitech professes the verifiability of its data to advertisers by referencing ComScore, an audience measurement and analytics firm that provides companies with information on digital media consumption and website audience demographics. Media agencies often use the ComScore software during the planning and consumer profiling phase to understand the kinds of websites a campaign's target audience visits. "ComScore is the Nielsen of digital," Andy explained. "They are a governing body, a third-party verification service that says, 'This person isn't fuckin' lying.'" A company like Hispanitech partners with ComScore to evaluate the demographics of the visitors to its Hispanic network websites from which it is collecting audience data. Using proprietary statistical methods to ascertain a website's "audience composition," ComScore has developed its own criteria for measuring Hispanic user identity online, which includes analyses of recruited users' Spanish-language web pages viewed, and of surnames.[37]

For Hispanitech, there is symbolic and economic value associated with ComScore's third-party verification of its audience data stock as authentically representing "Hispanic" users. Authenticity, or an affective state of being considered original, trustworthy, and thus reliable, pervades contemporary marketing discourse with the notion that brands can be arbiters of human connection despite the "the crassness of capital exchange."[38] An "authentic" brand is one that is perceived as genuinely embodying the product it represents—one whose use value and social value align with customers' expectations, reinforcing its credibility and market appeal.

Hispanitech draws on racial authenticity rhetoric to market and sell its audience data to advertisers as representing "verified" Hispanic consumers, implying that there is both an objective and a quantifiable way to measure and ascertain Hispanic identity. Racial authenticity discourse reduces race to a set of predefined characteristics, framing it as an essentialized category, ignoring its reality as a historically contingent and political construct. Anthropologist John L. Jackson, drawing on philosopher K. Anthony Appiah, critiques racial authenticity discourse for "reducing people to little more than objects of racial discourse, [or] characters in racial scripts" that create and enforce boundaries of racial belonging—a kind of "social incarceration."[39] Hispanitech's claim that Hispanic identity can be distilled into discrete processable data points uses racial authenticity as both a marketing tool and a mechanism for surveillance. By classifying and scrutinizing internet users based on their "algorithmic fit" to its proprietary models of Hispanic identity, Hispanitech establishes and sells its own criteria for racial classification.[40] Data-driven advertising companies like Hispanitech transform "Hispanic" identity into an algorithmically derived commodity, detaching it from personal subjectivity and stripping it of political history, instability, and its inherent complexities and contradictions.

The racialization of internet users for advertising purposes occurs through the "disembodied gaze" of data companies, which are empowered by lax US regulations to collect, analyze, and sell vast amounts of personal data for profit, often with minimal transparency or accountability.[41] Crucially, in the United States, the audience data generated from user behavior do not belong to those being monitored but are treated as the property of the corporations that collect and monetize this data for advertisers.[42]

While companies like Hispanitech claim to sell "verifiable Hispanics" to advertisers, it is important to note that this classification is not static. Machine learning models are continuously modified, allowing the definition of "Hispanic" to shift over time. Through constant surveillance of user activities—such as browsing history, social media engagement, purchasing behavior, and app usage—these models perpetually reanalyze and reclassify users. As one's digital interactions change, so too does their classification, making it possible for a user to be categorized as "Hispanic" one month and not the next. With new data inputs and algorithmic refinements, the model's inference of Hispanic identity can change.

Yet, by marketing Hispanic data within the epistemic authority of machine learning and data science, companies like Hispanitech extend the legacy of racial science from previous centuries, reinforcing notions of racial differences by presenting these categories as objective and computationally derived. Predictive models not only reproduce existing racial categories but also redefine them, as algorithms ascribe racial identity through invisible back-end processes rather than historical visual markers. Science and technology studies scholar Beth Coleman observes how computer modeling and genetic mapping software re-present racial difference at the microcomputational level. Similarly, online advertising functions as a new form racial anthropometry where "there is no cranium to measure, but rather tendrils of information."[43] Visual markers and physical bodies are proverbially removed from the equation; instead, only digital traces matter. "What used to be a matter of flesh and blood is now highly abstracted data. Race has been made information," reconfigured through algorithmic surveillance and predictive analytics.[44]

Although digital advertising companies like Hispanitech profess the racial authenticity of their audience data, research has shown how dubious and overblown these claims of accuracy can be.[45] In fact, data companies often classify users into audience segments with which they might not self-identify.[46] Because models infer identity based on probabilities, any internet user who exhibits the behaviors deemed "Hispanic" by a given company could be classified as such even though it might not be a category with which the individual subjectively identifies. During my internship at Vista, I witnessed this routine racial misclassification happen firsthand. Several of the digital strategists who did not self-identify as "Hispanic" would joke about frequently receiving Spanish-language online ads meant for US Hispanic consumers while browsing the internet on their work laptops. They attributed this to the high volume of Spanish-language search terms and websites they had to visit when doing research for planning Hispanic targeted online advertising campaigns. Indeed, the supposedly tried-and-true measurement and classification methods of the digital advertising industry, which looks to web behavior as a proxy for racial identity, tend to lead to a great deal of user misclassification, which can prove problematic for companies investing marketing budgets in this form of racial profiling. "Digital targeting is an inexact science," admitted one of Vista's digital strategists, a self-identified Nigerian American who also received Spanish-language Hispanic targeted ads on his work computer. "There's just no way to ever achieve 100 percent anything. Our job is to get us as close to that 100 percent as possible and to work diligently to identify gaps where we can."

The rise of digital advertising has raised concerns within the multicultural marketing industry, as the shift toward behavioral rather than demographic segmentation threatens to diminish the utility of racially targeted marketing. A Miami-based Hispanic marketing agency executive warned in *Forbes* that advertisers are mistaken if they believe "behavioral segmentation makes cultural segmentation irrelevant," noting that while "behavioral segmentation tends to focus on what consumers do," cultural segmentation addresses "*why* they do it" and what messages and visuals resonate with different racial groups.[47] Despite multicultural marketers' efforts to control, rationalize, and predict consumer behavior, the process is subject to miscalculation and obfuscation. From the vantage point of multicultural marketing leaders in particular, these are business problems that must be solved.

DATA REPRESENTATION MATTERS

In 2019, fourteen senior marketing executives from the likes of Procter & Gamble, Target, General Mills, and Wells Fargo signed an open letter addressed to the audience data industry expressing their concerns about the "underrepresentation of multicultural consumers."[48] In the letter, published by the trade group Alliance for Inclusive and Multicultural Marketing (AIMM), the marketers expressed concerns that third-party data companies frequently underrepresent and misclassify multicultural consumers in the audience data they sell, thus making it difficult for advertisers to effectively conduct racially targeted digital advertising campaigns. "We strongly believe in the power of diversity and believe we have a responsibility to serve diverse consumers in the best possible way with our brands," penned the executives. "We call upon every major data provider—whether engaged in classifying consumers by ethnicity/race directly or whether they rely on a third-party source for classifying their own data—to join our efforts for greater transparency."[49]

Leaders in the multicultural marketing industry lament that "big data has a big diversity problem," often characterizing the market for multicultural audience data as "supply constrained."[50] A 2019 study conducted by AIMM on six US-based audience data companies revealed significant shortcomings in the multicultural data available for sale, finding that African Americans, Hispanics, and Asians were underrepresented relative to their proportions in the US population.[51] Additionally, among the companies audited, less than half of the data records were assigned a race or ethnicity.[52] Industry insiders attribute racial data issues to the outdated methodologies employed by data companies to classify records and internet users by race—methods which rely on analyses of surnames and web browsing behavior, with an emphasis on language preferences and consumption of culturally specific content.[53]

Another explanation for the dearth of multicultural audience data connects to emerging consumer data privacy legislation across several US states, as well as operational shifts within digital media platforms. In 2017, journalists at ProPublica exposed evidence that the social media platform Facebook/Meta permitted advertisers to include and exclude users from seeing housing and employment ads based on inferred racial identity, a practice that violated the Civil Rights Act and the Fair Housing Act.[54] In response, the company was sued by several states, leading it to discontinue "multicultural affinity targeting." Jose Villa, CEO of the multicultural advertising agency Sensis, reacted in *Digiday*, stating, "In the last few years, [digital multicultural marketing] has become a little more challenging, because a lot of the big players—particularly like social media platforms—have made it a lot more difficult to target people based on ethnicity."[55]

Public policy shifts are also a concern for multicultural marketers, particularly the patchwork of state-level consumer data privacy laws. States such as California, Colorado, Virginia, and Connecticut designate race and ethnicity as "sensitive information," requiring explicit consumer consent for data processing. These laws also mandate that consumers in these states have the right to opt out of tracking, further restricting marketer access to multicultural audience data.[56]

Multicultural marketing professionals express concern that racial audience data underrepresentation and inaccuracy is a critical inflection point for the industry. As Carlos Santiago, a multicultural market research executive and cofounder of the AIMM trade group, explained in *Advertising Age*: "If we cannot see multicultural segments with accuracy, then obviously the relevant messages infused with culture are going to fall short of the very careful creative process they were intended to create."[57] Santiago and others worry that without scalable audience data to target multicultural consumers with digital advertising, the intended consumers for those campaigns will neither see nor click on the ads made for them, undermining the effectiveness of multicultural marketing.

The 2019 AIMM report echoed warnings of the ripple effect that racial audience data underrepresentation could have on the multicultural marketing industry, emphasizing that if data companies misclassify Hispanic consumers, for example, their perceived economic value as a market demographic will diminish in the eyes of advertisers. "A 74 percent accuracy rate means that the value of the Hispanic consumer segment is being undervalued by about one-fourth. That could easily be the difference between the target audience being evaluated as profitable and worthy of investment, or not," the report stated.[58] In digital advertising, measurement of the return on investment (ROI) for campaigns is critical for determining success; if clicks, site visits, and sales cannot be measured and attributed to multicultural internet users, it becomes impossible to close the feedback loop for measuring the effectiveness of multicultural marketing online. For industry leaders, accurate and accessible racial audience data are essential to ensuring these groups—as well as the expertise of multicultural marketers—are recognized as worthy of advertiser attention and spending. As the majority of marketing budgets shift to digital advertising, racial data underrepresentation threatens to render the multicultural marketing business obsolete. "If we don't unite as a multicultural entity and advocate to address this problem with a balanced solution, our industry will only get more marginalized than it currently is," warned Gloria Constanza, a media buying executive at d'expósito & Partners.[59]

Industry leaders position the issue of racial audience data underrepresentation as a matter of social justice, often describing it as a form of "algorithmic bias"—a technological manifestation of the marginalization that people of color face in the marketplace and American society as a whole. In tones reminiscent of activist groups and social service agencies, some marketers suggest that the lack of racially classified audience data represents a form systemic disadvantage. David Queamante, an executive at the media agency UM, remarked that "diverse audiences are disadvantaged in a programmatic system," referring to the automated process of buying and selling digital ads, which heavily relies on audience data.[60] The "disadvantage" Queamante is purporting is multicultural consumers' limited exposure to racially targeted marketing, which he deems to be in and of itself inherently valuable. Positioning the underrepresentation of racial data as a form of erasure, executives like Queamante advocate for greater diversity in audience data to combat the marginalization of multicultural consumers in the media landscape, understanding this exclusion as a social harm. "The biggest challenge facing the industry is data privacy, and how removing race and ethnicity attributes from marketing data 'erases' people of color from the narrative," Queamante commented in 2024.[61]

Calls for racially inclusive audience data reached a head during the global racial justice movements of 2020, which brought increased scrutiny to racism in the advertising and media industries' employment practices and cultural production as well as in the market for advertising and media services.[62] This period also saw a resurgence of "buy Black" campaigns aimed at circulating capital within Black communities, reminiscent of Richard Nixon's post–civil rights era Black capitalism strategy, which sought to address urban social unrest through market-driven solutions.[63] In 2020, several advertisers and agencies launched public relations campaigns claiming to financially support Black-owned media companies through dedicated digital media buys, positioning these efforts as a form of economic reparations that could rectify racial disparities in media representation and advertising investment.

One popular initiative adopted across several US media agencies was the creation of curated "inclusion"-themed digital advertising marketplaces, also known as private marketplaces (PMPs). A PMP is a private digital advertising auction that combines the exclusivity of private marketplaces with automated ad-serving technology. In inclusion PMPs, publishers invite select advertisers to bid on premium ad-space inventory in publications targeting "diverse" consumers. Procter & Gamble, known for its industry-leading multicultural marketing initiatives, collaborated with the ad tech company The Trade Desk to develop a private programmatic marketplace aimed at connecting advertisers with Black-owned digital media publishers and their audiences.[64]

Mindshare, a leading media agency, in collaboration with feminine hygiene brand Kotex, launched the "Black Community PMP," designed to "amplify Black stories and voices across journalism and the arts and promote real inclusivity in media."[65] This effort claimed to redirect advertising funds to Black-owned digital media outlets, which suffered revenue declines due to widespread keyword blocking of terms like *George Floyd* and BLM and advertisers' concerns about placing ads near potentially polarizing Black Lives Matter protest content.[66]

Book publisher Penguin Random House was the first advertiser to participate in the ad tech company MediaMath's multicultural marketplace. MediaMath marketed its initiative as a form of economic support for racial justice, urging brands to invest in Black- and Hispanic-owned businesses by purchasing digital ad space targeting these audiences online. "It was a way for [Penguin Random House] to reach their target audience, while putting money back in the minority community," said a MediaMath executive about the book publisher's use of the multicultural PMP.[67] "Brands can also expand their reach and communicate their solidarity on key issues with the use of tools that provide audiences of consumers who have self-identified as supporting cultural movements, such as Black Lives Matter," relayed the adtech company in a press release.[68]

MediaMath's multicultural marketplace monetized Black Lives Matter by turning it into a data point for audience segmentation, transforming political support for racial justice into a consumer attribute for targeted digital marketing. The rise of inclusion PMPs and multicultural audience marketplaces promoted racial representation in online advertising as a premium ad-tech service, while simultaneously offering advertisers the chance to gain social prestige for supporting diversity and inclusion — especially at a time when racial justice was a prominent issue framed as top of mind for coveted consumer demographics like Gen Z.

The multicultural marketing industry's advocacy for producing more plentiful and accurate racial audience data is aligned with the rousing "representation matters" rhetoric that has become prevalent across popular discourse, which espouses increased media visibility of people of color as an urgent social justice imperative and a reflection of social standing. For marketers and consumers alike, this emphasis on a "cultural politics of recognition and media visibility" hinges on an "assumption [that] equate[s] greater visibility with political power," based on the belief that "increased visibility might in turn effect some measure of cultural justice, including empathy and sensitivity on the part of the powerful and the dominant groups to lives of poor, marginal, and dominated people," observes media theorist Herman Gray.[69]

What, then, are we to make of the multicultural marketing industry's emphasis on the cultural politics of representation as a justification for increased corporate surveillance, where people are profiled and targeted by companies under the guise of promoting racial justice through consumer capitalism? Sociologist Ruha Benjamin, in her analysis of global efforts to diversify law enforcement's facial recognition software datasets, calls attention to the potential pitfalls of data inclusion. She asks, "While inclusion and accuracy are worthy goals in the abstract, given the encoding of longstanding racism in discriminatory design, what does it mean to be included, and hence more accurately identifiable, in an unjust set of social relations?"[70]

Multicultural marketing's advocacy for more plentiful and accurate racial marketing data potentially subjects people racialized as multicultural to "the wrong kinds of attention," as legal scholar Anita Allen notes.[71] From predictive policing and criminalization, to the targeted promotions of predatory payday loans, unhealthy foods, and "illusory money-making schemes," there are numerous downsides to racial digital inclusion that "reproduce, harness, and entrench racially exploitative processes and systems."[72]

Indeed, the customers for racialized consumer data extend beyond marketers selling shampoo or cell phones. Commercial audience data is also sold to government and law-enforcement agencies. Investigative reports have revealed that the Department of Homeland Security, Immigration and Customs Enforcement (ICE), and the Department of Defense have purchased location data from marketing companies, harvested from mobile apps, used to track Muslims and Arab communities both within the United States and in the Middle East, as well as to surveil and apprehend undocumented migrants at the US–Mexico border.[73]

Yet marketing industry advocates for more racially inclusive audience data contend that the surveillance inherent in digital advertising offers valuable trade-offs for consumers, such as exposure to more relevant and engaging media and marketing, as well as free access to online content. Scott McKinley, CEO of the data company TruthSet, acknowledged in a trade press op-ed that while concerns about the collection of race and ethnicity data in relation to privacy and discrimination are "valid and warranted," excluding such data could further disadvantage multicultural communities by limiting their enjoyment of marketing, goods, and services that could benefit their lives.[74] He argues that without accurate racial data, brands risk delivering generic messaging that not only fails to reach the right consumer, resulting in lost revenue, but also fails to affirm the value of these consumers in society, leading to further social marginalization. "A beauty brand may want to target a variety of consumers—men and women, darker and lighter skin tones, etc.—with specific messaging. Losing ethnicity data means you're potentially delivering the same message to a Hispanic man as you are to an Asian-American woman."[75] McKinley framed the use of racialized surveillance in online advertising as a positive social force, arguing that race and ethnicity data could help address "systemic discrimination in marketing" by ensuring people of color receive tailored messages for products aligned with their specific interests and needs. A recurring narrative in these discussions frames targeted digital advertising as a social imperative, implying that being surveilled is almost akin to a right, reinforcing the notion that personalized marketing is essential for inclusion and equality in both the marketplace and American society at large. This dynamic is emblematic of what sociologist Tressie McMillan Cottom identifies as the fundamentally predacious dimensions of racialized digital capitalism; the incorporation of racialized populations into consumer capitalism is celebrated for its "ostensibly democratizing" potential but is ultimately enacted "on extractive terms."[76]

Multicultural marketing's focus on racial inclusion in audience data prioritizes corporate interests while overlooking the harms of tracking people as marketing targets. Commercialized racial profiling blurs the line between consumerism and criminalization, leaving people susceptible not only to marketing exploitation but also to discriminatory forms of corporate and state surveillance. Sociologist Anna Hoffmann's critique of the dating app Tinder's expansion of gender categories provides a fitting example of how the celebratory tone around making marketing data more diverse and inclusive can both naturalize and "neutralize" critical discussions about whether such data should be collected in the first place.[77]

"Racism has always been about predicting, about making certain racial groups seem predisposed to do bad things and justifying controlling them," observes legal scholar Dorothy Roberts.[78] The commercialization of racialized surveillance exposes the underlying desire for prediction and control at the core of advertising's racial information system. Multicultural marketing often frames the heightened visibility of people of color in surveillance advertising as empowering and beneficial, emphasizing audience data as valuable for providing economic opportunities for people of color and relevant content while ensuring efficient marketing spends for brands.

Although digital ad technology and behavioral data are relatively new, the racial epistemologies of tracking and measurement that underpin these techniques are not. These processes rely on surveillance and the transformation of humans' digital behavior and data—such as clicks, likes, and locations—into audience profiles that are bought and sold to the highest bidder in digital advertising auctions.

In the digital advertising landscape, race and ethnicity are theorized as comprised of behavioral tendencies assumed to be shared within groups. These racial "affinities," packaged and sold as audience data, are evaluated and verified by companies for their authenticity, accuracy, and efficacy for advertisers. When used to sell a phone plan in a banner ad, these techniques may seem rather benign. However, as law enforcement agencies develop surveillance technologies to monitor and criminalize populations globally, we must be vigilant about the broader applications of racial consumer data inclusion.[79] The future of multicultural advertising may rely on racial inclusion in digital audience data, but for the rest of us, the concern should be how—and to what ends—the new racial science of online advertising will be used for *and* against us.

4 THE TOTAL MARKET TURN / US CENSUS PROJECTIONS AND MAKING THE NEW MAINSTREAM CONSUMER

In 2017, Toyota launched the marketing campaign for its signature midsize sedan, the Camry. "The goal of the campaign is to introduce people to an inspiring, more emotional, more exciting driving experience that will make every driver feel special," read Toyota's press release about the vehicle.[1] To reach "every driver," the company released four commercials, each tailored to a different racial market. At first glance, Toyota's marketing strategy was emblematic of any other multicultural marketing campaign: four different agencies were hired to produce an ad to reach their designated market. What Toyota claimed was unique about this campaign, however, was that the company directed the agencies to work together on the same strategy, which focused on the notion of "sensations."

The Chicago-based ad agency Burrell Communications produced the advertisement for the African American market (figure 4.1). Over a jazz-inflected hip-hop track, the ad depicts a Black man racing through city streets in a red Camry on a thrilling adventure to pick up a pizza. While attracting the attention of onlookers, the car's engine emits a billow of flames, followed by a quick cutaway shot of a peacock spreading its iridescent feathers. "What we found with African-Americans is style really comes to the forefront in how we look at vehicles," explained Lewis Williams, the agency's chief creative officer at the time, in a *New York Times* article about the campaign.[2] To capture that cultural referent, the agency relied on an allusion to "peacocking," or the notion that African Americans engage in bold displays of style as acts of resistance against social marginalization in a racist society.

The California- and Texas-based ad agency Intertrend produced the advertisement targeted to Asian American consumers (figure 4.2). For their part, Intertrend opted to "highlight a not-often-seen behavior" in Asian American families, which the agency claimed was an affectionate father-daughter relationship.[3] In the ad, an East Asian man tenderly locks eyes with his daughter, dressed in a softball uniform, through the Camry's rear-view mirror. Her eyes widen in amazement as he navigates the winding back roads of a small town.

Also choosing to capture the theme of familial connections, the agency Conill produced Spanish and English commercials for the Hispanic market featuring a man so consumed with racing down a desolate roadway in his Camry that he commits what the agency characterized as an ultimate act of transgression in the Hispanic community—declining a phone call from one's mother (figure 4.3). Saatchi & Saatchi, Toyota's primary agency of record, was assigned with targeting the "transcultural mainstream." Their ad depicted a montage of mostly white and lighter-skinned people gleefully gripping the Camry's steering wheel as their loose hair is blown back in ecstatic motion by the exhilaration of a car ride (figure 4.4). Their "transcultural" approach emphasized the agency's role in engaging a broader US consumer base that, unlike the narrower focus of multicultural agencies, is not defined by race but transcends it.

Before 2014, when Toyota adopted the "total market" approach, its roster of multicultural and general market agencies created targeted campaigns for their respective racial markets based on completely different strategies and themes. For Edward Laukes, Toyota's then-vice president of performance and guest experience, there was nothing necessarily wrong with that approach. "This is how we've done it for years. And, frankly, it was very successful. But it was—and is—not sustainable. This is not an effective way to reach your *total market* that will continue to change."[4]

Under its T2 "total market" model, Toyota's roster of advertising agencies collaborates from the outset to develop a unified campaign strategy for the company's US marketing. For the promotion of the 2023 Grand Highlander SUV, Toyota once again applied its T2 approach, enlisting Burrell, Intertrend, Conill, and Saatchi to produce ads emphasizing the vehicle's role in creating meaningful family moments. "The cohesive marketing approach speaks to how some brands are trying to break down silos between

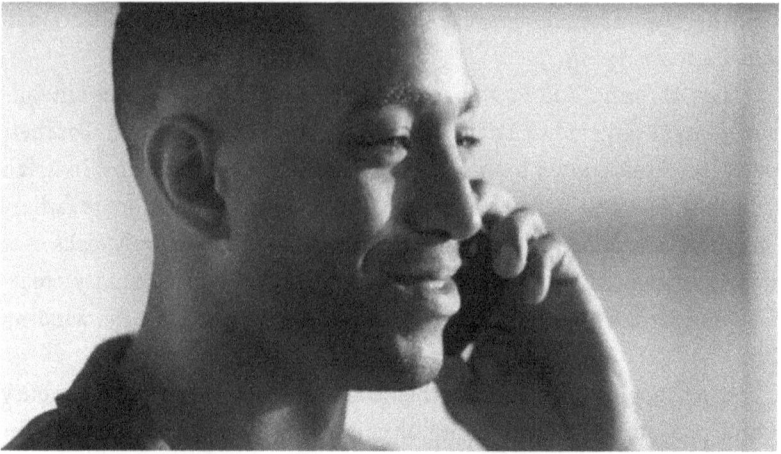

4.1 A scene from an advertisement in Toyota's 2017 Toyota Camry Campaign, created by Burrell Communications, targeted to the African American market.

4.2 A scene from an advertisement in Toyota's 2017 Toyota Camry Campaign, created by Intertrend, targeted to the Asian American market.

4.3 A scene from an advertisement in Toyota's 2017 Toyota Camry Campaign, created by Conill, targeted to the Hispanic market.

4.4 A scene from an advertisement in Toyota's 2017 Toyota Camry Campaign, created by Saatchi & Saatchi, targeted to the "transcultural mainstream."

their mainstream campaigns and those tailored to specific demographics as diversity and inclusion become bigger mandates in the industry," explained a trade press article about the campaign.[5]

Toyota's shift to a *total market* approach reflects broader changes in the US marketing landscape, driven by demographic trends captured in US Census data. As a cornerstone of American marketing's racial information system, census data has long provided statistical justification for multicultural marketing, reinforcing its economic appeal to corporate America. US Census data show a continued decline in the non-Hispanic white population, with people of color now comprising over half of the nation's population under age eighteen.[6] By 2050, non-white groups—particularly Hispanics, who are projected to make up one-quarter of the US population—will constitute the nation's majority.[7]

For decades, US marketing industry standards have entrenched a practice where the lead agency of record, implicitly centered on a white audience, guided the entire marketing process—from research and strategy to the creative brief and media plan. Only after the general market brief was finalized—and if the advertiser decided—would a multicultural marketing strategy be developed. However, racial demographic projections have called this over half-a-century-long practice into question, leading to the proposed development of new processes to racially integrate the separate "general market" and "multicultural" market segments into a unified vision of the American consumer public. "The shifting population proves we need to attract new customers to our brand, which will come directly from ethnic targets," explained Toyota's US marketing division.[8] A presentation by Laukes at a 2018 multicultural marketing conference illustrated the brand's redefinition of the US market—one that envisions a "transcultural mainstream" where representations of all racial segments are included while still maintaining targeted advertising appeals (figure 4.5).

The total market concept has been at the center of contentious debate among multicultural marketing leaders about the future of their industry, weighing the potential for lucrative business opportunities as well as formidable challenges. While US Census racial forecasts that project a "majority-minority" future have bolstered multicultural marketing's claim to corporate indispensability, they have also sparked fears that advertisers may abandon targeted campaigns in favor of broad, diversity-oriented strategies—empowering general market agencies to replace them once again. The American marketing industry is also contending with the ingrained racial segregation of advertising, media, and creative services,

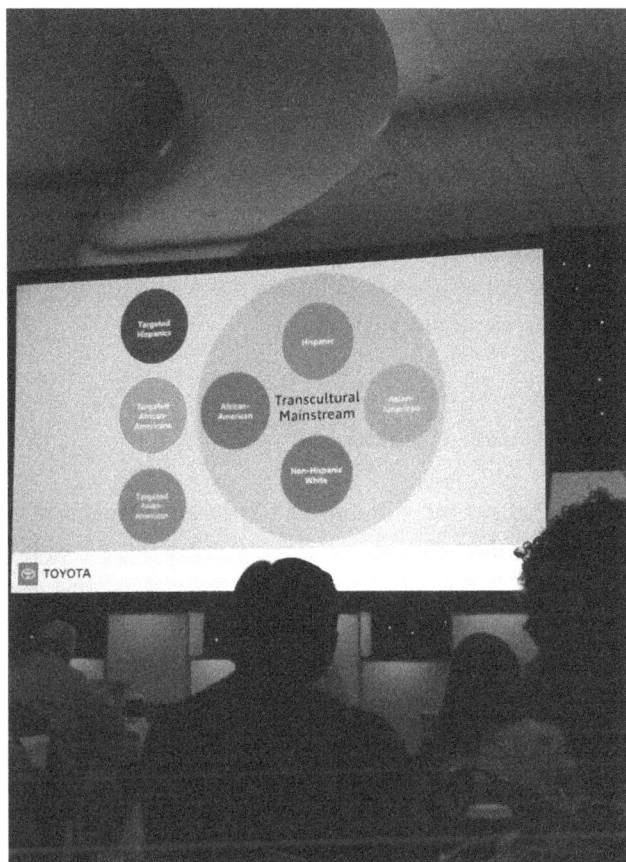

4.5 A slide from a presentation delivered by Toyota's North American vice president Edward Laukes, titled "Case for a Shift: How Toyota Sees the Total Market," at the 2018 ANA Multicultural Marketing and Diversity Conference, Miami, Florida. Photo by the author.

raising questions about the current structure's relevance and viability for business in the long run.

This chapter explores the emergence of the "total market" approach in the US advertising industry's racial information system and how it has sparked debates over the industry's racial epistemology and business practices. US ad industry deliberations about total market are closely tied to long-standing debates about "mainstream" American identity and perceptions of racial difference as either a unifying or divisive force in national culture. Embedded in advertising industry conversations about the "total market" are also political-economic struggles over who holds the epistemic authority to reimagine an American mainstream where whiteness is no longer the assumed norm. In this struggle for recognition and access to marketing budgets they believe they are rightly owed, multicultural advertising professionals have simultaneously capitalized on, challenged, and undermined the total market concept. Regardless of their stance, all have had to contend with large-scale demographic and cultural shifts and their implications for the racial politics of national belonging in American marketing's racial information system.

A NEW AMERICA DAWNING

"Out of the crucible of America's cultural and demographic melting pot, a new and profoundly different day is dawning. For brands looking to capture the hearts and minds of American consumers, that new day must start today." These are opening lines of a 2014 market research report by The Futures Company, titled *The Roadmap to the New America*.[9] For over two decades, the American marketing industry has been anticipating a "new mainstream" consumer revolution, citing the US Census projection of a 2043 tipping point, when the United States is expected to become a "majority-minority" nation.[10] The industry's anticipation of and preparation for this racial demographic shift are well documented across trade news outlets and other commentaries. In his 2005 book *The New Mainstream*, marketer Guy Garcia describes the cultural implications of these changes, envisioning a scenario where "the Old Mainstream—and the Eurocentric, agroindustrial values that go with it" have in the twenty-first century been eclipsed by a "new cultural movement" born from the "convergence of America's creative and multicultural classes."[11] Referring to this emerging new mainstream consumer group as "explorers" and "tastemakers," Garcia posits that they "tend not only to be tolerant of communities and cultures that are not their own but are more likely to find value in—and actively seek out—experiences and customs that add flavor, variety, and diversity to their lives."[12] Garcia's optimistic perspective on the changing racial demographics in the United States highlights these shifts as key drivers of a new mainstream marketplace, defined by its diversity and emphasis on social harmony, largely fostered through consumer culture.

When hair care and beauty company SheaMoisture launched in 2016, the company positioned itself in the marketplace as a brand tailor-made for the diverse new American mainstream. Its first ad campaign, Breaking Down the Walls, confronted the racialized segregation of beauty products in American retail stores, where "ethnic" haircare items—implicitly designated for non-white consumers—are physically separated from products labeled simply as "beauty." The advertisement depicted a Black woman with natural curly hair perusing the hair care section of a store, her expression pensive and anxious as she navigates divided aisles. As the sequence progresses, product shelves begin to collapse as if an earthquake is happening, and shampoo bottles crash to the floor. As the chaos settles, the protagonist's eyes open and there before her appears a new product aisle, featuring shelves full of SheaMoisture products. The ad concludes with non-white women of various skin tones and hair textures confidently browsing the newly integrated section of the store, accompanied by a voice-over stating that SheaMoisture "can be found in the beauty aisle—where we all belong."[13]

From melting pots to salad bowls, symphonies, and mosaics, a variety of metaphors have been used over the years to allude to varying theories about how culturally diverse groups become integrated into, and form a part of, what is considered a dominant culture and national identity. With every US Census projection about the "browning" population comes a growing popular fascination with what this future American could possibly look like. In November 1993, *Time* magazine published a special issue, "The New Face of America," featuring a racially ambiguous cover model who was not even a real person but a computer-generated composite "created from a mix of several races," as the cover copy stated. Exactly two decades later, in September 2013, *National Geographic* came out with its own special issue titled "The Changing Face of America," spotlighting the increasing number of people in the United States who identify as "multiracial." As journalist Doreen St. Félix observes about that *National Geographic* issue, the image of the future average American as a "multiracial person, who breaks the rules of the caste system, has become the subject of liberal, cross-racial desire, vaunted as diviners of social progress, or of apocalypse."[14]

This ongoing fixation on anticipating the new mainstream American is deeply intertwined with racial population politics that have influenced prevailing notions of national identity and particularly its association with white demographic dominance. The first US Constitution aspired to a populace made up of mostly people racialized as white or, as the Census Bureau put it in 1852, "the governing race."[15] Sociologists Richard Alba and Victor Nee posit the "American mainstream" as "that part of society within which ethnic and racial origins have at most minor impacts on life chances or opportunities."[16] They trace the origins of the American mainstream "to the early colonial settlers from Northern Europe" but note a significant shift in recent decades away from equating the mainstream exclusively with whiteness. They argue that *"interrelated institutional structures and organizations"*—such as immigration legislation, antidiscrimination policies, and civil rights laws—have "lowered the barriers to entry into the mainstream for nonwhites." This shift, they claim, is reflected in rising rates of interracial marriage and the growing presence of nonwhite people in higher-status positions in government and business.[17]

Yet Alba and Nee's optimistic view of an expanding and more inclusive mainstream warrants critique in the context of persistent racial oppression and xenophobia in the United States.[18] Policymakers and brand marketers alike have been theorizing about the impact of racial demographic shifts on the nation's cultural dynamics, particularly when population dominance has long been used to rationalize the concentration of power with people racialized as white. Heightened by the far right's resurgence in American politics, the ongoing culture war over the "mainstream" is not just about demographics but about power. As Jonathan Rosa observes, "When one is racialized as non-White . . . one's potential to be American or contribute to Americanness can perpetually be called into question."[19] Indeed, ongoing conflicts about immigration and DEI initiatives are driven by efforts to preserve a racially exclusionary notion of the American mainstream.

US Census racial data have long been central to the cultural narrative building about the American mainstream's present and future. As an instrument of enumeration and governance, the US Census not only manages and tracks racialized populations through data collection but also actively makes and unmakes racial classifications.[20] America's "statistical races," as sociologist Kenneth Prewitt points out, stem from the typological color-based schemes of human classification developed by eighteenth-century natural scientists.[21] With each decennial count, the US Census and the press attention around it contribute to storytelling about the nation as an "imagined community."[22] Population forecasts, a key statistical technique, are part of a discourse that anticipates changes in the nation's racial composition over time, claiming to offer glimpses into its envisioned demographic future.

"Racial forecasts are not neutral; they are politically charged," sociologists G. Cristina Mora and Michael Rodríguez-Muñiz assert.[23] The framing and interpretation of racial demographic forecasts depends largely on who is interpreting the data and for what purpose. When the 2010 Census projections were released, media coverage was flooded with dramatic metaphors of tsunamis, tidal waves, and diversity "explosions" depicting demographic shifts as an overwhelming and transformative force. "Forecasting tells a story about the future, what it means, and how one should feel about it," observes Rodríguez-Muñiz.[24] In *Figures of the Future*, Rodríguez-Muñiz explores how Latino civil rights groups have framed the 2010 US Census data to highlight Hispanics' political and social potential. He shows how these "figures of the future" become more than mere statistics — they are infused by these organizations with emotive language, emphasizing "strength and potential," so that Latinos are narrativized as an asset rather than a threat to the nation.[25]

The American marketing industry also participates in narrativizing US Census racial projections, often framing them with optimism and anticipation and emphasizing how brands can capitalize on these trends for growth and market expansion. US Census data have for decades been instrumental in shaping marketing strategies, guiding the placement of retail locations and influencing product development, often down to the zip code level.[26] However, for the multicultural marketing sector in particular, census racial data have an emphasized symbolic significance.[27] As an authoritative form of biopolitical enumeration, the census plays a crucial role in the American advertising industry's racial information system by providing detailed and officially sanctioned data on the size, income, and geographic concentration of various racial groups.[28]

In multicultural marketing presentations and public relations campaigns, Census racial data are frequently used to highlight the "size of the opportunity" and the "extended customer lifetime value" of multicultural markets in comparison to an aging, slow-growing, and rapidly declining non-Hispanic white population. A marketing report by Geoscape and the Chief Marketing Officer (CMO) Council, titled *Activating the New American Mainstream*™ (figure 4.6), emphasizes that "a marketer who believes he or she is 'American-centric' simply needs to look at the demographic trends to see that more than one-third of American people are from the three largest ethnic sub-segments (Hispanic, African American, and Asian)."[29] The report highlights that these racial groups, due to their younger age, family-building patterns, and growing household incomes, are driving spending growth and commanding increasing market share.

Marketers from some of the most well-known brands have imbued the projected rise of the "majority-minority" American population with anticipatory and positive sentiments, remarking on a demographic future

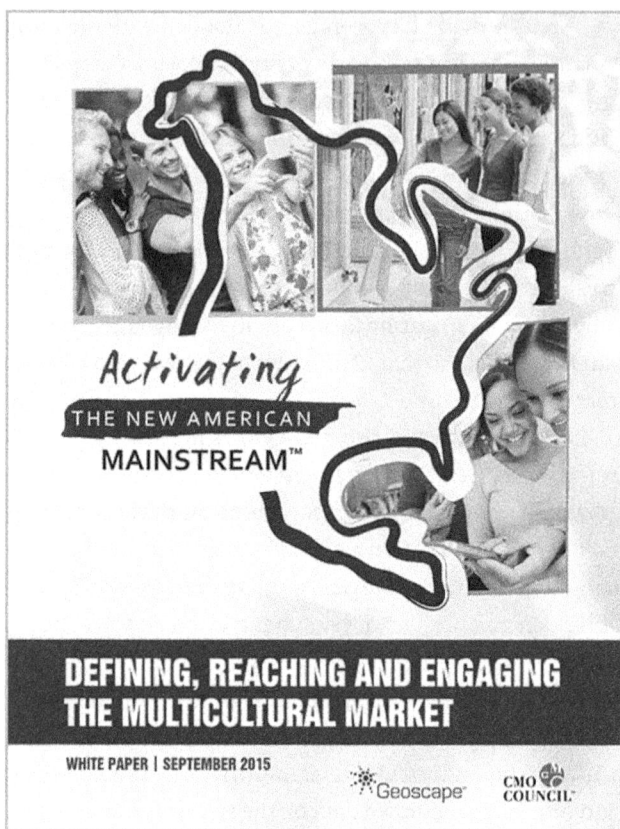

4.6 Front cover of *Activating the New American Mainstream*™:
Defining, Reaching and Engaging the Multicultural Market, a 2015
report by Geoscape and the CMO (Chief Marketing Officer)
Council, displaying the rise of trademarked approaches aiming
to help advertisers navigate shifting US racial demographics.

that companies can capitalize on with the right expertise and preparation. During his tenure as the senior vice president of brand marketing
at Walmart stores, Tony Rogers highlighted this shift in perspective, stating, "The [2010 US] Census really is changing the way a lot of people look
at multicultural [marketing]. It's suddenly on the radar of a lot more people."[30] Marc Pritchard, chief brand officer of Procter & Gamble, expressed
his optimism about US Census racial projections and the role population changes will play in driving sustained economic success for P&G and
other businesses, as well as benefiting American society through economic

growth. In a company blog post Pritchard noted, "According to the 2020 United States Census, 100% of the population growth in the past decade came from increases in the Black, Hispanic, Asian, Pacific Islander, Native, Indigenous, multi-racial, and multi-ethnic segments of the population. Market growth is the most important driver of business growth. When markets grow, all brands rise—new users enter the market, consumption increases, and innovation flourishes with new offerings that drive greater usage and potential for premium pricing. When done well, this results in increased income and wealth, which translates to more purchasing power."[31]

Pritchard predicts that racial demographic shifts will fuel market expansion and business innovation, creating a virtuous cycle that benefits consumers, American society, and businesses alike. His perspective positions racial markets as the backbone of an expanding consumer economy and welcomes the browning of America as an opportunity for increased consumption and higher-priced goods. Within this framework, people of color's social standing and well-being are directly linked to their virtues as consumers. This narrative, which celebrates rising multicultural market numbers for their perceived economic potential, is echoed by audience measurement firm Nielsen. Citing Census projections, Nielsen enthusiastically describes growing multicultural markets as the nation's "super consumers"—"an emerging consumer force in the country" who are "product enthusiasts, fueled by an emotional and very often a cultural connection."[32] Embedded in this optimistic framing of US Census racial projections is the marketing industry's embrace of "diversity" as an economic asset. As anthropologist Shalini Shankar observes, this business perspective is often "future-looking, unwilling to get mired in a complicated past, and highly attuned to where the United States is going."[33]

For the financial services company Wells Fargo, the anticipatory sentiments that permeate racial demographic projections have influenced major marketing changes. Jamie Moldafsky, former chief marketing officer of Wells Fargo, spoke at the 2015 Brand Masters Conference with urgency about the increasing number of American cities that are dominated by a rising majority of "multicultural" consumers: "We need to understand our consumers at a much different level . . . we're working very hard to make sure we're incorporating—in real time—the diversity change that's happening."[34] US Census racial data projections prompted the company to revamp its marketing strategy, adopting what they refer to as a "total market approach" that combines previously separate multicultural and general market strategies into unified, racially integrated advertising.

To an audience of fellow marketing executives, Moldafsky presented an advertisement titled "First Paycheck," which aired exclusively on English-language media networks, as being a quintessential example of the bank's total market direction. The bilingual commercial tells the story of a millennial Hispanic woman proudly sharing news of her first paycheck with her multigenerational family, including her cousins, parents, and, of course, her *abuela*, who lovingly congratulates her with a warm embrace and kiss on the cheek. Moldafsky explained that the ad was inspired by the brand's quest to "tap into the universal appeal and cultural cues reflective of Hispanic culture" while avoiding a simplistic "collage of ethnic images."[35] Wells Fargo adopted a strategy of incorporating non-white actors and Hispanic cultural references into its advertisement while airing it on English-language networks rather than restricting it to Spanish-language media. The goal was to make these once-niche multicultural elements broadly appealing, integrating them into mainstream marketing while ensuring they did not alienate white consumers.[36] Moldafsky shared that she couldn't "see any other way forward for Wells Fargo. . . . We're having great success in acquiring the customers we want."[37]

Moldafsky's presentation on Wells Fargo's total market strategy was delivered against the backdrop of the bank's ongoing controversial history of racially discriminatory and predatory banking practices. In 2017, Wells Fargo was fined by the US government after revelations that employees had opened millions of unauthorized bank and credit card accounts.[38] Testimonies from former employees indicated that undocumented Hispanic immigrants were specifically targeted as part of these aggressive sales tactics. During initiatives like "Hit the Streets Thursday," Wells Fargo employees, notably of Hispanic descent, sought out potential clients at construction sites and outside factories, exploiting the financial needs of undocumented workers and persuading them to open new accounts.[39]

Amid these controversies, Nydia Sahagún, then the senior vice president of segment marketing at Wells Fargo, highlighted at the 2018 Association of National Advertisers' conference the minimal impact of the bank's scandals on consumer loyalty, suggesting that its total market focus helped maintain trust among multicultural consumers despite the wider brand crisis. Sahagún stated, "What I would tell you is that, in the wake of this brand crisis, we've actually seen far less impact with multicultural consumers than we have with the general population. And what we attribute that to is really our commitment to diversity."[40]

Wells Fargo's avowed "commitment to diversity" involves adopting a total market strategy, aimed at targeting the evolving mainstream in response to US Census projections of shifting racial demographics. This strategy not only seeks to capitalize on the social currency of diversity but also serves as a veneer to conceal and perpetuate long-standing forms of "predatory inclusion," where people from marginalized groups are superficially granted access to markets like banking and mortgage lending, only to encounter conditions that further exacerbate exploitation and inequality.[41] Wells Fargo's total market strategy, cloaked under the progressive guise of "embracing diversity," invokes inclusive advertising as a façade to perpetuate discriminatory financial practices while aiming to boost its image with the "new mainstream." This contradiction is evident in a 2021 advertisement the company released targeting Spanish-speaking audiences, which features a diverse array of Hispanic people of varying ages, genders, sexual orientations, and skin colors. Set against the backdrop of emotive classical music, the ad conveys a message of Hispanic empowerment and future potential, aligning the bank with the aspirations of the Hispanic population. The ad's on-screen message unfolds over a sequence of images: "Eres más de lo que superas / Eres tradición / Eres orgullo / determinación / y presente / Eres el futuro / Te celebramos" (You are more than what you have overcome / You are tradition / You are pride / determination / and now / You are the future / We celebrate you).[42] The ad positions the bank as a supportive ally, tapping into feel-good politics that leverage diversity and inclusion rhetoric with "the pleasures of consumption" to portray Latino consumers as valuable assets in American capitalism's present and future.[43]

As companies like Wells Fargo opportunistically use racial demographic projections of the US Census to exploit racial markets under the guise of inclusion, the total market approach itself was a highly debated topic within the advertising industry's racial information system. Central to this debate were questions about the role of multicultural marketing and racial expertise in the future of American advertising—specifically, who holds the authority and expertise to redefine the mainstream American consumer for advertisers.

With racial demographic projections of the US Census predicting a future where previously classified "racial minorities" become the "new majority," the total market concept emerged as a key focus for marketers, prompting discussions about the impact of these demographic shifts on Madison Avenue's business structures and the traditional division of the American marketplace into racially segmented multicultural (MC) and general market (GM) strategies. Across trade publications, industry conferences, and beyond, debates ensued over the definition and relevance of the total market approach. While some rejected the concept outright, others sought to define, brand, and claim proprietary expertise. "Total Market is a little like high school sex—everyone seems to be talking about it, and no one seems to be doing it perfectly well," mused Gilbert Dávila, a multicultural market research executive and cofounder of the industry trade group Alliance for Inclusive and Multicultural Marketing.[44]

The origins of the total market concept have been the subject of various theories regarding its inception and underlying motivations. One prominent theory I learned from my research interlocutors suggests that the concept originated not from a genuine effort by advertisers to engage a diverse American consumer base but rather as a cost-saving measure during the 2008 recession. The financial turmoil of that period severely impacted the advertising industry, leading many brands to drastically reduce their advertising budgets and disrupt the traditional "agency of record" business model with shorter term, project-based contracts accompanied by lower fees.[45] In the more extreme case, some brands eliminated their agency partnerships altogether and brought their advertising functions in-house.[46] This restructuring inevitably unsettled the industry. In the decade following 2008, several of the global advertising holding companies responded to the economic hardship with cutbacks and mergers.[47] During this period of financial strain, marketing budgets were reduced, leading some industry professionals to suggest that the total market strategy was designed by advertisers to maintain relevance amid shifting racial demographics while maximizing efficiency by consolidating the number of agencies on their rosters. As one industry insider noted: "I think 'total market' was born out of the recession. I don't think it was a specific vertical or industry. Companies were hurting in 2008. Is it just a coincidence that this 'great new idea'—Total Market—emerges right after a recession and marketing budgets are cut? I don't think so. It's as if advertisers were justifying decreasing spend, particularly for multicultural markets, by branding it as a 'total market' innovation."[48]

Mary, a multicultural marketing researcher and strategist, posited that the growing popularity of the total market concept was heavily influenced by the post-racial rhetoric that followed the 2008 presidential election where commentators hailed Barack Obama's victory as evidence of the power of a multiracial coalition or a "new progressive majority."[49] In this context, Mary observed that multicultural marketing expertise was increasingly viewed as unnecessary in a nation perceived as having transcended racial divisions: "I think [total market] became popular when the census started announcing that America was going to be a 'majority minority.' We saw a big shift in its popularity when Barack Obama won the presidency in 2008.... People felt that we were a post-racial society, and total market fit right in there. One message, to reach everybody, because we are finally post-racial."[50]

As the total market idea gained traction across US marketing industry discourse during the latter part of the 2010s, some leaders in the multicultural marketing industry expressed concern over the threat it posed to their business sector. As Vince from the multicultural agency Soar put it, "Clients are asking everyone to come to the table to find a 'universal insight.' Brands are starting to say, 'Why bother with multicultural marketing?'"[51]

Brands' shift toward total market campaigns, rather than racially segmented ones, suggested to some multicultural marketing industry leaders that their value proposition—rooted in their expertise with racialized populations' cultural differences—was being consolidated and appropriated by better-resourced general market agencies. "It definitely wasn't the multicultural agencies driving total market. They wouldn't come up with an idea that's going to decrease their revenue," remarked a multicultural advertising market researcher I spoke with.[52]

Another of the perceived threats to multicultural marketing that emerged from the total market concept was the rise of advertising agencies positioning themselves as one-stop shops for reaching the new mainstream. Agencies like Translation, founded by hip-hop music executive Steve Stoute, exemplify this trend. In his book *The Tanning of America*, Stoute presents his racial theory of contemporary American culture, which he calls "tanning." "Today's consumer is a mindset, not a race—and when businesses get it right and have a proper understanding of tanning, success is imminent. The 'tanning' phenomenon has given rise to the first generation of consumers who share the same 'mental complexion' based on shared experiences and values," lauds the book's cover. He theorizes that "tanning," born from the globalization of hip-hop and the surge in social media and technology, represents a cultural and cognitive habitus shared by Millennials who are "no longer confined to a literal definition or location" but transcend these boundaries. Published during President Obama's first term, *The Tanning of America* embodies that era's overly optimistic ethos of post-racial, color-blind rhetoric, suggesting that Americans are defined by something greater than race: brands.

Other ad agencies publicly announced their plans to overhaul the advertising industry's entrenched racial segmentation paradigm in response to projected population shifts. Anomaly made headlines in early 2016 by placing a two-page spread in *Advertising Age*, declaring their ambition "to tear down the last silo: the Hispanic marketing silo." The imagery of an imposing grain storage silo, commonly used as a metaphor for the rigid divisions between general market and multicultural market service sectors, was central to their message: "As we look to the future, we cannot help but be inspired by the changed dynamics of America today. We are creating a very different mission—a mission to make Anomaly a company that can credibly and relevantly communicate with everyone in America. Equally."[53] Anomaly's PR strategy adopted a self-righteous tone, implicitly likening their mission to the civil rights movement's fight for racial desegregation while also framing "tearing down the Hispanic silo" as an economically beneficial move for advertisers.

In response to the 2010 US Census projections, one of the largest global ad agencies, Ogilvy & Mather Worldwide, launched a new unit called OgilvyCulture, focusing on "cross-cultural marketing." John Seifert, chairman and chief executive of Ogilvy & Mather North America, explained to the *New York Times*, "This starts from the kind of firm we want to be in the future. . . . Instead of thinking of discrete segments in a multicultural world, we're saying the new reality is that it's more of a cross-cultural world, a mash-up of cultures."[54]

OgilvyCulture's then senior partner and managing director, Jeffrey L. Bowman, soon became a prominent and sometimes controversial advocate of the total market concept. Bowman, an African American marketer who had previously held executive-level positions at companies like Sears, Pepsi, and Dell, left his post at OgilvyCulture in 2012 to found Reframe Consulting, a consultancy and software platform aimed at preparing brands for economic success in the new majority marketplace.

"Eighty percent of U.S. growth is projected to come from the minority majority, but the business and marketing models for reaching them have gone unchanged since the 1960s," Bowman warned in the book *Reframe the Marketplace*.[55] His definition of total market was rooted in the belief that a fundamental overhaul of the American advertising business infrastructure was needed for corporations to grow sales and deepen their connections with America's new mainstream consumers.[56] "The buying approach and structure that Corporate America and Madison Avenue engage in is like 'redlining,'" Bowman claimed.[57]

Bowman's version of the total market strategy integrates McKinsey's "change management" framework to advocate for a restructuring of how marketing and communications services are managed—"not separated by ethnic walls nor driven solely by ethnic-specific decisions."[58] This transformation would involve changes in marketing strategies, including more comprehensive market research, as well as overhauls to internal corporate structures, including hiring, so that staff better reflect population shifts.

In the multicultural marketing industry, one of the leading voices opposing Bowman's vision of total market was the Association of Hispanic Advertising Agencies (AHAA; now called the Hispanic Marketing Council). The trade group led a public relations offensive against Bowman's vision of the total market concept. In an email to its members, AHAA critiqued an op-ed Bowman had published in which he criticized the US marketing industry for operating on a "segregated model in which the general market is separate from multicultural."[59] The AHAA email lambasting Bowman read as a call to action that emphasized multicultural marketers' vital role in "help[ing] brands navigate the nuances that tug at both the heart and the wallet."[60]

Some multicultural marketing professionals sought to discredit the total market concept altogether, with one calling it "total bullshit" in a LinkedIn post.[61] In 2017 the trade publication *Hispanic Market Overview* ran a satirical public-service-announcement-style ad reminiscent of *National Enquirer* tabloids, criticizing advertisers for their ineffectiveness and shortsightedness for abandoning multicultural marketing (figure 4.7). The headline "60 Million Hispanics Vanish from Client Radars!" is accompanied by an image of a presumably non-Hispanic white marketing executive shrugging nonchalantly and thinking, in a speech bubble, "One universal insight: how hard can it be?" The image was a pointed reference to a common critique of the total market approach from multicultural marketers, who argue that advertisers' attempts to reach a new mainstream without the help of multicultural advertising experts overlook the cultural nuances that are consequential to connecting with and persuading multicultural

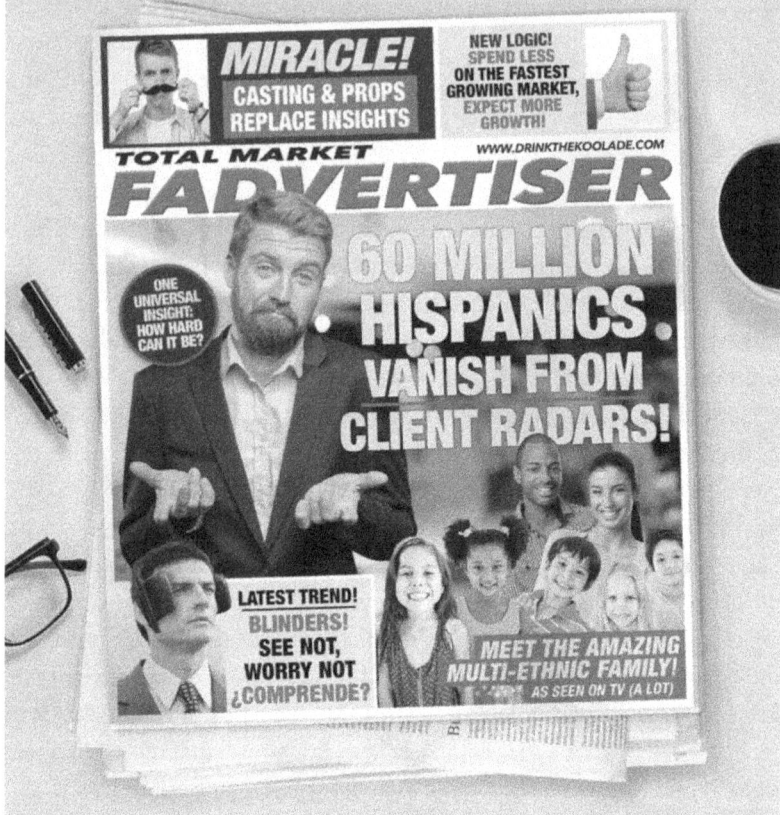

4.7 Public service announcement meets satirical advertisement in this critique of the "total market" idea by leaders in the Hispanic advertising industry. Produced by the Adam R. Jacobson Multicultural Consultancy, published in *Hispanic Market Overview* (2017), and distributed by the trade outlet HispanicAd.com.

consumers. The tension boiled down to the concerns of an industry facing possible obsolescence, and deliberations about how to rearticulate its reason for being at a time when they should be needed the most by advertisers. "There was a lot of virulent debate," recalled Stacy, a multicultural advertising strategist at a shopper marketing agency. "It got nasty out there. When people feel their livelihoods are being threatened, they get scared and they attack."[62]

Against the backdrop of shifting racial dynamics and slashed marketing budgets, Bowman distilled the stakes of the total market debate into a single, pointed question at one of his Total Market Summits that I attended in New York City in 2017: "Who is going to give up power?" Bowman described a scenario resembling a turf war between multicultural agencies and general market agencies, along with the battle for brand advertising budgets that are already fiercely guarded. Bowman anticipated that the multicultural advertising industry would meet the total market approach "with resistance and pushback."

A number of multicultural ad industry professionals expressed resentment toward the structural changes proposed by Bowman's notion of the total market approach, believing that the established segmentation model, which included multicultural agencies as subject matter experts, was "never given a fair shot at success."[63] Some multicultural marketing professionals have pointed out that these agencies have historically operated on miniscule budgets compared to their general market counterparts. Consequently, they have been forced to disproportionately allocate their limited resources toward justifying their very existence to advertisers. Aaron Walton, CEO of the multicultural advertising agency Walton Isaacson, echoed these concerns in an *AdAge* op-ed titled "The Total Market Approach Isn't Just Offensive, It's Dangerous." He argued that the total market approach was attractive to advertisers because it promised an "efficient" strategy to reach the multicultural emerging majority without their needing to expend budget on specialty agencies' expertise. Walton stated, "Total Market became an efficiency play that played right into the hands of larger organizations, those who could showcase just the right dose of diversity: 'Look at us, we talk to everyone.'"[64] Rather than advertisers empowering multicultural marketing agencies as experts in a new mainstream by increasing their budgets, Walton lamented that the total market strategy reinforced the existing power of larger general market agencies. Critics of the total market approach viewed it as a form of color-blind racism that once again marginalized racial markets and the specialized ad agencies that served them.

The debates about the total market approach highlight the social processes involved in "entrenching a theory" within an institution.[65] Bowman and AHAA were engaged in an epistemological struggle over the "right" way to imagine the American mainstream marketplace anew. Although many multicultural advertising professionals mounted formidable resistance against the entrenchment of the total market concept, in order to remain competitive in the advertising industry, some also chose to adopt and adapt it. Several multicultural agencies have since rebranded themselves to advertisers, moving away from marketing their services according to racial segment-specific expertise and toward trademarked reinterpretations of the total market approach. For example, d'expósito & Partners, a legacy Hispanic advertising firm based in New York City, now refers to itself as the "New American Agency," promoting the hallmarks of a "Total Relevance" approach (figure 4.8). Similarly, Miami-headquartered agency The Community positions itself as "the creative partner for the new mainstream," embracing the term "cross-culture." BeautifulBeast explains their stance on their website: "While our DNA is Hispanic, we are a cross-cultural agency." This foray into total market territory, with a focus on cross-cultural approaches, is seen by some multicultural marketing industry leaders as essential for the economic viability of multicultural advertising moving forward. As the creative chairman of the Miami-based Hispanic creative agency Alma remarked, "The agencies that are able to transition from a pure Hispanic focus to a real multicultural, upstream total market approach will continue to drive results for smart clients who understand that the country has changed."[66]

As advertising agencies across the board continue to merge or close, brand marketers bring their advertising work in-house, and general market firms shift toward more diverse audience strategies, multicultural advertising is rebranding itself to find its footing. When I started my research in 2014, the total market bonanza was reaching a head. By the time of completing this book in 2024, the term has mostly fallen out of favor in industry discourse.

Despite its brief circulation, the total market approach left a lasting impact. According to Mary, an African American consumer research strategist, total market discourse "financially devastated [the multicultural marketing] business," elaborating that the rise of total market strategies was "about power—and money too."[67] Mary pointed out that general mar-

4.8 New York City–based multicultural ad agency d'expósito & Partners markets its trademarked "Total Relevance" approach for a new mainstream market, 2017.

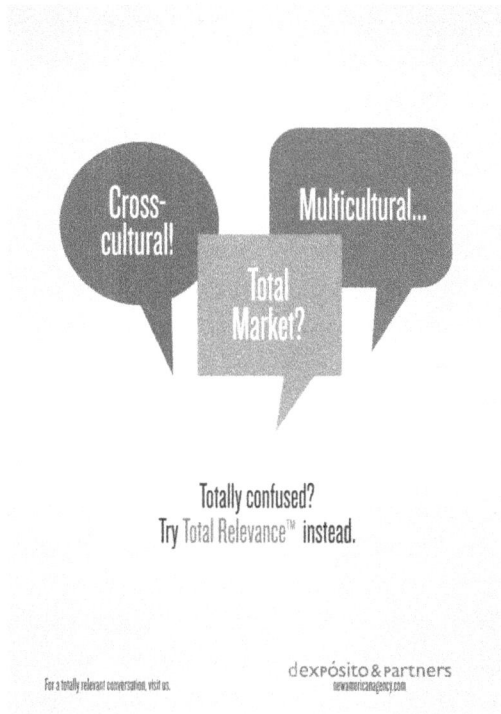

Cross-cultural!

Multicultural...

Total Market?

Totally confused?
Try Total Relevance™ instead.

For a totally relevant conversation, visit us.

d·expósito & partners
newamericanagency.com

ket agencies were its primary beneficiaries, as they could compete for work traditionally handled by multicultural agencies, therefore encroaching on their territory and budgets. "For years and years and years, [multicultural marketers] were like lepers to mainstream marketers. They didn't want to touch us. And now they've come for our business, and they've taken it over. And it's been horrible for all of us. It was swift, and it was quick. There are some brands that just completely converted to total market. So they just stopped investing. The Black agency budgets moved over to mainstream. *Just like that.*"[68]

During my internship at Soar, I asked Vince what impact he believed the total market debate had on the multicultural advertising industry. His response was marked by a sense of ambivalence, underpinned by a foreboding certainty that more multicultural firms would soon be absorbed into larger entities. "For good or for bad, multicultural marketing soon won't exist. I'm not passing judgment on that but if you follow the crumbs, that's where we're going. I feel conflicted because if we do our job right, that *should* happen—for all marketers to serve the audience that they need to."[69] Vince's words highlighted a paradox that has long troubled the multicultural marketing sector: If the new mainstream is non-white, then all ad agencies should be capable of reaching these audiences, thereby rendering their companies obsolete.

Vince's prediction about multicultural ad agencies being "absorbed and accounted for" by general market firms proved to be prescient in his case. Just months after my internship at Soar ended in 2018, I received an email from him informing me that he had been laid off. Vince's job became a casualty of holding company cutbacks, and his multicultural agency was "absorbed" into the general market agency Blue.

The industry debate surrounding the total market highlights the interconnections between advertising, the population politics of racial classification, and the role of US Census projections in shaping perceptions of the nation as a consumer market. Advertisers and agencies are grappling with how to represent a new vision of American national identity, driven by projections and perceptions of shifting racial demographics. These changes have prompted a reconsideration of the American consumer and led key industry players to reform institutionalized practices of racially segmented business services. For multicultural advertising, which has long operated on the distinction between white and non-white markets, the total market approach—seeking to merge racial differences into "universal" messages— has effectively signaled the decline of their industry. The struggle to define total market terminology reflects a broader contest over power and authority within the US advertising economy.

This book has explored the American advertising industry's role in shaping perceptions of humanity through the lens of racial difference. In the wake of the 2020 racial justice movements, many brands publicly committed to anti-racism and broader diversity initiatives. The conclusion examines how the advertising industry's racial information system has incorporated anti-racist rhetoric—revealing the paradoxes and ambivalence of these efforts amid the ever-shifting pendulum of racial reckoning and retrenchment.

CONCLUSION /
INTERSECTIONALITY,
INC. / ANTI-RACISM AS
CONSUMER FANTASY

The summer of 2020 will be remembered as a flash point in US history, marked by the convergence of a global pandemic and a racial reckoning that sparked the largest anti-racism demonstrations since the civil rights movement. Calls for justice spread from the streets to social media and into corporate boardrooms nationwide. Netflix made it known to its followers that "to be silent is to be complicit. Black Lives Matter." Doritos, the Frito-Lay brand typically known for its playful marketing of cheesy tortilla chips, shifted to a more austere tone with its #AmplifyBlackVoices campaign, featuring a TV commercial, murals advocating racial justice in several major cities painted by Black artists, and a $150,000 pledge to the Black Lives Matter organization (figure C.1). Doritos' parent company, PepsiCo, committed millions of dollars to its "Journey to Racial Equality" while Walmart launched its own Center for Racial Equity. Long-standing consumer packaged goods brands like Aunt Jemima and Uncle Ben's, with mascots rooted in racist stereotypes, underwent significant rebranding. Meanwhile, McDonald's publicly declared in a video posted across its social media accounts that Trayvon Martin, George Floyd, Atatiana Jefferson, and other African Americans killed by law enforcement were "one of us," adding, in the fast-food chain's signature red and mustard-yellow brand colors: "It's why we stand for them and any other victims of systemic oppression and violence. Today we stand with Black communities across America" (figure C.2).

The American marketing industry's momentary racial reckoning in 2020 forced a confrontation with the structural racism embedded in corporate practices, from marketing and hiring to "implicit bias" in workplace

C.1 One of Doritos' out-of-home advertisements in Brooklyn, New York, from its #AmplifyBlackVoices campaign, released at the height of the summer 2020 racial justice protests. Photo by Ali Rosa-Salas.

Trayvon Martin. Michael Brown. Alton Sterling.
Botham Jean. Atatiana Jefferson. Ahmaud Arbery. George Floyd.

He was one of us. She was one of us. They were all one of us.
We see them in our customers. We see them in our crew members. We see them in our franchisees.
And this is why the entire McDonald's family grieves.
It's why we stand for them and any other victims of systemic oppression and violence.
Today we stand with Black communities across America.
Which is why we're donating to the National Urban League and the NAACP.
We do not tolerate inequity, injustice, or racism.

Black lives matter.

M

C.2 McDonald's June 2020 advertisement titled "They Were One of Us," sharing the names of Black Americans who died in police custody or because of racial violence. Created by the agency Wieden + Kennedy, New York.

culture, prompting companies to publicly pledge reforms, donations, and a commitment to do better. As consumer expectations for corporate support of racial justice movements have risen, some companies have grappled with how to integrate this support into their brand messaging and business operations.

Throughout this book, I have explored how the American advertising industry is involved in shaping and perpetuating the production of racial knowledge—or, in other words, the frameworks through which US society perceives, classifies, and assigns meaning to race as a way of understanding what it is to be human. Central to my analysis has been the concept of the American advertising industry's *racial information system*—the intersection of processes, professionals, institutions, ideologies, and artifacts that coalesce to commodify and reproduce ideas about racial difference for corporate profit. At the core of the advertising industry's racial information system is the long-standing assumption that Americans racialized as white and of economic means represent the prototypical "general market" consumer. This belief, rooted in racialized constructs of American citizenship that have been codified by law and entrenched in custom, has shaped marketing practices for over a century, resulting in the division of the US marketplace and advertising business infrastructure into "general" (implicitly white) and "multicultural" (racially distinct and otherized) sectors.

Multicultural advertising's production of racial knowledge is solidified through the specialized labor of advertising strategists and media planners who deploy data collection, analysis, and quantification to highlight their theories about the distinct cultural practices of multicultural market segments and the economic value they present to advertisers. In the digital age, commercialized racial knowledge production has become even more extensive, through the utilization of surveillance technologies and machine learning to predict, influence, and monetize human behavior on the internet. As digitization advances and US Census data reflects shifting racial demographics, the US advertising industry faces growing debates about how the emerging "new mainstream" marketplace will impact legacy business practices, marketing budgets, and segmentation models.

Multicultural marketing has traditionally carried an implicit social justice mission aimed at amending exclusionary and racially stereotypical portrayals in American advertising. By offering specialized racial expertise to corporate America, multicultural marketing professionals often situate their work as a social good by depicting people of color as valuable, loyal consumers and, by extension, productive contributors to American society. In this framework, being acknowledged by a brand as a desirable consumer becomes a proxy for social status and political equality.

I conclude this book by reflecting on how the marketing industry's racial information system has embraced and then rather quickly abandoned the rhetoric of anti-racism, suggesting that racial justice can be achieved through market-driven approaches—primarily by enhancing the visibility and representation of people of color to make them "feel seen" or validated, respected, and affirmed by corporations. This shift embodies what scholars Felice Blake and Paula Ioanide describe as "anti-racist incorporation," where rather than ignoring or minimizing the reality of systemic racism, as have most rhetorics of color-blindness and diversity, anti-racist incorporation is a discourse that "openly articulates the problem of racism and racial justice" while simultaneously neutralizing its insurgent potential.[1]

From the popularity of intersectionality as a marketing strategy to calls for increased racial diversity and inclusion in advertising, the evolution of anti-racism rhetoric in consumer culture may appear to signal progress. Yet, this phenomenon also is revelatory of the false promises, ambivalences, and the many contradictions inherent in US capitalist culture, where enthusiasm for and investment in racially inclusive advertising coexists with escalating racialized violence, systemic oppression, and state-sanctioned exclusion. It is telling that, as political tides shift, anti-racism marketing initiatives are being abandoned as quickly as they were adopted, discarded under the pressure of right wing backlash.

INTERSECTIONALITY AS MARKETING STRATEGY

Sony Motion Pictures' North American division made an unprecedented move in 2019 by appointing its first senior vice president of "intersectional marketing." An internal memo penned by the company's US marketing director to studio employees clarified that the role aims to "establish holistic multicultural and inclusion-based strategies for all [Sony] films . . . to ensure our campaigns achieve maximum exposure to the widest possible audiences."[2] Intersectionality, framed by Sony executives as a savvy business move toward inclusivity and efficiency, has made its way from critical race theory and into press releases about corporate marketing strategy.

Legal scholar and activist Kimberlé Crenshaw introduced the term *intersectionality* in two seminal academic articles published in 1989 and 1991 to illuminate how US legal and social structures have failed to address the compounded vulnerabilities and violence experienced by women of color in the confluence of racism, sexism, and struggles for citizenship status.[3] Her work emphasizes that the interconnected nature of systemic oppression is frequently overlooked not only by the American legal system but also by feminist and anti-racist movements. As Crenshaw explained to Vox in 2019, "Intersectionality was a prism to bring to light dynamics within discrimination law that weren't being appreciated by the courts. In particular, courts seem to think that race discrimination was what happened to all black people across gender and sex discrimination was what happened to all women, and if that is your framework, of course, what happens to black women and other women of color is going to be difficult to see."[4]

To be sure, the concept of interconnected structural oppressions has deeper historical roots in the "unnamed border spaces between activism and academia"—tracing back to Sojourner Truth's "Ain't I a Woman?" speech, the Black feminist radicalism of the Combahee River Collective, and Gloria Anzaldúa's "new mestiza" consciousness.[5] Nevertheless, Crenshaw's conceptualization has been profoundly impactful in highlighting "the significance of social structural arrangements of power, how individual and group experiences reflect those structural intersections, and how political marginality might engender new subjectivities and agency," observes Patricia Hill Collins.[6]

Since the 1990s, intersectionality has operated "at the crossroads of multiple interpretive communities,"[7] from academia, activism, policymaking, and, as I will demonstrate, the US marketing industry, where it has recently been imbued with "undeniable intellectual, political, and moral capital."[8] Sociologist Sirma Bilge highlights that although intersectionality has gained widespread circulation and acclaim within academia in particular, its incorporation into the "market-driven and state-sanctioned governmentality of diversity" has also exposed the limitations of the academy in fostering meaningful anti-oppressive social change.[9] Bilge criticizes some feminist academics for turning intersectionality into a form of "marketable expertise" that sidelines Black feminist scholarship and critical analyses of race. She argues that as academic careerism fixates on abstract theoretical debates, intersectionality has been tokenized and disconnected from the political struggles and material realities of oppression it was originally intended to address.[10] Crenshaw has similarly pointed out the problematic misappropriation of intersectionality within academic settings, where she observes how women-of-color theorists are systematically marginalized from being viewed as experts on a topic meant to center their lives and struggles. Crenshaw remarked at a 2017 conference at Tulane University that "intersectionality has been gentrified, in the sense that the people it was initially designed to recognize have been pushed out of the discourse."[11]

Intersectionality has gained significantly more public attention outside the academy since Donald Trump's first presidential election—a time marked both by the resurgence of brazen and overt white nationalism as well as growing public discourse and protests about systemic racism and gendered oppression. Social media and digital platforms have been instrumental in amplifying ideas related to critical race theory. However, as social movements have gained traction, backlash against diversity, equity, and inclusion (DEI) initiatives has intensified, with several US states either proposing or enacting legislation to restrict the teaching of critical race theory in public schools, government institutions, and workplaces. Conservative commentators have focused on mischaracterizing intersectionality as a "new caste system"[12] based on a "hierarchy of victimhood" that marginalizes heterosexual white men.[13]

Intersectionality's growing prominence across various fields raises important questions about epistemic power. As Patricia Hill Collins notes, "Epistemic power is part of how domination operates," highlighting how political and social forces shape what is considered authoritative knowledge and whose perspectives are valued in producing it as such.[14] As intersectionality moves from academia to industries like marketing, a prudent question remains: "Who gets to tell intersectionality's story? And what story will they tell?"[15] Examining the epistemic power at play in the marketing industry's anti-racist incorporation of intersectionality requires scrutinizing how marketers are defining the concept, the purposes for which it is deployed, and who ultimately benefits from its application.

The US marketing industry's racial information system has leveraged a definition of intersectionality as a strategy to create products and advertisements that resonate with marginalized groups, recognizing them as consumers who seek visibility, representation, and validation from corporate power structures. Consumer culture scholar Francesca Sobande observes that contemporary brands are navigating stances on morality more than ever to maintain their status as "good" and "cool."[16] Intersectionality as a brand strategy is embedded within the intensification of "commodity activism," where companies position racial justice as a theme that can be addressed through individual consumption choices.[17] During the summer of 2020, amid widespread racial justice protests, advertisers took center stage as the public demanded greater accountability from corporations in advancing racial justice through financial commitments and public advocacy. As Richard Edelman, CEO of the public relations and market consultancy firm Edelman, had noted, "Brands are now being pushed to go beyond their classic business interests to become advocates. It is a new relationship between company and consumer, where purchase is premised on the brand's willingness to live its values, act with purpose, and if necessary, make the leap into activism."[18] A June 2020 survey conducted by Edelman with two thousand Americans found that the majority of respondents expected brands to play a central role in addressing racial oppression; over half reported that brands must also take on a leading role in educating the public on anti-racism.[19]

A report from the market research firm System1 further underscores a shift in the marketing industry's incorporation of racial justice rhetoric in response to consumer demand. The company noted that "brands today look to show a level of understanding and inclusion of diverse customers that goes much deeper, telling unique not generic stories, and raising awareness of problems rather than trying to camouflage them. Brands want to go beyond diversity and into inclusion and demonstrating real allyship."[20] System1 advises that impactful marketing today should not avoid referencing issues like oppression and anti-racism as thematic content but rather see them as opportunities for brands to be at the forefront of cultural discourse.

The first time I encountered intersectionality in a marketing context was during my internship at the Hispanic advertising agency Soar. One day I was invited to observe a practice run for a new business pitch. During the team's dynamic presentation, one of the agency's executives explained that today's American society is shaped by the convergence of several cultural forces: "global transculturalism," "advances in technology," and "intersectionality." Intersectionality was introduced as an area of marketing expertise useful for comprehending and rationalizing human identities increasingly recognized as multilayered and complex.

Across the advertising and media industry trade press, intersectionality has been reimagined as a theory to refine market segmentation and branding strategies, aiming to make advertising more impactful, "nuanced" and persuasive with "diverse" consumers. When *Deadline*, the Hollywood industry magazine, reported on Sony's North American intersectional marketing executive position, it defined intersectionality as a way that marketers can "acknowled[ge] the nuances of various identity classifications like class, race, sexuality, gender, and age as interwoven yet distinct factors that create unique individual experiences."[21] A *Forbes* business journalist echoed this view of intersectionality, noting, "Rather than viewing diversity as appealing to many individual constituencies, brands that do it right realize that consumers have multiple, overlapping identities—and they expect to see this complexity reflected in their product advertising."[22] In advertising's racial information system, intersectionality, often used interchangeably with the term *diversity*, has become a marketable business asset for identifying distinct consumer lifestyle segments and blending demographics in hybrid ways. "Intersectionality acknowledges all the parts of ourselves that make us different," explained the chief diversity officer at the ad agency BBDO, "and through inclusive advertising, we are able to tap into human truths that connect us despite those differences."[23] Marketers have repurposed intersectionality as a tool to deepen consumer capitalism's influence on personhood, shifting the term away from its activist roots toward a focus on individual consumer choice and market appeal.

Positioning intersectionality as a marketing strategy, mega retailer Amazon's advertising division highlighted its potential to achieve both economic efficiency and emotional effectiveness by helping advertisers span multiple demographics with a single marketing initiative. In an advertorial titled "Why Inclusivity Matters," placed by Amazon Ads in the trade magazine *Adweek* in 2024, the company promoted a campaign it launched in collaboration with financial services company Mastercard, which featured Black women entrepreneurs: "In the U.S., the activation started during Black History Month in February and continued into Women's History Month in March, bringing to life the intersectionality of the campaign," explained Amazon.[24]

Some advertising agencies have framed intersectionality as a surefire route to brand relevance and customer loyalty with youth demographics. R/GA, a digital advertising agency based in New York City, referenced that "an understanding of intersectional identity politics" is a defining character trait of the coveted Gen Z demographic cohort—who are, as the agency noted, also "the most diverse and gender nonbinary of the generations." As the agency put it in a 2021 market research report, intersectionality "result[s] in a multitude of identities that open up possibilities rather than close them down."[25] Like other market segmentation approaches such as psychographics, which orient the creation of consumer markets around shared psychological characteristics, attitudes, and lifestyles and the five-factor OCEAN model of personality borrowed from psychology, advertising agencies' reinterpretation of intersectionality claims to offer advertisers a more precise alternative to traditional demographic targeting that orients markets around single categories. As one media agency executive put it, intersectionality can help marketers think outside of the conventional demographic box: "I think that in the [advertising] industry, and society in general, we have gotten to a place where we end up in buckets that are boxes. And they don't consider any of the intersectionality that makes any of us unique."[26]

Intersectionality's influential contribution to contemporary discourse on identity emphasizes the multiplicity of oppressions that shape subjectivity, social belonging, and the politics of classification.[27] Within marketing's racial information system, however, intersectionality is conceived of as an individualized trait, where people are envisioned as composites of distinct, bounded categories combined in a bespoke manner to be leveraged for brand appeal.

The marketing industry's impulse to rationalize and even quantify intersectionality as a technique of consumer measurement was promoted by the US advertising agency UM in a survey it commissioned to give a quantitative "confirmation of intersectionality" for its brand clients. Their survey claimed that "the average U.S. consumer identifies himself or herself 9.3 different ways, while Hispanic respondents placed into 10.3 different segments and Black audiences into 10 segments."[28] Indeed, advertising's fixation with interpreting intersectionality as a tool for creating, measuring, and objectifying populations into market segments diverges from Crenshaw's original intent for the term. In a 2016 speech at London's Southbank Centre, she underscored that intersectionality is not necessarily a theory of identity but is a critique of how political structures render certain identities both a consequence of and a vehicle for marginalization.[29]

Corporate America's widened embrace of intersectionality can be seen in its invocation as a focal point at key industry events like the 2020 AdColor Conference, one of the leading diversity and inclusion trade conferences for the American marketing, media, and entertainment industries. Crenshaw participated in the conference on a panel titled "Intersectionality 2.0," where she was in conversation with Google's chief diversity officer Melonie Parker to discuss how the concept of intersectionality could help corporate leaders develop better HR strategies, particularly for advancing Black women and women of color in corporate marketing fields. Crenshaw emphasized the critical role that advertising plays in societal storytelling, with its power to shift social consciousness. She urged the audience of marketing and media professionals to prioritize creating representations that honestly reflect American society's challenges with structural oppression rather than presenting only aspirational images of equality already achieved:

> We want to be that society, but to become that society, we've got to tell the stories of when we're not. . . . We have to fill it with content, with narrative, with more honest portrayals of people, of what this world actually looks like and what their various challenges are. If we fill it with these substantive stories and ideas, then we are able to consistently build on this picture of reality rather than starting from a fiction that none of this stuff matters anymore because we are a society that really embraces equality and justice for all.[30]

Intersectionality's anti-racist incorporation in brand marketing discourse has not simply been a top-down process of corporate co-optation. With help of the pro bono arm of the global public relations firm FleishmanHillard, Crenshaw has collaborated directly with brands, using their financial resources and far-reaching platforms to raise awareness about the #SayHerName campaign, founded in 2014 by her organization the African American Policy Forum, to increase visibility and legal redress for Black women and girls impacted by state violence and police brutality in the United States.

Following the murder of Breonna Taylor by Louisville, Kentucky, police, the WNBA partnered with Crenshaw's organization and dedicated the 2020 season to Taylor and other Black women victims of police brutality. The season opener featured a televised moment of silence, with players wearing #SayHerName and "Breonna Taylor" jerseys and digital displays of the phrase on the courts.[31] Crenshaw described the WNBA partnership as "game changing" for raising public awareness about intersectional feminism, especially considering the league's viewership notably increased that year.[32] Her organization has also collaborated with luxury brand Gucci and its Chime for Change corporate social responsibility program to produce a digital zine featuring essays, poetry, art, and audiovisual testimonies that centered Black women in discussions of structural racism, gender violence, and police brutality.[33] The zine was promoted across Gucci Chime's social media platforms (figure C.3).

Crenshaw's direct engagement with brand culture as a strategy to spread the political teachings of intersectionality to wider audiences high-

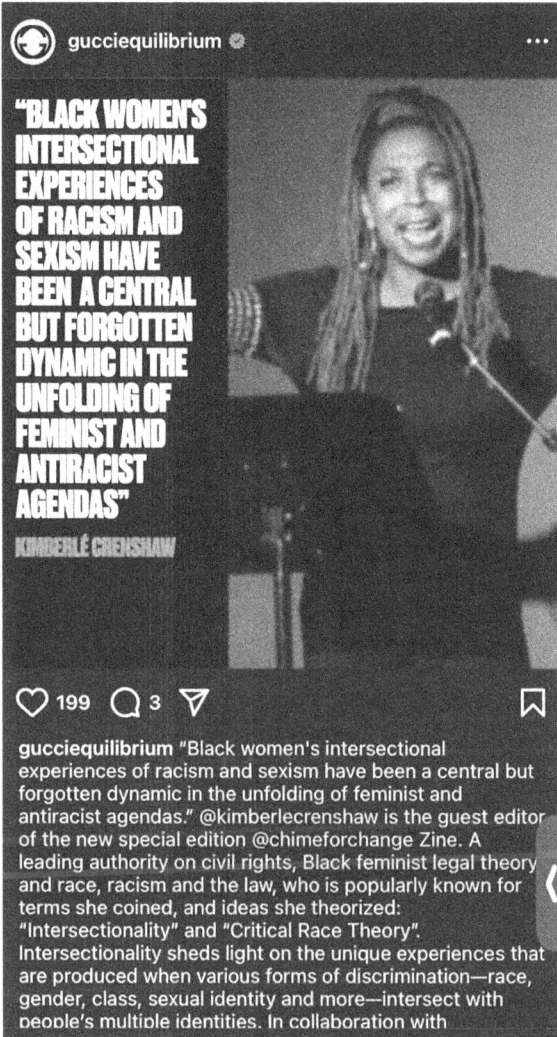

gucciequilibrium ✓ ···

"BLACK WOMEN'S INTERSECTIONAL EXPERIENCES OF RACISM AND SEXISM HAVE BEEN A CENTRAL BUT FORGOTTEN DYNAMIC IN THE UNFOLDING OF FEMINIST AND ANTIRACIST AGENDAS"

KIMBERLÉ CRENSHAW

♡ 199   ◯ 3   ◁   ◻

gucciequilibrium "Black women's intersectional experiences of racism and sexism have been a central but forgotten dynamic in the unfolding of feminist and antiracist agendas." @kimberlecrenshaw is the guest editor of the new special edition @chimeforchange Zine. A leading authority on civil rights, Black feminist legal theory and race, racism and the law, who is popularly known for terms she coined, and ideas she theorized: "Intersectionality" and "Critical Race Theory". Intersectionality sheds light on the unique experiences that are produced when various forms of discrimination—race, gender, class, sexual identity and more—intersect with people's multiple identities. In collaboration with

C.3 Gucci Equilibrium's 2020 Instagram post promoting the "Chime for Change #SayHerName Zine" guest-edited by Kimberlé Crenshaw and the African American Policy Forum.

C.4 The cover of *Adweek*'s August 2020 issue, featuring Patrisse Cullors, Alicia Garza, and Opal Tometi—the founders of the Black Lives Matter hashtag and movement.

lights the complex and ambivalent dynamics of contemporary social activism within neoliberal capitalism, where advocates can strategically try to leverage corporate marketing platforms in an effort to shift social consciousness and also secure financial support. Amid the marketing industry's 2020 racial reckoning, the advertising industry trade magazine *Adweek* featured Patrisse Cullors, Alicia Garza, and Opal Tometi—the founders of the Black Lives Matter hashtag and movement—on its cover and awarded them the Beacon Award for "driving significant change in diversity, equity, and inclusion" (figure C.4).[34] In the accompanying article, Patrisse Cullors humorously reflected on the proliferation of corporate brand messaging in support of #BlackLivesMatter, highlighting the unexpected endorsement from General Mills' Gushers candy brand. She remarked, "Gushers put up some tweets that were totally in support of BLM, and it was the funniest shit ever. . . . It was almost like the public pressure had them like, 'We've gotta say something, we can't be the only ones not saying something!' That's when I knew. I was like, 'OK, we've done our job.'"[35]

Cullors's statement celebrates the adoption of Black Lives Matter by brands as a signal of the movement's evolution from a grassroots initiative to a viral media moment, positioning brand marketing acknowledgment as a triumph for the social acceptance of anti-racism discourse in wider US culture. By featuring the BLM founders on its cover, *Adweek* implicitly framed the movement as a cultural media phenomenon that brands could learn from and actively participate in to shape consumer sentiment. Brand recognition, hailed as a milestone of social acceptance, is indeed playing a pivotal role in "telling intersectionality's story" to the public.

While the incorporation of anti-racist-themed messages and rhetoric in marketing can be seen as a victory for discursive and ideological change by bringing concepts from critical race theory, such as intersectionality, into wider awareness, this type of advertising often proves more effective at promoting the image of progress as a form of aspiration. In a 2021 speech marking the 100th anniversary of the Tulsa Race Massacre, President Joe Biden highlighted the increasing presence of interracial couples in TV ads as a symbol of social progress, remarking, "For those of you who are over 50—how often did you see advertisements on television with Black and white couples? . . . Today, two to three out of five commercials feature mixed-race couples. That's not by accident. They're selling soap, man."[36] The notion that advertising accurately reflects political reality overlooks the fact that it is a refraction, shaped by the perceptions and objectives of marketing elites who are not only selling products but also projecting desires, and what they believe consumers want to see. Biden's perspective obscures how social justice–themed advertising is not done out of benevolence but is intended to align with corporate interests, surreptitiously reinforcing existing power structures through the symbols and discourse of insurgent politics.

When Doritos positions itself as a "megaphone for change" in the realm of racial justice, it does so as a coercive force, with the aim of shaping human behavior and perceptions in its favor.[37] Although anti-racism has gained prominence as a marketing theme, and corporations have recognized people of color as valuable target consumers, this heightened acknowledgment exists alongside the harsh reality that these groups continue to endure the harmful outcomes of a society structured by intersecting oppressions.

TARGETING EL PASO

On the morning of August 3, 2019, the Cielo Vista Walmart store in El Paso, Texas, bustled with shoppers starting their day. Located in the southwestern part of the state, El Paso shares a border with the Mexican city of Juárez and has a population that is over 81 percent Hispanic.[38] Walmart, as one of the nation's largest retailers, boasts store locations within ten miles of 90 percent of the US population.[39] In 2023, the company spent over $4 billion advertising its "Save Money. Live Better" brand message to American consumers. "One hundred percent of the growth [in sales] is going to come from multicultural customers," was a point highlighted by the brand's senior vice president of brand marketing at a major multicultural advertising conference.[40]

Given El Paso's demographic makeup, the city's residents are a prime target for Walmart's Hispanic marketing efforts. "We're striving to integrate Hispanics into every step of our marketing process, and beyond to merchandising and operations," said Tony Rogers, Walmart's former senior vice president for brand marketing in 2011.[41] Speaking of cities in the United States undergoing minority-majority demographic change, Rogers observed at an industry conference, "Places that were traditionally in the top 20 like Baltimore, Milwaukee and Boston are now giving way to new growth centers like El Paso, Texas."

At many of the industry trade conferences and events I attended, Walmart was celebrated as a leader in multicultural marketing, praised for investing in long-term business relationships with several multicultural advertising agencies, including Hispanic agency Lopez Negrete Communications in Houston, Texas, and African American agency Burrell Communications in Chicago, Illinois. Walmart has also received awards for its targeted Hispanic marketing efforts, ranking among the top brands with the most "culturally relevant" ads that also encourage "purchase intent," according to advertising reception studies.[42]

One of Walmart's winning "culturally relevant," multicultural marketing campaigns in 2019, made by Lopez Negrete, depicts a lively scene of young, mostly olive-skinned, dark-haired twenty-somethings jubilantly

C.5 The closing shot from Walmart's 2019 Hispanic-market advertisement, created by Lopez Negrete Communications, for which Walmart won an industry award from the Association of National Advertisers as one of the most "culturally relevant" brands.

preparing a summer meal together at a backyard barbecue. Set against a rhythmic reggaeton soundtrack, the ad rotates through and features symbols drawn from tropes of Hispanic pan-ethnicity routinely used in the multicultural market. There is a close-up shot of a habanero pepper being seared by an even hotter flame (the pepper is used to make salsa, of course); a curly-haired woman dances coquettishly around a simmering pot of beans; a group of friends giggles over a pan of frying empanadas. Everyone is happy and dancing (figure C.5). Alex Lopez, head of Lopez Negrete, responded to the accolades for the campaign by emphasizing the instrumental role of his agency's multicultural marketing expertise in producing advertising that authentically reflects Hispanic cultural distinctiveness, making consumers feel affirmed, valued, and thus more loyal to the Walmart brand. Lopez stated: "Imbuing cultural insights and elements into an ad or any piece of content is a subtle art form with very powerful results. Authenticity comes from articulating a shared perception and a willingness *to be seen* and recognized accordingly."[43]

Lopez's remarks mirror the sentiments of Walmart's own marketing executives, who also attribute the company's success with Hispanic consumers to their dedication to making them "feel seen." "We build trust with our consumers by delivering on our brand promise of enhancing their lives," said the company's chief marketing officer William White in a 2022 address after receiving an award for being the most "Culturally Inclusive Brand in the United States." "This involves ensuring that everyone feels seen, heard, and welcomed in every interaction—whether in-store, online, or through our marketing."[44]

In the American advertising industry's racial information system, the phrase "feeling seen" has become increasingly emphasized in marketing briefs, research, and trade publications. The term is used to refer to the emotional experience of recognition, validation, respect, and affirmation that people of color should feel when they perceive themselves as accurately represented in marketing campaigns. To "feel seen" is to be interpellated by an advertiser—hailed as a valued consumer subject, recognized as important, worthy, and deserving of a message crafted just for them. In the United States, this desire reflects the market's deep influence on shaping subjectivity, intertwining consumerism with broader aspirations for social equity, respect, and political inclusion.

"When you don't see yourself reflected [in advertising], when you are not feeling seen, it says you are invisible, you are not important, and you don't matter," notes Ty Heath, a marketing executive at the social networking platform LinkedIn.[45] Inclusive advertising is increasingly viewed not only as essential to corporate responsibility and societal fairness but also as a business imperative. "It is our responsibility as marketers to ensure that people are portrayed and that in doing so the portrayal is fair, accurate and realistic," continued Heath.

A wealth of market research highlights the importance of "feeling seen," which is considered particularly significant for people of color who have historically been subjected to stereotypical portrayals and exclusion in mass advertising. Market research firm Kantar reports that 64 percent of Hispanic consumers seek out brands that acknowledge their culture and unique traditions.[46] Similarly, a 2024 survey by Google claimed that Black millennials in the United States are more likely to support brands that positively reflect "Black culture," with 70 percent stating they are "more likely to buy from a brand that takes a stand on race-related issues."[47] Marketing is being increasingly recognized and held accountable as an institutional force that shapes ideological perceptions of racial groups, with growing expectations from consumers for greater responsibility in this role.

"Feeling seen" is also theorized about by businesses as a powerful tool for cultivating customer loyalty and profitability among America's new mainstream consumer groups. In today's increasingly fragmented digital-first marketing landscape, the "positive emotional response" of "feeling seen" in an ad "is the number one element that determines its potential to make a long-term impact on brand growth," note marketers at the firm System1.[48]

"Feeling seen" as a marketing strategy raises critical questions about who truly benefits from this heightened commercial visibility. Sarah Banet-Weiser argues that today's neoliberal brand culture operates within a digitally mediated "economy of visibility," where public discourse on social justice is increasingly shaped by corporate platform engagement metrics— likes, shares, and follows. Resultantly, the types of feminism most easily branded through a market logic, such as those that focus on individual self-improvement, confidence and competence, and social justice through consumption, prevail. Brands like Dove, celebrated for critiquing sexism in the beauty industry, and Always, with its #LikeAGirl campaign, promote a popular feminism that prioritizes inclusion and visibility as symbols of social justice in and of themselves. Banet-Weiser critiques this heightened focus on visibility, arguing that it "does not describe a political process, but rather assumes that visibility itself has been absorbed into the economy; indeed, that absorption is the political."[49] As a result, this "economy of visibility" fosters a form of popularized feminism that does not challenge the underlying power structures oppressing women. Instead, it ties women's identities and politics to consumer culture, where categories like race and gender are increasingly valued for their presence in prevailing power structures rather than for their ability to address the underlying systems of oppression shaping their manifestation. Francesca Sobande further observes that the intersectional "femvertising" from advertisers like Nike and Pepsi exemplifies how marketers making more overt references to systemic oppression as advertising themes do so in ways that still emphasize notions of social change through consumption and individualism as opposed to any form of collective resistance.[50]

Walmart's 2020 marketing campaign "A Different Kind of Membership," which was launched during the American football season to promote the membership delivery service Walmart+, featured a TV ad with twenty-two families representing "the diversity of America," including Asian American, Black, Hispanic, white, and multiracial families, as well as new and single parents, multigenerational households, and people with disabilities. In a press release, Walmart described the commercial as capturing "a snapshot into [the families'] authentic, chaotic, and beautiful lives."[51] Advertisers like Walmart position themselves as agents of change by offering "authentic" representations of diversity and difference, generating positive brand associations and framing visibility in advertising as routes to social change. However, the rhetoric of "feeling seen" in American advertising ultimately "obscures the ways in which that aesthetic representation is not an analogue for the material positions, means, or resources of those [marginalized] populations."[52]

Walmart's marketing department is not the only institution focused on targeting Hispanics in El Paso, Texas. The city has also been a testing ground for the US government's immigration enforcement initiatives, including the surveillance, criminal prosecution, and separation of migrant children and families along the US–Mexico border.[53] As companies like Walmart embrace multicultural marketing strategies, conservative politicians and commentators are raising xenophobic alarms about the "great replacement"—a perceived threat implying a decline in non-Hispanic-white influence on American politics and culture due to immigration and birth-rate trends.

So, on the morning of August 3, 2019, when a twenty-one-year-old white nationalist drove nearly eleven hours to the Cielo Vista Walmart store in El Paso and killed twenty-three shoppers and injured twenty-two more, the store became the target of a racially motivated massacre, the deadliest on Hispanic people in modern US history: most of the victims were Mexican American and several were Mexican nationals from Juárez. Twenty minutes before the attack, the shooter published a white supremacist manifesto on the popular extremist message board 8chan, citing his crime as "a response to the Hispanic invasion of Texas." "They're taking our jobs, they're coming to replace us. . . . If we can get rid of enough people, then our way of life can be more sustainable," he wrote in his four-page screed. Upon being taken into police custody, the shooter flatly stated his ambitions to authorities: "I came here to kill Mexicans."[54]

The El Paso Walmart mass shooting starkly illustrates the contradictory ways Hispanics are perceived and targeted in the US today: as a desirable, loyal consumer market; as criminalized subjects of government surveillance and detainment; as threats to national security; and as victims of racial violence. This paradox exists in a cultural and political climate where "the state capitalizes on the mass detainment and deportation of non-white immigrants while claiming to celebrate diversity and multiculturalism."[55] Whether Hispanics are framed as a threat or as loyal consumers, racial ideologies are flexible and mobilized to serve different projects and agendas. Indeed, an underlying commitment remains to the category

itself, and the construction, assignment, and enforcement of such categories to maintain power hierarchies and regulate social, political, and economic life.

In the years since the summer of 2020, marketing's anti-racism moment has proven to be fleeting and largely symbolic—a brief public relations spectacle. The billions of dollars pledged by corporate America
following George Floyd's murder have had a minimal measurable impact.
According to a *Washington Post* analysis, of the nearly $50 billion pledged by
the fifty largest public companies to racial justice initiatives, over 90 percent consisted of loans or investments from which the companies could
profit.[56] Meanwhile, as journalist Pamela Newkirk highlights in her book
Diversity, Inc., corporate diversity policies have historically functioned as
mechanisms to protect organizations from costly employment discrimination lawsuits.[57]

Diversity was a celebrated virtue in the post–civil rights era and was
subsequently deployed by capitalism as a business imperative—tied to
profitability and product innovation. However, the pendulum has swung
the other way, especially following Donald Trump's 2024 presidential victory, with a conservative backlash sweeping state, federal, and corporate
arenas. The Supreme Court's 2023 decision to overturn affirmative action
in college admissions catalyzed widespread legal scrutiny of DEI initiatives
across the public and private sectors.

Many of the same companies that championed racial justice in their
2020 marketing campaigns are now reversing course. Some have even
cited DEI as a "risk factor" in securities filings, acknowledging the potential
legal and financial repercussions of prioritizing diversity in an increasingly
hostile right-wing political climate.[58] Walmart shuttered its Center for Racial Equity, while McDonald's pointed to the "shifting legal landscape" in
its decision to phase out DEI programs in executive leadership and sup-
plier relationships. In a 2025 press release, Target announced the end of
its Racial Equity Action and Change initiative, which was launched in 2020
to support Black-owned businesses. Despite these rollbacks, the company
maintains that it seeks to "create joyful experiences through an assortment
of products and services that help all guests *feel seen* and celebrated."[59]

Multicultural advertising agencies are seeing their budgets slashed by
clients who once rushed to signal their commitment to racial equality in
the marketplace. As one managing partner of a Black-owned marketing
agency told *Digiday*, "We've seen many clients completely eliminate their
DEI budgets"—a stark contrast to the flood of inquiries that followed the

racial justice uprisings of 2020, when "phones were ringing off the hook."[60] The advertising industry, which once helped solidify *diversity* as a marketable asset, now grapples with the term's volatile positioning at the heart of America's cultural and political wars. DEI has become an expendable business practice, readily abandoned under the weight of political retribution.

Despite heightening racial tensions in the United States and an intensifying conservative backlash against DEI, the multicultural marketing professionals I observed during my research still approach their work with a profound sense of purpose. For them, their work is not just about economic gain. In a nation where *citizen* and *consumer* are nearly synonymous, one of the long-standing principles of multicultural marketing has been the imperative to craft commercial narratives that challenge racial stereotypes and affirm the worth of people of color as American consumer-citizens.

Yvonne, a Hispanic multicultural marketing strategist, views her profession as a way to advocate for people of color within corporate America. As she puts it, "I get to tell people about my story. I get to tell brands how important it is to speak to Black and Brown [people]. If [companies] want to get into my pockets, they have to reach me authentically and in a way that feels genuine."[61] For Yvonne, multicultural marketing is deeply personal, as she draws from her lived experiences to inform the advertising strategies she helps create, infusing them with racial expertise. This sentiment, shared by Yvonne and many of my research participants, highlights the driving force behind these professionals: the desire to create a sense of feeling seen, recognized, and respected in the marketing messages that brands convey. When corporations are positioned as arbiters of societal value, multicultural marketing takes on an activist dimension.

For Vince, head of strategy at Soar, multicultural marketing represents a powerful avenue for economic self-determination for Hispanic entrepreneurs like himself. "I take pride in building a career rooted in my identity, in what I experience as a human on this earth. I can support my family through an economy created by my own people."[62] Vince reflects on the pivotal role that multicultural advertising agencies have played, serving as what historian Jason Chambers calls an "economic on-ramp" for people of color to own means of production in the American advertising industry.[63] In this sense, racial expertise is both "enabling and constraining" for the political aims of those working within it.[64] It is enabling because it turns racial subjectivity into a source of professional opportunity within capitalism, providing economic self-sufficiency and granting industry professionals a degree of control over how people of color are represented in the media. Yet, it is also constraining, as these professionals are often compelled to reify race in ways that naturalize racial categories and endorse a cultural narrative that conflates consumer buying power with political power.

American advertising's racial information system has long defined the value of people of color as consumers through quantitative data, from US Census projections to market research that measures their economic influence in terms like gross domestic product (GDP). As one marketer put it, "The U.S. multicultural population is an economic powerhouse, with the GDPs of the African American and Hispanic populations each surpassing those of all but thirteen countries in the world, and Asian buying power exceeding the GDP of all but sixteen countries."[65] This move to economize racialized life through the concepts of GDP and buying power promotes a misleading narrative about consumer capitalism's potential to foster racial equality. Communications theorist Jared Ball argues that the notion of "Black buying power" promotes a narrow and misleading definition of power as the ability to consume goods rather than achieve social and economic equality.[66] Marketing narratives that celebrate "buying power" as a marker of consumer citizenship perpetuate the myth that purchasing power is equivalent to equal protection under the law.

Total Market American provides a perspective on the US advertising industry's ongoing efforts to mold and persuade human beings for profit, shedding light on how knowledge production about racial difference underpins the foundations of American business—and, by extension, contemporary capitalism. Multicultural marketing and the racial expertise it produces and commodifies reveal the entanglement of consumer culture with ideological investments designed to keep us ensnared in its logic. This process reflects deeply ingrained notions of essential racial difference, rooted in centuries of history, while simultaneously contributing to their perpetuation and evolution.

The book also examines the struggles experienced by the multicultural marketing industry to gain acceptance and validation for its expertise and the racial markets it represents. These struggles highlight the paradoxes of racism within the American marketplace, where the value of people of color is often questioned by advertisers despite the economic potential that such targeted marketing could possibly provide.

"If race lives on today, it can do so only because we continue to create and re-create it in our social life, continue to verify it, and thus continue to need a social vocabulary that will allow us to make sense, not of what our ancestors did then, but of what we ourselves choose to do now," reflects historian Barbara Fields.[67] Advertising professional discourse, as an institutionalized form of knowledge made for commercial interests, plays a part in re-creating racism's influence on how we understand what it means to be human. The social categories racism creates, meant to divide and partition people for domination and extraction, are reflected, refracted, and reinforced through marketing practices.

Advertising's power has always rested on its capacity to interpellate us into its matrix of meanings, where in our market society, we look to it as a domain that can validate the sanctity of our humanity. For decades, the advertising industry has transfused the supposed virtues of consumerism into popular culture representations and political stump speeches about American exceptionalism, conflating democratic freedoms with free market aims. These narratives designed to entice become infused—whether we like it or not—into our own life narratives, seeping into our conceptions of who we are and where we belong.

Multicultural marketing's normative politics aim to rectify the legacy and continued relevance of racist mass media, marketplace segregation, and exclusion. Through avowed strategic nuance, data, and market research, industry professionals deploy racial knowledge production as a means of restoring dignity, framing target marketing budgets as a measure of social standing. Yet, as Sut Jhally notes, "The falsity of advertising is not in the appeals it makes, but in the answers that it provides."[68] Multicultural marketing's answer siphons anti-racism through the visuality and, increasingly, the surveillance of consumer culture.

When we rely on marketing to convey anti-racist discourse, we cede the power to corporations to define what anti-racism means and which rights are worth protecting. The right to exist, to dream, and to belong becomes bounded by what we can buy and how corporations measure our value to them. This dynamic leaves us vulnerable: When corporate priorities shift, as we're seeing in case of DEI, the recognition and visibility we sought through these avenues may vanish. Where does that leave us?

In the end, brands won't save us—they never could. Only by confronting the contradictions of consumer capitalism and dismantling its false promises can we break free from the illusive reality that the advertising industry's racial information system seeks to dream for us.

ACKNOWLEDGMENTS

I often refer to this book as my third baby, as I became a mother (twice) while writing it. Without the support of my family, it simply wouldn't exist. My mother, G. Rosa Rey, always there for me when I need her, was also the first to tell me, "If there's a book you want to read but hasn't been written, you need to write it." Since childhood, she always encouraged me to question authority. My sister, Ali Rosa-Salas, is my lifelong companion and an unwavering source of support and grounding. To my father, Alfonso Salas—thank you for always believing in me.

Along the way, my husband, Michael L. Thomas Jr., offered loving provocations and encouragement. And my children, Ezra and Soleil, are my life's biggest teachers.

I am fortunate to have had mentors along my journey who have engaged with my ideas at all stages, offering invaluable guidance and inspiration throughout the various stages of research, writing, and revision. My doctoral training in cultural anthropology at New York University was shaped by the influence of Arlene Dávila, whose groundbreaking work, *Latinos, Inc.*, was the first to show me that the research I wanted to do could be done. Her honesty, attentiveness, and care have been a gift to me. Helena Hansen's compassionate mentorship and the invaluable opportunity to be a research assistant for her project on multicultural pharmaceutical marketing provided crucial pre-fieldwork experiences and connections. I am also fortunate to have learned greatly from Faye Ginsburg, David Crockett, and Safiya Noble, whose sage insights played a crucial role in bringing this work to fruition.

Throughout my educational journey, I have been lucky to have come across educators who have influenced my approach as a scholar and have inspired and encouraged me along the way. Thank you to John L. Jackson Jr., Tanji Gilliam, Dorothy Roberts, Deborah A. Thomas, Donald Bogle, and the late Phoebe Search for their mentorship over the years.

Dear friends and colleagues have also been integral to this process. Their brilliance, feedback, and support—delivered always with care—helped see me and this work through. I owe special thanks to Julia Chan, Victor Peterson II, Isabel Attyah Flower, Kiran Samuel, Ethiraj Gabriel Dattatreyan, Amelia Herbert, Olufemi Leverett, and Chasson Gracie. Thanks to Alexis Van Eyken for facilitating connections, as well as Edward Timke and Martin Vega for sharing articles. I also extend endless gratitude to Charlie Monlouis Anderle and Adwoa Duncan Williams for being trusted caregivers to Ezra, allowing me precious daylight hours to work on these pages.

It has been a dream to work with Duke University Press. I am grateful for Ken Wissoker for believing in this work and supporting it through the years it has taken me to shape it into what I envisioned. Many thanks are due to Ryan Kendall, Michael Trudeau, Livia Tenzer, and the entire production and design team at Duke, as well as the anonymous reviewers whose enthusiasm and generative feedback have helped make this book the best it can be.

A special thank you to the research librarians at Duke University's David M. Rubenstein Rare Book and Manuscript Library for their assistance in sourcing images, and Muhammad Aakif Khan for his diligence and attention to detail in completing my citations and bibliography. I am grateful to Paula Durbin-Westby for her work on the index. I learned a great deal from my tutoring sessions with Dr. Jody-Ann S. Jones on digital advertising and machine learning.

Over the years, I have had the privilege of presenting parts of this book to audiences whose engagement and questions have helped shape it into what it is today. I would like to thank the organizers and participants of the Race in the Marketplace Research Forum (2018), the Latinx Project at NYU's Digitizing Race Conference (2018), the USC Annenberg Summer Doctoral Institute on Difference in Media and Culture (2019), the Columbia University Sociology Department's Critical Race and Digital Studies Working Group (2020), Data and Society (2020), Harvard's Berkman Klein Race and Media Working Group (2021), the University of Cincinnati's Department of Anthropology Colloquium (2021), the Chicago Consumer Culture Community Working Group (2021), the Mary E. Junck Research Colloquium at the University of North Carolina at Chapel Hill (2024), and the students in Arlene Dávila's media and race courses at NYU and Zeynep Sertbulut's Global Media Worlds course at Haverford College.

Fieldwork for this book was made possible by the generous support of the Wenner-Gren Foundation and the Ford Foundation Predoctoral Fellowship. I wrote the first draft of this manuscript in Madrid, Spain, in 2018 as part of NYU's Global Research Initiative Fellowship.

Lastly, though I cannot name them here due to the anonymity maintained throughout the book, I owe a profound debt of gratitude to the advertising industry professionals whose openness and willingness to share their experiences with me about their profession are central to this work. Their collaboration, insights, and generosity are the core of this project, and I am grateful for their trust.

NOTES

1   Dímelo is a pseudonym.
2   "US Multicultural Media Spend to Grow." In 2023, advertisers spent over $34 billion on advertising targeted to Hispanic, African American, and Asian American markets, accounting for over 5 percent of overall advertising and marketing spending.
3   Frey, "US Will Become 'Minority White'"; Vespa, Medina, and Armstrong, *Demographic Turning Points*, 7.
4   "Marc Pritchard"; Pritchard, "New Habits for Multicultural Growth."
5   See Lears, *Fables of Abundance*; Marchand, *Advertising the American Dream*; McGovern, *Sold American*; Ewen, *Captains of Consciousness*.
6   Turow, *Breaking Up America*.
7   For the construction of a child-oriented market with the rise of the television network Nickelodeon, see Banet-Weiser, *Kids Rule!*; on the commodification of feminist politics in the twenty-first century, see Banet-Weiser, *Empowered*; about the role of anti-Black racial discrimination in US retail settings, see Austin, "'A Nation of Thieves'"; for an anthropological exploration of African American consumers through the lives of children, see Chin, *Purchasing Power*, and O'Barr, *Culture and the Ad*. Outside the American context, anthropologists have examined advertising agencies in nations like Sri Lanka, Trinidad, and India and have documented industry professionals' processes of imagining audiences as they navigate global advertisers' expectations for locally resonant campaigns. See Kemper, *Buying and Believing*; Mazzarella, *Shoveling Smoke*; Miller, *Capitalism*.
8   Dávila, *Latinos, Inc.*; Shankar, *Advertising Diversity*.
9   Dávila, *Latinos, Inc.*, chap. 2.
10 Shankar, "Nothing Sells like Whiteness."
11 Napoli, *Audience Evolution*, 30.
12 Ang, *Desperately Seeking the Audience*, 32, 35.

13 Bowker and Star, *Sorting Things Out*.

14 Chatelain, *Franchise*, 18. For another important book on the racial politics of fast food marketing, see Kwate, *White Burgers, Black Cash*.

15 Quoted in Helm, "Ethnic Marketing."

16 Quoted in Helm, "Ethnic Marketing."

17 WARC, "McDonald's Eyes Ethnic Consumers."

18 York, "Ethnic Insights Form."

19 WARC, "McDonald's Eyes Ethnic Consumers."

20 McDonald's Corporation, "Black and Golden."

21 Taylor, "Leaked Memo."

22 Sender, *Business, Not Politics*, 141.

23 See Robinson, *Black Marxism*, for historical background on the role of racial
thinking in the structure of capitalism's economic and social hierarchies,
with antecedents in feudal Europe. See also Melamed, "Racial Capitalism";
Jenkins and Leroy, introduction to *Histories of Racial Capitalism*.

24 In *Racecraft: The Soul of Inequality in American Life*, historians Karen Fields
and Barbara Fields critique these enduring epistemologies for miscon-
struing the products of racist power structures as racial traits. They pro-
pose the concept of "racecraft," a cognitive illusion akin to witchcraft,
which obscures the fact that racism is the creator of race as a construct
of what it means to be human shaped by political structures designed to
justify inequality and exploitation.

25 Goldberg, "Racial Knowledge," 154–55.

26 Hall, *Race: The Floating Signifier*.

27 Goldberg, "Racial Knowledge," 155.

28 Bhattacharyya, *Rethinking Racial Capitalism*, 7.

29 Roberts, *Fatal Invention*; Elias and Feagin, *Racial Theories in Social Science*.

30 Graves and Goodman, *Racism, Not Race*, 23.

31 "Linnaeus and Race."

32 Smedley, *Race in North America*, 170.

33 "Linnaeus and Race."

34 Appiah, *Lies That Bind*, 26.

35 Morton and Combe, *Crania Americana*. For the refutation of Morton and
other eugenics, including scientific racism, see Gould, *Mismeasure of Man*.

36 Du Bois's *Philadelphia Negro* used data to link African American struggles
to social conditions. In 1885, Anténor Firmin's *The Equality of the Human
Races* refuted racial science with anthropological evidence.

37 Muhammad, *The Condemnation of Blackness*.

38 Although Franz Boas and his students are credited with challenging scientific racism with cultural relativism, historians have shown the ways
in which anthropologists of the early twentieth century "promoted a vision of race rooted in both bodies *and* cultures," as Tracy Teslow writes
in *Constructing Race: The Science of Bodies and Cultures in American Anthropol-*

ogy (3). Teslow observes that this framing not only naturalized race but embedded racial logics in the culture concept itself, leaving a lasting legacy in the theorization of human differences within anthropology and wider society. See also Baker, *Anthropology and the Racial Politics*; Baker, "Racist Anti-Racism"; Trouillot, "Adieu, Culture."

39   Rutherford, *How to Argue with a Racist*.

40   Smedley and Smedley, "Race as Biology Is Fiction."

41   Smedley, *Race in North America*, 33.

42   On Black athleticism, see Schultz, "Racialized Osteology"; on race-based medicine, see Kahn, *Race in a Bottle*; on the idea of "the Black vote," see Johnson, "How the Black Vote Became."

43   Pegg et al., "Revealed: International 'Race Science' Network."

44   While on the 2024 campaign trail, Donald Trump drew a direct link between Latin American immigration, violent crime, and genetics, stating, "We got a lot of bad genes in our country right now." See Oza, "Trump's Talk of 'Bad Genes.'"

45   Hammonds and Herzig, "Introduction to the End of Race," 311.

46   McDonald's Corporation, *McDonald's 2021–2022*.

47   Pepviz, *Circle of Joy*, 6.

48   Bowker and Star, *Sorting Things Out*, 321.

49   Scholars like Cedric Robinson have pointed out that racialism—or the categorization and hierarchical treatment of people based on traits believed to be inherent and immutable—was not exclusive to the emergence of capitalism but was already present in Europe during the feudal and medieval periods. See Robinson, *Black Marxism*.

50   Kern-Foxworth, *Aunt Jemima, Uncle Ben*; Kennedy, "Marketing Goods," 621–22.

51   Davis, "Selling Whiteness?"; Kennedy, "Marketing Goods."

52   "Commodity racism" is a term developed by Anne McClintock in her 1995 book *Imperial Leather*, where she examined how turn-of-the-twentieth-century soap advertising in imperial England was suffused with symbolism about cleanliness that functioned to normalize ideologies of white supremacy. In Elizabeth Chin's 2015 article "Commodity Racism," she broadens the definition of "commodity racism" to refer "racist modes of the commodification of people," which include slavery but also advertising's repertoire of media where racial logics are embedded.

53   hooks, *Black Looks*, 21–39.

54   Wilson, "Race in Commodity Exchange and Consumption," 587.

55   Weems, *Desegregating the Dollar*, 2.

56   Chang, *Who We Be*; Melamed, *Represent and Destroy*.

57   Ferguson, *Reorder of Things*, 66.

58   Frank, *Conquest of Cool*, 25.

59   Ferguson, *Reorder of Things*, 73.

60 Turow, *Breaking Up America*.

61 Purpose Brand. "Black Lives Matter Sparks Marketing Response."

62 Featherstone, *Divining Desire*.

63 Dávila, *Latinos, Inc.*, 19.

64 Shankar, *Advertising Diversity*, 30.

65 US Census Bureau, "Hispanic Heritage Month."

66 Lopez, Krogstad, and Passel, "Who Is Hispanic?" Morales, *Latinx*, argues that those classified as "Latinx" occupy an in-between space that challenges the US Black/white racial binary. Yet, in marketing contexts, I've observed this "mixedness" still framed in racialized terms.

CHAPTER 1. THE "GENERAL MARKET": ON THE COMMERCIAL CONSTRUCTION OF AMERICAN WHITENESS

This chapter draws on my chapter "Making the Mass White: How Racial Segregation Shaped Consumer Segmentation," in *Race in the Marketplace: Crossing Critical Boundaries* (New York: Palgrave MacMillan, 2019), edited by Guillaume D. Johnson et al.

1   Maheshwari, "Different Ads."

2   Personal communication with the author, 2016.

3   Personal communication with the author, 2016.

4   Personal communication with the author, 2018.

5   Personal communication with the author, 2018.

6   Personal communication with the author, 2018.

7   Hartigan, *Racial Situations*, 191.

8   Dyer, *White*.

9   Allen, *Invention of the White Race*.

10 Mills, *Racial Contract*, 61; Morris, "Standard White," 952.

11 Dyer, "Matter of Whiteness," 10.

12 Haney-López, *White by Law*; Harris, "Whiteness as Property."

13 In a 2005 implicit association study at an American university, psychologists Thierry Devos and Mahzarin Banaji found that most of the student participants unconsciously understood the categories of "American" and "white" as synonymous. See Devos and Banaji, "American = White?"

14 Mehaffy, "Advertising Race," 133.

15 Mehaffy, "Advertising Race," 133.

16 Manring, *Slave in a Box*, 36.

17 McGovern, *Sold American*, 106.

18 Marchand, *Advertising the American*, 64.

19 McGovern, *Sold American*, 97.

20 McGovern, *Sold American*, 119.

21 Jacobson, *Whiteness of a Different Color*.

22 Heinze, *Adapting to Abundance*.
23 Snyder, "European Americans."
24 Diner and Diner, "Jews and American Advertising."
25 Ewen, *Captains of Consciousness*, 64.
26 Diner and Diner, "Jews and American Advertising."
27 Turow, *Breaking Up America*, 23.
28 Painter, *History of White People*.
29 Frankenberg, *White Women*, 203.
30 Igo, *Averaged American*, 88, 86.
31 Douglas, *How Institutions Think*, 59.
32 Marchand, *Advertising the American*, 64.
33 Marchand, *Advertising the American*, xvii.
34 Fox, "Epitaph for Middletown," 119; quote from Igo, "From Main Street," 244.
35 Igo, *Averaged American*, 57.
36 Fox, "Epitaph for Middletown," 119.
37 Halvorson and Reno, *Imagining the Heartland*.
38 Marchand, *Advertising the American*, 64.
39 Marchand, *Advertising the American*, 64.
40 Ward, "Capitalism," 210.
41 Zunz, *Why the American Century?*, 60.
42 Wayland-Smith, *Angel in the Marketplace*, 95.
43 Davis, "Realizing Marketplace Opportunity," 475.
44 Rothstein, *Color of Law*.
45 Cohen, *A Consumers' Republic*.
46 Lipsitz, *Possessive Investment*, 7.
47 Harris, *Little White Houses*, 16.
48 Chambers, *Madison Avenue*, chap. 5.
49 Mora, *Making Hispanics*; Dávila, *Latinos, Inc.*
50 Shankar, "Nothing Sells like Whiteness."
51 Cohen, *A Consumers' Republic*, 325.
52 Mora, *Making Hispanics*, 126–27.
53 Mora, *Making Hispanics*, 126.
54 Mora, *Making Hispanics*, 129.
55 Personal communication with the author, 2018.
56 Burgos and Mobolade, *Marketing to the New Majority*.
57 Grue and Heiberg, "Notes on the History of Normality."
58 Reisdorf, "Significance of Race."
59 Wynter, "Unsettling the Coloniality."
60 Ferguson, *Out There*, 11.
61 Personal communication with the author, 2018.
62 Robinson, "Sharecropping on Madison Avenue."
63 Rittenhouse, "Agencies Owned."

64 Morris, "Standard White," 975.

65 Personal communication with the author, 2015.

66 Personal communication with the author, 2017.

67 Personal communication with the author, 2017.

68 Personal communication with the author, 2018.

69 Abu-Lughod, "Writing Against Culture," 143.

70 Frankenberg, *White Women*, 202–3.

71 Frankenberg, *White Women*, 197.

72 Personal communication with the author, 2018.

73 Personal communication with the author, 2018.

74 Crockett, "Marketing Blackness," 256.

75 Personal communication with the author, 2017.

76 Frankenberg, *White Women*, 197–98; quote from Mora and Rodríguez-Muñiz, "Latinos, Race," 43.

77 Hautzinger, "How Tom Burrell Convinced Corporations," emphasis added.

78 Personal communication with the author, 2017.

79 Personal communication with the author, 2018.

80 Personal communication with the author, 2018.

81 Mills, "White Ignorance."

82 Personal communication with the author, 2018.

83 Hansen, Netherland, and Herzberg, *Whiteout*, 32.

84 Hansen, Netherland, and Herzberg, *Whiteout*, 11.

85 Personal communication with the author, 2017.

86 Personal communication with the author, 2017.

87 Personal communication with the author, 2018.

88 Personal communication with the author, 2018.

89 Personal communication with the author, 2018.

90 Bruell and Vranica, "Trump's Win."

91 Bruell and Vranica, "Trump's Win."

92 Maheshwari, "After Election Surprise."

CHAPTER 2. MULTICULTURAL STRATEGY AND THE PRODUCTION OF RACIAL EXPERTISE

1 A shopper marketing agency is a specialty type of marketing firm that is hired by retailers and brands to help them figure out an in-store and online shopping experience for customers that can maximize sales.

2 Emba, "'Black Panther.'"

3 Personal communication with the author, 2018.

4 Personal communication with the author, 2018.

5 As of 2019, the social media site Infoscout is now known as Numerator.

6 Napoli, *Audience Evolution*, 30, 51.

7   Dávila, *Latinos, Inc.*

8   Sender, *Business, Not Politics*, 145.

9   Ang, *Desperately Seeking the Audience*, 32.

10 Nancy Leong defines the concept of identity entrepreneurship as when "out-group members leverage their out-group status to derive social and economic value for themselves." Leong, "Identity Entrepreneurs," 1334. See also Leong, *Identity Capitalists.*

11 Feldwick, "Account Planning," 193.

12 Personal communication with the author, 2018.

13 Galbraith, *Affluent Society*, 127.

14 Personal communication with the author, 2018.

15 Personal communication with the author, 2018.

16 Bernays, *Propaganda.*

17 See Steel, *Truth, Lies, and Advertising.*

18 Baskin and Pickton, "Account Planning," 417.

19 Personal communication with the author, 2018.

20 Bhattacharyya, *Rethinking Racial Capitalism*, 157.

21 Personal communication with the author, 2018.

22 Resonate, "Understanding the Nuances."

23 Quoted in "Reimagining 'Multicultural.'"

24 Weems, *Desegregating the Dollar*, 32.

25 Davis, "Realizing Marketplace Opportunity," 475, commenting on H. A. Haring, "The Negro as Consumer," *Advertising and Selling*, September 3, 1930, 21.

26 Gandy, "Audience Construction," 20.

27 Davis, "Realizing Marketplace Opportunity," 474.

28 For a history of Pepsi's marketing to Black consumers, see Capparell, *Real Pepsi Challenge*. For a closer look at Coca-Cola's efforts, see Greer, *Represented.*

29 Weems, *Desegregating the Dollar*, 33.

30 Davis, "Realizing Marketplace Opportunity," 482.

31 Davis, "Realizing Marketplace Opportunity," 481.

32 Langston, dir., *Secret of Selling.*

33 Ball, *Myth and Propaganda*, 29.

34 Weems, *Desegregating the Dollar*, 75; Saunders, *Negro Handbook.*

35 Ferguson, *Reorder of Things*, 73.

36 Wailoo, *Pushing Cool*, 16–17, 22.

37 Patton, *Under the Influence.*

38 Dávila, *Latinos, Inc.*, 70.

39 Dávila, *Latinos, Inc.*, 73.

40 "HMC Strategic Excellence Awards."

41 Personal communication with the author, 2017.

42 Sender, *Business, Not Politics*, 154.

43 Sender, *Business, Not Politics*, 163.

44 Featherstone, *Divining Desire*.

45 NBC Universal Telemundo, *200%ers: Power of Bi-Cultural/Bi-Lingual Hispanics*.

46 Dávila, *Latinos, Inc.*, 76.

47 Napoli, *Audience Evolution*, 52.

48 "National Consumer Study," MRI-Simmons, https://www.mrisimmons .com/our-data/national-studies/national-consumer-study/ (accessed July 16, 2024). As the company's website explains, in 2021 it merged its National Consumer Study with its Survey of the American Consumer to create MRI-Simmons-USA, "the most comprehensive truth set on American consumers."

49 MRI-Simmons, "Hispanic Acculturation Segmentation."

50 Simmons Sales Representative, phone communication with the author, October 2019.

51 MRI-Simmons, "Hispanic Acculturation Segmentation."

52 See Todd et al., "Ethnicity and Analgesic Practice"; Todd, Samaroo, and Hoffman, "Ethnicity as a Risk Factor"; Wailoo, *Pain*.

53 Rodríguez-Muñiz, *Figures of the Future*, 85.

54 Ang, *Desperately Seeking the Audience*, 35.

55 Ang, *Desperately Seeking the Audience*, 35.

56 Saha, *Race and the Cultural Industries*, 138.

57 Saha, *Race and the Cultural Industries*, 128.

58 Zuberi, *Thicker than Blood*, 120.

59 Sender, *Business, Not Politics*, 154.

60 See James, "Making Sense of Race"; Zuberi, *Thicker than Blood*.

61 Nielsen, *La Oportunidad Latinx*, 48.

62 Ohmer, *George Gallup in Hollywood*, 7.

CHAPTER 3. REACHING "VERIFIED HISPANICS": THE RACIAL SCIENCE OF DIGITAL ADVERTISING

1 Cramer-Flood, "US Ad Spending 2023."

2 Boerman, Kruikemeier, and Borgesius, "Online Behavioral Advertising," 364.

3 Crain, *Profit over Privacy*, 1.

4 Cheney-Lippold, *We Are Data*, 45.

5 *Digiday*, "WTF Is Identity," 14; collection of the author. This article is no longer online.

6 Sivanandan, "Demographics Are Dead."

7 Personal communication with the author, 2018.

8 Blake, "Hispanic Ad Market Morphs."

9   Zuboff, *Age of Surveillance*, 6.

10   Gandy, *Panoptic Sort*, 16, 29.

11   Facebook, "Difference Diversity Makes."

12   Vidal, "Inclusion as Personalization."

13   Darmandrail, "Audience Data."

14   Lotame, "Lotame Data Exchange."

15   Acxiom, "Acxiom Personicx® Hispanic."

16   Browne, *Dark Matters*, 16.

17   Browne, *Dark Matters*, 91.

18   Browne, *Dark Matters*, 42.

19   On forecasting crime, see Richardson, Schultz, and Crawford, "Dirty Data." On suppressing racial justice movements, see Cagle, "Facebook"; Arrigo and Shaw, "De-Realization of Black Bodies." On overpolicing of marginalized communities, see OpenMIC, "Surveillance Capitalism."

20   Browne, *Dark Matters*, 109.

21   Chaar López, *Cybernetic Border*.

22   Amrute, "Sounding the Flat Alarm."

23   Turow, *Niche Envy*.

24   Sweeney, "Discrimination in Online Ad Delivery."

25   Noble, *Algorithms of Oppression*, xvi.

26   McGuigan, *Selling the American People*, 167.

27   Phan and Wark, "What Personalisation Can Do for You!"

28   Personal communication with the author, 2018.

29   In *Cybertypes* Lisa Nakamura uses the term *menu-driven identity* to refer to how digital interfaces, particularly drop-down menus, limit self-expression by enforcing predefined categories that reflect and reinforce racialized boundaries.

30   Hispanitech is a pseudonym.

31   Cheney-Lippold, *We Are Data*, 108–9.

32   Cheney-Lippold, *We Are Data*, 45.

33   Gordon, *Assimilation in American Life*, 72.

34   McGuigan and Rosa-Salas, "Model Consumers."

35   Dávila, *Latinos, Inc.*, 249.

36   Gandy, *Panoptic Sort*, 30.

37   ComScore, "ComScore Unified Digital Measurement™."

38   Banet-Weiser, *Authentic™*, 5.

39   Jackson, *Real Black*, 15, 13.

40   Cheney-Lippold, *We Are Data*.

41   Browne, *Dark Matters*, 110.

42   In "The Algorithm Knows I'm Black," Daniel Meyerend reflects on Black consumers' growing awareness and criticism of racialized personalization on platforms like Netflix.

43   Coleman, "Race as Technology," 193.

44 Coleman, "Race as Technology," 193.

45 Hwang, *Subprime Attention Crisis.*

46 Neumann, Tucker, and Whitfield, "How Effective Is Third-Party?"

47 Mizrahi, "7 CMOS Myths."

48 Sylvester, Santiago, and Spaeth, "Addressing Biases in Multicultural," 6.

49 Sylvester, Santiago, and Spaeth, "Addressing Biases in Multicultural," 6.

50 Carrasco, "Big Data Has a Big Diversity Problem."

51 Sylvester, Santiago, and Spaeth, "Addressing Biases in Multicultural," 8.

52 Sylvester, Santiago, and Spaeth, "Addressing Biases in Multicultural," 12.

53 Sylvester, Santiago, and Spaeth, "Addressing Biases in Multicultural," 5, 7.

54 Angwin, Tobin, and Varner, "Facebook (Still) Letting Housing Advertisers."

55 Siu, "Media Agencies."

56 Miller, "Data Privacy Laws."

57 Neff, "9 Companies and Agencies."

58 Sylvester, Santiago, and Spaeth, "Addressing Biases in Multicultural," 14.

59 Portada, "Leaders at PHD, UM and D'exposito Urge for Solutions."

60 Portada, "Do DSPs Have Racist Behavior?"

61 Portada, "Leaders at PHD, UM and D'exposito Urge for Solutions."

62 AdAge, "How Brands and Agencies Responded."

63 Hutchinson, *Myth of Black Capitalism*; Baradaran, *Color of Money.*

64 Schiff, "P&G's Programmatic Strategy."

65 Mandese, "Mindshare Launches Black 'Inclusion PMP.'"

66 VICE Media Group, "VICE Media Announces."

67 Sluis, "Penguin Random House."

68 MediaMath, "MediaMath Expands."

69 Gray, "Subject(ed) to Recognition," 788–89, 791.

70 Benjamin, *Race After Technology*, 124.

71 Allen, "Dismantling the 'Black Opticon,'" 927.

72 Quotation from Arnett, "Data, the New Cotton," 5. On the use of digital data in policing and criminalization, see Richardson, Schultz, and Crawford, "Dirty Data"; on the promotion of payday loans, see Hawkins and Penner, "Advertising Injustices"; on unhealthy foods, see Chester, Kopp, and Montgomery, "Does Buying Groceries Online Put SNAP Recipients at Risk"; on money-making schemes, see Allen, "Dismantling the 'Black Opticon,'" 925; and on the general downsides, see Gangadharan, "Downside of Digital Inclusion."

73 See Cox, "How the U.S. Military Buys Location Data"; Tau and Hackman, "Federal Agencies Use Cellphone Location."

74 McKinley, "Why Removing Ethnicity."

75 McKinley, "Why Removing Ethnicity."

76 McMillan Cottom, "Where Platform Capitalism," 443.

77 Hoffmann, "Terms of Inclusion," 3548.

78 Haymarket Books, "Policing Without the Police."
79 Roberts, "Digitizing the Carceral State."

CHAPTER 4. THE TOTAL MARKET TURN: US CENSUS PROJECTIONS AND MAKING THE NEW MAINSTREAM CONSUMER

1   Toyota, "All-New Toyota Camry Ignites."
2   Maheshwari, "Different Ads."
3   Maheshwari, "Different Ads."
4   Precourt, "Toyota Makes 'Total Market.'"
5   Adams, "Toyota Unifies Multicultural."
6   Frey, "New 2020 Census Results."
7   Frey, "Census Shows America's Post-2020."
8   Precourt, "Toyota Makes 'Total Market.'"
9   Futures Company, "Roadmap to the New America."
10 US Census Bureau, "U.S. Census Bureau Projections."
11 Garcia, *New Mainstream*, xii.
12 Garcia, *New Mainstream*, xii.
13 "SheaMoisture: Break the Walls."
14 St. Félix, "National Geographic Twins."
15 US Census Office, *History and Statistics of the State of Maryland*, quoted in Rodríguez, *Changing Race*, 76.
16 Alba and Nee, *Remaking the American Mainstream*, 12.
17 Alba and Nee, *Remaking the American Mainstream*, 284.
18 Mora and Rodríguez-Muñiz, "Latinos, Race," 44.
19 Rosa, *Looking Like a Language*, 21.
20 Nobles, *Shades of Citizenship*, 1.
21 Prewitt, *What Is "Your" Race?*
22 Anderson, *Imagined Communities*.
23 Mora and Rodríguez-Muñiz, "Latinos, Race," 45.
24 Rodríguez-Muñiz, *Figures of the Future*, 85.
25 Rodríguez-Muñiz, *Figures of the Future*, 89, 98.
26 Edmonston and Schultze, *Modernizing the U.S. Census*, 292.
27 Chambers, *Madison Avenue and the Color Line*, 45–46; Mora, *Making Hispanics*, 112–14. Census data itself has led to the burgeoning of entirely new ethnoracial market segments. For example, the 1980 US Census data—the first to include a question about Hispanic ethnicity—was absolutely crucial to the rise of the Hispanic advertising industry. Census data allowed for Spanish-language media networks, consumer researchers, and advertising executives to demonstrate—with the official imprimatur of the state—the existence of a growing "Hispanic popu-

lation" that spanned the entire nation. Relatedly, anthropologist Shankar's scholarship details the ways that US Census data are central to the existence of Asian American advertising agencies. Shankar shows how US Census racial data, combined "with data from market research, demography and history," coalesce in industry practice "to construct the category of Asian American for advertising" in a manner that meets the industry's financial imperatives. Shankar, *Advertising Diversity*, 8 and 59.

28 Shankar, *Advertising Diversity*, 150.

29 Geoscape and CMO Council, *Activating the New American Mainstream™*, 9.

30 Precourt, "Walmart's Multicultural Strategy."

31 Pritchard, "New Habits for Multicultural Growth."

32 Nielsen, "Making of a Multicultural Super Consumer."

33 Shankar, "Nothing Sells like Whiteness," 114.

34 Precourt, "Wells Fargo Builds Total-Market Insights."

35 Odell, "Wells Fargo's Total Market Approach Journey."

36 Johnson and Grier, "Targeting Without Alienating."

37 Precourt, "Wells Fargo Builds Total-Market Insights."

38 US Department of Justice, "Wells Fargo Agrees to Pay $3 Billion."

39 Phillips, "Wells Fargo Targeted Undocumented Immigrants."

40 WARC, "Wells Fargo Boosted by Multicultural Strength."

41 Taylor, *Race for Profit*.

42 For the ad, see "Apoyamos con orgullo."

43 Ahmed, *On Being Included*, 69.

44 Jacobson, "Total Market," 27.

45 Hsu, "Advertising Industry Has a Problem."

46 "Nothing to Shout About."

47 Rittenhouse, "More Agency Consolidation."

48 Personal communication with the author, 2018.

49 Phillips, *Brown Is the New White*, 3.

50 Personal communication with the author, 2018.

51 Personal communication with the author, 2018.

52 Personal communication with the author, 2018.

53 Círculo Creativo USA, "Anomaly Takes Aim at the 'Last Silo.'"

54 Elliott, "Ogilvy and Mather Unit Tries."

55 Bowman and Katz, *Reframe the Marketplace*, 65. See also Bowman, *Whitewashing of the Total Market*.

56 Bowman credits the origins of the *total market* terminology to a 1966 paper published by the management consulting firm McKinsey & Company (Louth, "Changing Face of Marketing"). According to Bowman, the phrase "Total Market opportunity" referred to the consequential profit opportunity available for businesses that addressed "the wants and needs of the upwardly mobile Negro." Bowman and Katz, *Reframe the Marketplace*, 25. The phrase "total market" appears in a section of the

McKinsey paper discussing the move away from mass marketing and the expansion of consumer segmentation: "Typically, a total market now comprises a series of submarkets. . . . For most companies, it is a gross error to develop a marketing program aimed at the 'average customer.'" Louth, "Changing Face of Marketing," 2.

57 Bowman, *Whitewashing of the Total Market*, 8.
58 Bowman, *Whitewashing of the Total Market*, 9.
59 Bowman, "Close the Gap."
60 AHAA email to Listserv Members, March 3, 2017.
61 Chitel, "Wake Up and Smell the Cafécito."
62 Personal communication with the author, 2018.
63 Miller, "'Total Market' Gets Lots of Buzz."
64 Walton, "Opinion."
65 Douglas, *How Institutions Think*, 45.
66 Jacobson, "Total Market," 20.
67 Personal communication with the author, 2018.
68 Personal communication with the author, 2018.
69 Personal communication with the author, 2018.

CONCLUSION. INTERSECTIONALITY, INC.: ANTI-RACISM AS CONSUMER FANTASY

The conclusion draws some of its ideas from my article "Waking Up from Advertising's 'Woke' Dreamscape: Reflections from a Marketing Professor," *Deem Journal*, no. 2 (2021); and from an article I coauthored with Francesca Sobande, "Hierarchies of Knowledge About Intersectionality in Marketing Theory and Practice," *Marketing Theory* 22, no. 2 (2022).

1   Blake and Ioanide, "Antiracism Incorporated," 22.
2   N'Duka, "Sony Pictures Hires Ellene V. Miles."
3   Crenshaw, "Mapping the Margins"; Crenshaw, "Demarginalizing the Intersection."
4   Coaston, "Intersectionality Wars."
5   Collins, *Intersectionality*, 126.
6   Collins, *Intersectionality*, 26.
7   Collins, *Intersectionality*, 128.
8   Bilge, "Intersectionality Undone," 408.
9   Bilge, "Intersectionality Undone," 407.
10 Bilge, "Intersectionality Undone," 410–15.
11 Fornof, Pierre, and Lopez, "Kimberlé Crenshaw Speaks at Tulane."
12 Bloch, "Intersectionality."
13 Ben Shapiro, quoted in a Vox interview; see Coaston, "Intersectionality Wars."

14   Collins, *Intersectionality*, 122.

15   Collins, *Intersectionality*, 122.

16   Sobande, *Big Brands Are Watching You*, 59.

17   Mukherjee and Banet-Weiser, *Commodity Activism*.

18   "Most Americans Expect Brands." Edelman made the statement in 2018 and was quoted in 2020.

19   Edelman, "Edelman Trust Barometer."

20   System1, *Feeling Seen USA*, 9.

21   N'Duka, "Sony Pictures Hires Ellene V. Miles."

22   Zalis, "Inclusion Imperative."

23   System1, *Feeling Seen USA*, 63.

24   Amazon Ads, "Why Inclusivity Matters."

25   Herman, "Gen Z."

26   Precourt, "GroupM Offers a Response."

27   Some scholars have critiqued Crenshaw's grid-like traffic-intersection metaphor for reinforcing binary and fixed notions of identity, arguing that this oversimplifies identity's fluid, processual, and dynamic nature. See Puar, "'I Would Rather Be a Cyborg,'" 50.

28   Rittenhouse, "UM Promotes Deidre Smalls-Landau."

29   Burden, "Kimberle Crenshaw Intersectionality."

30   Crenshaw and Parker, "You Belong Here."

31   FleishmanHillard, "African American Policy Forum."

32   Petri, "At the W.N.B.A."

33   Equilibrium, "Chime for Change."

34   Granatstein, "Editor's Letter."

35   Miller, "*Adweek* Interviews the 3 Women."

36   PBS NewsHour, "Watch Live."

37   Frito-Lay, "Doritos Amplifies Black Voices."

38   El Paso Economic Development Department, "Population Demographics."

39   Faria, "Wal-Mart Stores, Inc."

40   Wentz, "Walmart's Tony Rogers."

41   Mast, "Walmart Plans for Growing U.S."

42   Alliance for Inclusive and Multicultural Marketing, "AIMM's New Metric."

43   Alliance for Inclusive and Multicultural Marketing, "AIMM's New Metric." Emphasis added.

44   Cultural Inclusion Accelerator, "Walmart."

45   System1, *Feeling Seen USA*, 1.

46   Pulido, "Creating Marketing Impact."

47   King, "Case for Diversity."

48   System1, *Feeling Seen USA*, 9.

49   Banet-Weiser, *Empowered*, 23.

50   Sobande, "Woke-Washing."

51   White, "Different Kind of Ad Campaign."

52   Lowe, "Imagining Los Angeles," 415.

53   FRONTLINE PBS, "Targeting El Paso."

54   Arango, Bogel-Burroughs, and Benner, "Minutes Before El Paso Killing."

55   Blake and Ioanide, "Antiracism Incorporated," 20–21.

56   Jan, McGregor, and Hoyer, "Corporate America's $50 Billion Promise."

57   Newkirk, *Diversity, Inc.*

58   Hudson and Setty, "Firms from KKR to Coors."

59   Target, "Belonging at the Bullseye."

60   McCoy, "'We Can't Cry About the Milk That's Spilled.'"

61   Personal communication with the author, 2019.

62   Personal communication with the author, 2018.

63   Chambers, *Madison Avenue and the Color Line*, 254.

64   Saha, *Race and the Cultural Industries*, 72.

65   Soto, *3.5 Trillion Advantage*, ch. 2.

66   Ball, *Myth and Propaganda*, 9–10.

67   Fields, "Slavery, Race and Ideology."

68   Jhally, "Image-Based Culture."

BIBLIOGRAPHY

Abu-Lughod, Lila. "Writing Against Culture." In *Recapturing Anthropology: Working in the Present*, edited by Richard G. Fox. School of American Research Press, 1991.

Acxiom. "Acxiom Personicx® Hispanic: Define and Deliver Culturally Relevant Communications." Acxiom.com, accessed March 4, 2025. https://www .acxiom.com/wp-content/uploads/2022/02/FS-Personicx_Hispanic_AC -2212-21.pdf.

AdAge. "How Brands and Agencies Responded to Racial Injustice in the First Month Following George Floyd's Death." AdAge.com, July 7, 2020. https:// adage.com/article/cmo-strategy/how-brands-and-agencies-responded -racial-injustice-first-month-following-george-floyds-death/2265626.

Adamczeski, Ryan. "Jack Daniel's and Harley-Davidson Drop DEI Programs After Conservatives Whine." *Advocate*, August 23, 2024. https://www.advocate .com/news/jack-daniels-harley-davidson-dei.

Adams, Peter. "Toyota Unifies Multicultural, Mainstream Messaging in Multi-Agency Campaign." Marketing Dive, September 12, 2023. https://www .marketingdive.com/news/toyota-grand-highlander-SUV-multicultural -automotive-marketing/693400.

Ahmed, Sara. *On Being Included: Racism and Diversity in Institutional Life*. Duke University Press, 2012.

Alba, Richard. "The Likely Persistence of a White Majority." *American Prospect*, January 11, 2016. https://prospect.org/civil-rights/likely-persistence-white -majority.

Alba, Richard, and Victor Nee. *Remaking the American Mainstream: Assimilation and Contemporary Immigration*. Harvard University Press, 2003.

Allen, Anita L. "Dismantling the 'Black Opticon': Privacy, Race Equity, and Online Data-Protection Reform." *Yale Law Journal Forum* 131 (2022): 907–58. https:// scholarship.law.upenn.edu/faculty_scholarship/2803.

Allen, Theodore W. *The Invention of the White Race*, volume 1: *Racial Oppression and Social Control*. 2nd ed. Verso, 2012.

Alliance for Inclusive and Multicultural Marketing. "AIMM's New Metric Reveals Top Performing Ads Among African-American, Hispanic, LGBTQ+; Gauges

Purchase Intent." ANA AIMM, November 7, 2019. https://www.anaaimm.net/press-release/aimms-new-metric-reveals-top-performing-ads-among-african-american-hispanic-lgbtq-gauges-purchase-intent.

Amazon Ads. "Why Inclusivity Matters." Adweek, August 17, 2023. https://www.adweek.com/sponsored/why-inclusivity-matters.

Amrute, Sareeta. "Sounding the Flat Alarm (Review of Shoshana Zuboff, *The Age of Surveillance Capitalism*)." *b2o: An Online Journal*, January 27, 2020. https://www.boundary2.org/2020/01/sareeta-amrute-sounding-the-flat-alarm-review-of-shoshana-zuboff-the-age-of-surveillance-capitalism.

Anderson, Benedict. *Imagined Communities: Reflections on the Origin and Spread of Nationalism*. Rev. ed. Verso, 1991.

Ang, Ien. *Desperately Seeking the Audience*. Routledge, 2006.

Angwin, Julia, Ariana Tobin, and Madeleine Varner. "Facebook (Still) Letting Housing Advertisers Exclude Users by Race." ProPublica, November 21, 2017. https://www.propublica.org/article/facebook-advertising-discrimination-housing-race-sex-national-origin.

"Apoyamos con orgullo a personas y organizaciones en la comunidad Latina." Advertisement, posted by Wells Fargo, August 23, 2021, YouTube. https://www.youtube.com/watch?v=FrKovmIqsaQ.

Appiah, Kwame Anthony. *The Lies That Bind: Rethinking Identity; Creed, Country, Color, Class, Culture*. Liveright, 2019.

Arango, Tim, Nicholas Bogel-Burroughs, and Katie Benner. "Minutes Before El Paso Killing, Hate-Filled Manifesto Appears Online." *New York Times*, August 3, 2019. https://www.nytimes.com/2019/08/03/us/patrick-crusius-el-paso-shooter-manifesto.html.

Arnett, Chaz. "Data, the New Cotton." Legal Studies Research Paper No. 2022–07, University of Maryland Francis King Carey School of Law, 2022. https://ssrn.com/abstract=4129512.

Arrigo, Bruce, and Olivia P. Shaw. "The De-Realization of Black Bodies in an Era of Mass Digital Surveillance: A Techno-Criminological Critique." *Theoretical Criminology* 27, no. 2 (2022): 265–82. https://www.doi.org/10.1177/13624806221082318.

Austin, Regina. "'A Nation of Thieves': Securing Black People's Right to Shop and to Sell in White America." *Utah Law Review* (1994): 147–77. https://scholarship.law.upenn.edu/faculty_scholarship/818.

Baker, Lee D. *Anthropology and the Racial Politics of Culture*. Duke University Press, 2010.

Baker, Lee D. "The Racist Anti-Racism of American Anthropology." *Transforming Anthropology* 29, no. 2 (2021): 127–42. https://www.doi.org/10.1111/traa.12222.

Ball, Jared A. *The Myth and Propaganda of Black Buying Power: Media, Race, Economics*. 2nd ed. Palgrave Macmillan, 2023.

Banet-Weiser, Sarah. *Authentic™: The Politics of Ambivalence in a Brand Culture*. New York University Press, 2012.

Banet-Weiser, Sarah. *Empowered: Popular Feminism and Popular Misogyny*. Duke University Press, 2018.

Banet-Weiser, Sarah. *Kids Rule! Nickelodeon and Consumer Citizenship*. Duke University Press, 2007.

Baradaran, Mehrsa. *The Color of Money: Black Banks and the Racial Wealth Gap*. Harvard University Press, 2017.

Baskin, Merry, and David Pickton. "Account Planning—from Genesis to Revelation." *Marketing Intelligence & Planning* 21, no. 7 (2003): 416–24. https://www.doi.org/10.1108/02634500310504250.

Benjamin, Ruha. *Race After Technology: Abolitionist Tools for the New Jim Code*. Polity Press, 2019.

Bernays, Edward L. *Propaganda*. Ig, 2004.

Bhattacharyya, Gargi. *Rethinking Racial Capitalism: Questions of Reproduction and Survival*. Rowman and Littlefield, 2018.

Bilge, Sirma. "Intersectionality Undone: Saving Intersectionality from Feminist Intersectionality Studies." *Du Bois Review: Social Science Research on Race* 10, no. 2 (2013): 405–24. https://www.doi.org/10.1017/S1742058X13000283.

Blake, Felice, and Paula Ioanide. "Antiracism Incorporated." In *Antiracism Inc: Why the Way We Talk About Racial Justice Matters*, edited by Felice Blake, Paula Ioanide, and Alison Reed. Punctum Books, 2019.

Blake, Matthew. "Hispanic Ad Market Morphs." *LA Business Journal*, June 28, 2018. https://labusinessjournal.com/news/weekly-news/hispanic-ad-market-morphs.

Bloch, Karen Lehrman. "Intersectionality: The New Caste System." *Jewish Journal*, February 27, 2019. https://jewishjournal.com/commentary/columnist/294500/intersectionality-the-new-caste-system.

Boerman, Sophie C., Sanne Kruikemeier, and Frederik J. Zuiderveen Borgesius. "Online Behavioral Advertising: A Literature Review and Research Agenda." *Journal of Advertising* 46, no. 3 (2017): 363–76. https://www.doi.org/10.1080/00913367.2017.1339368.

Bowker, G. C., and S. L. Star. *Sorting Things Out: Classification and Its Consequences*. MIT Press, 2000.

Bowman, Jeffrey L. "Close the Gap: The State of the 'Total Market' Industry." Campaign Live, February 24, 2017. https://www.campaignlive.com/article/close-gap-state-total-market-industry/1425286.

Bowman, Jeffrey L. *The Whitewashing of the Total Market Approach and Why It Matters to Black Lives: A Call to Action to Reframe Madison Avenue*. Reframe, October 2022. https://getreframe.com/wp-content/uploads/2022/10/Reframe-The-Marketplace-The-Whitewashing-of-the-Total-Market-Approach_103022.pdf.

Bowman, Jeffrey L., and Jeremy Katz. *Reframe the Marketplace: The Total Market Approach to Reaching the New Majority*. Wiley, 2015.

Browne, Simone. *Dark Matters: On the Surveillance of Blackness*. Duke University Press, 2015.

Bruell, Alexandra, and Suzanne Vranica. "Trump's Win Has Ad Agencies Rethink How They Collect Data, Recruit Staff." *Wall Street Journal*, November 21, 2016. https:// www.wsj.com/articles/advertisers-search-for-middle -america-1479687543.

Burgos, David, and Ola Mobolade. *Marketing to the New Majority: Strategies for a Diverse World*. St. Martin's, 2011.

Cagle, Matt. "Facebook, Instagram, and Twitter Provided Data Access for a Surveillance Product Marketed to Target Activists of Color." ACLU Northern California, October 11, 2016. https://www.aclunc.org/blog/facebook -instagram-and-twitter-provided-data-access-surveillance-product -marketed-target.

Capparell, Stephanie. *The Real Pepsi Challenge: The Inspirational Story of Breaking the Color Barrier in American Business*. Free Press, 2007.

Carrasco, Mario. "Big Data Has a Big Diversity Problem." MediaPost, February 4, 2016. https://www.mediapost.com/publications/article/268300/big-data -has-a-big-diversity-problem.html.

Chaar López, Iván. *The Cybernetic Border: Drones, Technology, and Intrusion*. Duke University Press, 2024.

Chambers, Jason. *Madison Avenue and the Color Line: African Americans in the Advertising Industry*. University of Pennsylvania Press, 2008.

Chang, Jeff. *Who We Be: A Cultural History of Race in Post–Civil Rights America*. Picador, 2016.

Chatelain, Marcia. *Franchise: The Golden Arches in Black America*. Liveright, 2020.

Cheney-Lippold, John. *We Are Data: Algorithms and the Making of Our Digital Selves*. New York University Press, 2017.

Chester, Jeff, Katharina Kopp, and Kathryn C. Montgomery. "Does Buying Groceries Online Put SNAP Participants at Risk? How to Protect Health, Privacy, and Equity." Center for Digital Democracy, July 16, 2020. https:// democraticmedia.org/reports/does-buying-groceries-online-put-snap -participants-risk.

Chin, Elizabeth. "Commodity Racism." In *The Wiley Blackwell Encyclopedia of Consumption and Consumer Studies*, edited by Daniel T. Cook and J. M. Ryan. Wiley-Blackwell, 2015.

Chin, Elizabeth. *Purchasing Power: Black Kids and American Consumer Culture*. University of Minnesota Press, 2001.

Chitel, David. "Wake Up and Smell the Cafécito, the Despacito and the 'Total' U.S. Hispanic Market." LinkedIn, August 29, 2017. https://www.linkedin.com /pulse/wake-up-smell-caf%C3%A9cito-despacito-total-us-hispanic-market -chitel.

Círculo Creativo USA. "Anomaly Takes Aim at the 'Last Silo'—Introduces Progressive Approach to Hispanic Marketing." Círculo Creativo, January 25, 2016. https:// www.circulocreativo.org/more-news/2016/1/25/anomaly-takes-aim -at-the-last-silo-introduces-progressive-approach-to-hispanic-marketing.

Coaston, Jane. "The Intersectionality Wars." Vox, May 28, 2019. https://www.vox .com/the-highlight/2019/5/20/18542843/intersectionality-conservatism-law -race-gender-discrimination.

Cohen, Lizabeth. *A Consumers' Republic: The Politics of Mass Consumption in Postwar America*. Alfred A. Knopf, 2003.

Coleman, Beth. "Race as Technology." *Camera Obscura* 24, no. 1 (2009): 177–207. https://www.doi.org/10.1215/02705346-2008-018.

Collins, Patricia Hill. *Intersectionality as Critical Social Theory*. Duke University Press, 2019.

ComScore. "ComScore Unified Digital Measurement™ Methodology." Comscore .com, accessed August 15, 2024. https://www.comscore.com/content /download/18013/file/Comscore_UDM_Methodology.pdf?inLanguage=eng -US&version=1.

Cox, Joseph. "How the U.S. Military Buys Location Data from Ordinary Apps." VICE, November 16, 2020. https://www.vice.com/en/article/us-military -location-data-xmode-locate-x.

Crain, Matthew. *Profit over Privacy: How Surveillance Advertising Conquered the Internet*. University of Minnesota Press, 2021.

Cramer-Flood, Ethan. "US Ad Spending 2023." Emarketer, May 5, 2023. https:// www.emarketer.com/content/us-ad-spending-2023.

Crenshaw, Kimberlé. "Demarginalizing the Intersection of Race and Sex: A Black Feminist Critique of Antidiscrimination Doctrine, Feminist Theory and Antiracist Politics." *University of Chicago Legal Forum* 1989, no. 1 (1989): 139–67. https://chicagounbound.uchicago.edu/uclf/vol1989/iss1/8.

Crenshaw, Kimberlé. "Mapping the Margins: Intersectionality, Identity Politics, and Violence Against Women of Color." *Stanford Law Review* 43, no. 6 (1991): 1241–99. https://www.jstor.org/stable/1229039.

Crenshaw, Kimberlé, and Melonie Parker. "You Belong Here: Intersectionality 2.0." AdColor 2020 Virtual Conference, September 9, 2020.

Crockett, David. "Marketing Blackness: How Advertisers Use Race to Sell Products." *Journal of Consumer Culture* 8, no. 2 (2008): 245–68. https:// www.doi .org/10.1177/1469540508090088.

Cultural Inclusion Accelerator. "Walmart: William White." Video interview, posted March 21, 2023. https://culturalinclusionaccelerator.com/walmart-william -white/.

Darmandrail, Santi. "Audience Data Is the Holy Grail for Hispanic Media Planning and Buying." Retargetly, January 1, 2020. https://retargetly.com/blog-en /audience-data-is-the-holy-grail-for-hispanic-media-planning-and -buying.

Dávila, Arlene. *Latinos, Inc.: The Marketing and Making of a People*. University of California Press, 2012.

Dávila, Arlene. *Latino Spin: Public Image and the Whitewashing of Race*. New York University Press, 2008.

Davis, Judy Foster. "Realizing Marketplace Opportunity: How Research on the Black Consumer Market Influenced Mainstream Marketers, 1920–1970." *Journal of Historical Research in Marketing* 5, no. 4 (2013): 471–93. https://www.doi.org/10.1108/JHRM-02-2013-0006.

Davis, Judy Foster. "Selling Whiteness? A Critical Review of the Literature on Marketing and Racism." *Journal of Marketing Management* 34, 1–2 (2018): 134–77. https://www.doi.org/10.1080/0267257X.2017.1395902.

Devos, Thierry, and Mahzarin R. Banaji. "American = White?" *Journal of Personality and Social Psychology* 88, no. 3 (2005): 447–66. https://www.doi.org/10.1037/0022-3514.88.3.447.

Diner, Eli, and Hasia Diner. "Jews and American Advertising." Race & Ethnicity in Advertising: America in the 20th Century, accessed July 14, 2024. https://raceandethnicity.org/exhibits/show/jews-and-american-advertising/jews-and-american-advertising.

Douglas, Mary. *How Institutions Think*. Syracuse University Press, 1986.

Du Bois, W. E. B. *The Philadelphia Negro: A Social Study*. With the assistance of Isabel Eaton. 1899. University of Pennsylvania Press, 2023.

Dyer, Richard. "The Matter of Whiteness." In *White Privilege: Essential Readings on the Other Side of Racism*, edited by Paula S. Rothenberg, 2nd ed. Worth, 2005.

Dyer, Richard. *White: Essays on Race and Culture*. Taylor and Francis, 2013.

Edelman. *Edelman Trust Barometer 2020: Special Report; Brands and Racial Justice in America*. Edelman.com, June 2020. https://www.edelman.com/sites/g/files/aatuss191/files/2020-06/2020%20Edelman%20Trust%20Barometer%20Specl%20Rept%20Brands%20and%20Racial%20Justice%20in%20America.pdf.

Edmonston, Barry, and Charles Schultze, eds. *Modernizing the U.S. Census*. National Academy Press, 1995.

Elias, Sean, and Joe R. Feagin. *Racial Theories in Social Science: A Systemic Racism Critique*. Routledge, 2016.

Elliott, Stuart. "Ogilvy and Mather Unit Tries New Marketing Approach." *New York Times*, July 18, 2011. https://www.nytimes.com/2011/07/18/business/media/ogilvy-mather-unit-tries-new-marketing-approach.html.

El Paso Economic Development Department. "Population Demographics." City of El Paso, accessed September 20, 2024. https://www.elpasotexas.gov/economic-development/economic-snapshot/population-demographics.

Emba, Christine. "'Black Panther' Is a Black Triumph: America Is Afraid of Those." *Washington Post*, February 16, 2018. https://www.washingtonpost.com

/opinions/black-panther-is-a-triumph-in-a-year-of-triumphs-for-people
-of-color/2018/02/16/080aaf24-1359-11e8-9065-e55346f6de81_story.html.

Equilibrium. "Chime for Change #SayHerName Zine." Gucci Equilibrium,
September 17, 2020. https://equilibrium.gucci.com/chime-for-change
-sayhername-zine.

Ewen, Stuart. *Captains of Consciousness: Advertising and the Social Roots of the Consumer Culture*. Basic Books, 1976.

Facebook. "The Difference Diversity Makes in Online Advertising." Facebook IQ,
March 8, 2021. https://www.facebook.com/business/news/insights/the
-difference-diversity-makes-in-online-advertising#How-can-online
-advertisers-take-action-to-accelerate-inclusive-representation.

Faria, Julia. "Wal-Mart Stores, Inc Advertising Costs Worldwide in the Fiscal Years
2014 to 2023." Statista, March 22, 2024. https://www.statista.com
/statistics/622029/walmart-ad-spend.

Featherstone, Liza. *Divining Desire: Focus Groups and the Culture of Consultation*. OR
Books, 2017.

Feldwick, Paul. "Account Planning: Its History and Its Significance for Ad Agencies." In *The SAGE Handbook of Advertising*, edited by Gerard J. Tellis and Tim
Ambler. SAGE, 2007.

Ferguson, Roderick A. *The Reorder of Things: The University and Its Pedagogies of Minority Difference*. University of Minnesota Press, 2012.

Ferguson, Russell, Martha Gever, Trinh T. Minh-ha, and Cornel West, eds. *Out
There: Marginalization and Contemporary Cultures*. MIT Press, 1990.

Fields, Barbara J. "Slavery, Race and Ideology in the United States of America."
New Left Review 1, no. 181 (1990): 95–118. https://newleftreview.org/issues
/i181/articles/barbara-jeanne-fields-slavery-race-and-ideology-in-the
-united-states-of-america.

Fields, Karen E., and Barbara J. Fields. *Racecraft: The Soul of Inequality in American
Life*. Verso, 2012.

Firmin, Anténor. *The Equality of the Human Races*. Translated by Asselin Charles.
University of Illinois Press, 2002.

FleishmanHillard. "African American Policy Forum: Reckoning #SayHerName
and Its Creators." FleishmanHillard.com, August 2, 2021. https://web
.archive.org/web/20241108212549/https://fleishmanhillard.com/work
/reckoning-sayhername/.

Flores, Tatiana. "'Latinidad Is Cancelled': Confronting an Anti-Black Construct."
Latin American and Latinx Visual Culture 3, no. 3 (2021): 58–79. https://www
.doi.org/10.1525/lavc.2021.3.3.58.

Fornof, Emily, Nile Pierre, and Canela Lopez. "Kimberlé Crenshaw Speaks at Tulane on the Erasure of Women of Color." Tulane Hullabaloo, October 4, 2017.
https://tulanehullabaloo.com/30450/intersections/kimberle-crenshaw-3.

Fox, Richard Wightman. "Epitaph for Middletown: Robert S. Lynd and the
Analysis of Consumer Culture." In *The Culture of Consumption: Critical Essays*

in American History, 1880–1980, edited by Richard W. Fox and T. J. Jackson Lears. Pantheon, 1983.

Frank, Thomas. *The Conquest of Cool: Business Culture, Counterculture, and the Rise of Hip Consumerism*. University of Chicago Press, 1997.

Frankenberg, Ruth. *White Women, Race Matters: The Social Construction of Whiteness*. University of Minnesota Press, 1993.

Frey, William H. "Census Shows America's Post-2020 Population Is Driven by Diversity Especially Among the Young." Brookings, July 24, 2024, https://www.brookings.edu/articles/census-shows-americas-post-2020-population-is-driven-by-diversity-especially-among-the-young/.

Frey, William H. "New 2020 Census Results Show Increased Diversity Countering Decade-Long Declines in America's White and Youth Populations." Brookings, August 13, 2021. https://www.brookings.edu/articles/new-2020-census-results-show-increased-diversity-countering-decade-long-declines-in-americas-white-and-youth-populations/.

Frey, William H. "The US Will Become 'Minority White' in 2045, Census Projects." Brookings, March 14, 2018. https://www.brookings.edu/articles/the-us-will-become-minority-white-in-2045-census-projects/.

Frito-Lay. "Doritos Amplifies Black Voices." Frito-Lay.com, accessed August 12, 2020. https://www.fritolay.com/doritos-amplifies-black-voices.

FRONTLINE PBS. "Targeting El Paso (Full Documentary)." Video posted July 19, 2022, YouTube. https://youtu.be/jHC6GouPjjU?si=sByl2BXdZh2XSTB2.

Futures Company. "The Roadmap to the New America." WARC.com, accessed August 21, 2024. With subscription: https://www.warc.com/content/paywall/article/the-roadmap-to-the-new-america/en-GB/106472.

Galbraith, J. K. *The Affluent Society*. 40th anniversary ed. Houghton Mifflin, 1998.

Gandy, Oscar H., Jr. "Audience Construction: Race, Ethnicity and Segmentation in Popular Media." Paper presented at the 50th Annual Conference of the International Communication Association, Acapulco, May 2000.

Gandy, Oscar H. *The Panoptic Sort: A Political Economy of Personal Information*. 2nd ed. Oxford University Press, 2021.

Gangadharan, Seeta Peña. "The Downside of Digital Inclusion: Expectations and Experiences of Privacy and Surveillance Among Marginal Internet Users." *New Media & Society* 19, no. 4 (2015): 597–615. https://www.doi.org/10.1177/1461444815614053.

Garcia, Guy. *The New Mainstream: How the Multicultural Consumer Is Transforming American Business*. HarperCollins, 2005.

Geoscape and CMO Council. *Activating the New American Mainstream™: Defining, Reaching and Engaging the Multicultural Market*. CMO Council, September 2015. https://www.cmocouncil.org/thought-leadership/reports/activating-the-new-american-mainstream.

Goldberg, David T. "Racial Knowledge." In *Theories of Race and Racism: A Reader*, edited by Les Back and John Solomos. Routledge, 1993.

Gómez, Laura E. *Inventing Latinos: A New Story of American Racism*. New Press, 2020.

Gordon, Milton M. *Assimilation in American Life: The Role of Race, Religion, and National Origins*. Oxford University Press, 1964.

Gould, Stephen Jay. *The Mismeasure of Man*. W. W. Norton, 1996.

Granatstein, Lisa. "Editor's Letter: Black Lives Matter Founders Are This Year's Beacon Award Honorees." Adweek, August 30, 2020. https://www.adweek.com/brand-marketing/black-lives-matter-founders-are-this-years-beacon-award-honorees.

Graves, Joseph L., Jr., and Alan H. Goodman. *Racism, Not Race: Answers to Frequently Asked Questions*. Columbia University Press, 2021.

Gray, Herman. "Subject(ed) to Recognition." *American Quarterly* 65, no. 4 (2013): 771–98. https://www.doi.org/10.1353/aq.2013.0058.

Greer, Brenna. *Represented: The Black Imagemakers Who Reimagined African American Citizenship*. University of Pennsylvania Press, 2019.

Grue, Lars, and Arvid Heiberg. "Notes on the History of Normality—Reflections on the Work of Quetelet and Galton." *Scandinavian Journal of Disability Research* 8, no. 4 (2006): 232–46. https://www.doi.org/10.1080/15017410600608491.

Grzanka, Patrick Ryan, Rajani Bhatia, Mel Michelle Lewis, et al. "Intersectionality, Inc.: A Dialogue on Intersectionality's Travels and Tribulations." *Atlantis: Critical Studies in Gender, Culture & Social Justice* 38, no. 1 (2017): 16–27. https://atlantisjournal.ca/index.php/atlantis/article/view/4769.

Hall, Stuart. "Conclusion: The Multi-Cultural Question." In *Un/settled Multiculturalisms: Diasporas, Entanglements, Transruptions*, edited by Barnor Hesse. Zed Books, 2000.

Hall, Stuart. "*Race: The Floating Signifier*: Featuring Stuart Hall." Film transcript. Media Education Foundation, 1997. https://www.mediaed.org/transcripts/Stuart-Hall-Race-the-Floating-Signifier-Transcript.pdf.

Halvorson, Britt E., and Joshua O. Reno. *Imagining the Heartland: White Supremacy and the American Midwest*. University of California Press, 2022.

Hammonds, Evelynn M., and Rebecca M. Herzig. "Introduction to the End of Race." In *The Nature of Difference: Sciences of Race in the United States from Jefferson to Genomics*, edited by Evelynn M. Hammonds and Rebecca M. Herzig. MIT Press, 2009.

Haney López, Ian. *White by Law: The Legal Construction of Race*. 10th anniversary ed. New York University Press, 2006.

Hansen, Helena, Jules Netherland, and David Herzberg. *Whiteout: How Racial Capitalism Changed the Color of Opioids in America*. University of California Press, 2023.

Harris, Cheryl I. "Whiteness as Property." *Harvard Law Review* 106, no. 8 (1993): 1707–91. https://harvardlawreview.org/print/no-volume/whiteness-as-property.

Harris, Dianne. *Little White Houses: How the Postwar Home Constructed Race in America*. University of Minnesota Press, 2013.

Hartigan, John, Jr. *Racial Situations: Class Predicaments of Whiteness in Detroit*. Princeton University Press, 1999.

Hautzinger, Daniel. "How Tom Burrell Convinced Corporations That 'Black People Are Not Dark-Skinned White People.'" WTTW, Playlist, June 28, 2018. https://www.wttw.com/playlist/2018/06/28/tom-burrell.

Hawkins, Jim, and Tiffany Penner. "Advertising Injustices: Marketing Race and Credit in America." *Emory Law Journal* 70, no. 7 (2021): 1619–57. https://scholarlycommons.law.emory.edu/elj/vol70/iss7/7.

Haymarket Books. "Policing Without the Police: Race, Technology and the New Jim Code." YouTube livestream, July 8, 2020. https://www.youtube.com/watch?v=tfonEQTLw04&t=1641s.

Heinze, Andrew R. *Adapting to Abundance: Jewish Immigrants, Mass Consumption, and the Search for American Identity*. Columbia University Press, 1992.

Helm, Burt. "Ethnic Marketing: McDonald's Is Lovin' it." Bloomberg, July 8, 2010. https://www.bloomberg.com/news/articles/2010-07-08/ethnic-marketing-mcdonalds-is-lovin-it.

Herman, Barbara. "Gen Z: Nonrebels with a Cause." R/GA, February 11, 2021. https://web.archive.org/web/20221205152256/https://www.rga.com/futurevision/articles/genz-nonrebels-with-a-cause.

Hirschfeld, Lawrence. "Natural Assumptions: Race, Essence, and Taxonomies of Human Kinds." *Social Research* 65 (1998): 331–49. https://www.researchgate.net/publication/299047482_Natural_assumptions_Race_essence_and_taxonomies_of_human_kinds.

"HMC Strategic Excellence Awards." Hispanic Marketing Council, accessed July 16, 2024. https://hispanicmarketingcouncil.org/strategic-excellence-awards/.

Hoffmann, Anna Lauren. "Terms of Inclusion: Data, Discourse, Violence." *New Media & Society* 23, no. 12 (2020): 3539–56. https://www.doi.org/10.1177/1461444820958725.

hooks, bell. *Black Looks: Race and Representation*. South End Press, 1992.

Hsu, Tiffany. "The Advertising Industry Has a Problem: People Hate Ads." *New York Times*, October 28, 2019. https://www.nytimes.com/2019/10/28/business/media/advertising-industry-research.html.

Hudson, Clara, and Riddhi Setty. "Firms from KKR to Coors Flag DEI as Business, Legal Risk (1)." Bloomberg Law, March 12, 2024. https://news.bloomberglaw.com/daily-labor-report/firms-from-kkr-to-coors-flag-dei-as-a-risk-to-their-bottom-lines.

Hutchinson, Earl Ofari. *The Myth of Black Capitalism*. 2nd ed. Monthly Review Press, 2024.

Hwang, Tim. *Subprime Attention Crisis: Advertising and the Time Bomb at the Heart of the Internet*. Farrar, Straus and Giroux, 2020.

Igo, Sarah. "From Main Street to Mainstream: *Middletown*, Muncie, and 'Typical America.'" *Indiana Magazine of History* 3 (2005): 239–66. https://

scholarworks.iu.edu/journals/index.php/imh/article/view/12137
/17982.

Igo, Sarah E. *The Averaged American: Surveys, Citizens, and the Making of a Mass Public*. Harvard University Press, 2007.

Jackson, John L., Jr. *Real Black: Adventures in Racial Sincerity*. University of Chicago Press, 2005.

Jacobson, Adam R. "Total Market: Unplugged—A Special Hispanic Market Overview Supplement for HispanicAd." *Hispanic Market Overview*, HispanicAd, August 7, 2017.

Jacobson, Matthew F. *Whiteness of a Different Color: European Immigrants and the Alchemy of Race*. Harvard University Press, 1999.

James, Angela. "Making Sense of Race and Racial Classification." *Race and Society* 4, no. 2 (2001): 235–47. https://www.doi.org/10.1016/S1090–9524 (03)00012–3.

Jan, Tracy, Jena McGregor, and Meghan Hoyer. "Corporate America's $50 Billion Promise." *Washington Post*, August 24, 2021. https://www.washingtonpost .com/business/interactive/2021/george-floyd-corporate-america-racial -justice.

Jenkins, Destin, and Justin Leroy. Introduction to *Histories of Racial Capitalism*, edited by Destin Jenkins and Justin Leroy. Columbia University Press, 2021.

Jhally, Sut. "Image-Based Culture: Advertising and Popular Culture." In *Gender, Race, and Class in Media: A Text-Reader*, edited by Gail Dines and Jean M. Humez, 2nd ed. SAGE, 2003.

Johnson, Guillaume D., and Sonya A. Grier. "Targeting Without Alienating: Multicultural Advertising and the Subtleties of Targeted Advertising." *International Journal of Advertising* 30, no. 2 (2011): 233–58. https://www.doi.org /10.2501/IJA-30-2-233-258.

Johnson, Theodore R. "How the Black Vote Became a Political Monolith." *New York Times*, September 16, 2020. https://www.nytimes.com/2020/09/16/magazine /black-vote.html.

Kahn, Jonathan. *Race in a Bottle: The Story of BiDil and Racialized Medicine in a Post-Genomic Age*. Columbia University Press, 2012.

Kemper, Steven. *Buying and Believing: Sri Lankan Advertising and Consumers in a Transnational World*. University of Chicago Press, 2001.

Kennedy, Deseriee. "Marketing Goods, Marketing Images: The Impact of Advertising on Race." *Arizona State Law Journal* 32 (2000): 615–94. https://digital commons.tourolaw.edu/scholarlyworks/199.

Kern-Foxworth, Marilyn. *Aunt Jemima, Uncle Ben, and Rastus: Blacks in Advertising, Yesterday, Today, and Tomorrow*. Greenwood, 1994.

"Kimberle Crenshaw Intersectionality NOT Identity." Video posted by Scott Burden, August 17, 2017, YouTube. https://www.youtube.com/watch?v =uPtz8TiATJY&ab_channel=ScottBurden.

King, Oona. "The Case for Diversity in Advertising." Thinking with Google, February 23, 2017. https://web.archive.org/web/20210226200252/https://www.thinkwithgoogle.com/marketing-strategies/video/diversity-in-advertising-black-millennials/.

Klara, Robert. "CMOs Have Lost Focus on DEI Initiatives, MediaLink Report Finds." Adweek, April 2, 2024. https://www.adweek.com/brand-marketing/cmos-have-lost-focus-on-dei-initiatives-medialink-report-finds.

Kwate, Naa Oyo A. *White Burgers, Black Cash: Fast Food from Black Exclusion to Exploitation*. University of Minnesota Press, 2023.

Langston, Wayne A., dir. *The Secret of Selling the Negro*. Documentary, 21 mins. Johnson Publishing, 1954.

"Latino Is Not a Race: Understanding Lived Experiences Through Street Race." Latino Policy and Politics Institute, UCLA, July 2024. https://latino.ucla.edu/wp-content/uploads/2024/07/Latino-is-Not-a-Race-Understanding-Lived-Experiences-through-Street-Race.pdf.

Lears, Jackson. *Fables of Abundance: A Cultural History of Advertising in America*. Basic Books, 1995.

Leong, Nancy. *Identity Capitalists: The Powerful Insiders Who Exploit Diversity to Maintain Inequality*. Stanford University Press, 2021.

Leong, Nancy. "Identity Entrepreneurs." *California Law Review* 104, no. 6 (2016): 1333–99. https://doi.org/10.15779/Z383G3M.

"Linnaeus and Race." Linnean Society of London, accessed September 3, 2020. https://www.linnean.org/learning/who-was-linnaeus/linnaeus-and-race.

Lipsitz, George. *The Possessive Investment in Whiteness: How White People Profit from Identity Politics*. Temple University Press, 2006.

Lopez, Mark Hugo, Jens Manuel Krogstad, and Jeffrey S. Passel. "Who Is Hispanic?" Pew Research, September 5, 2023. https://www.pewresearch.org/short-reads/2023/09/05/who-is-hispanic.

Lotame. "Lotame Data Exchange: World's Largest 2nd- and 3rd-Party Data Marketplace." Lotame Resources, accessed September 13, 2024. https://web.archive.org/web/20221128073732/https://resources.lotame.com/hubfs/2020%20LDX%20Marketing/LDX_HispanicSegments_final2020.pdf.

Louth, John D. "The Changing Face of Marketing." *McKinsey Quarterly*, September 1966. https://www.mckinsey.com/capabilities/growth-marketing-and-sales/our-insights/the-changing-face-of-marketing#/.

Lowe, Lisa. "Imagining Los Angeles in the Production of Multiculturalism." In *Mapping Multiculturalism*, edited by Avery F. Gordon and Christopher Newfield. University of Minnesota Press, 1996.

Lynd, Robert S, and Helen Merrell Lynd. *Middletown: A Study in American Culture*. Harcourt Brace, 1929.

Maheshwari, Sapna. "After Election Surprise, Marketers Rethink How to Study Consumers." *New York Times*, November 14, 2016. https:// www.nytimes.com

/2016/11/15/business/media/advertisers-look-to-an-era-of-increased-data
-and-fewer-facts.html.

Maheshwari, Sapna. "Different Ads, Different Ethnicities, Same Car." *New York
Times*, October 12, 2017. https://www.nytimes.com/interactive/2017/10/12
/business/media/toyota-camry-ads-different-ethnicities.html.

Mandese, Joe. "Mindshare Launches Black 'Inclusion PMP,' Intends to Overcome
Programmatic Bias." MediaPost, July 16, 2020. https://www.mediapost
.com/publications/article/353730/mindshare-launches-black-inclusion
-pmp-intends.html?edition=119131.

Manring, M. M. *Slave in a Box: The Strange Career of Aunt Jemima*. University Press of
Virginia, 1998.

Marchand, Roland. *Advertising the American Dream: Making Way for Modernity, 1920–
1940*. University of California Press, 1985.

"Marc Pritchard: Chief Brand Officer." Procter & Gamble, accessed July 4, 2024.
https://us.pg.com/leadership-team/marc-pritchard.

Mast, Carlotta. "Walmart Plans for Growing U.S. Hispanic Population." New
Hope, March 30, 2011. https://www.newhope.com/retailers/walmart-plans
-for-growing-u-s-hispanic-population.

Mazzarella, William. *Shoveling Smoke: Advertising and Globalization in Contemporary
India*. Duke University Press, 2003.

McClintock, Anne. *Imperial Leather: Race, Gender, and Sexuality in the Colonial Contest*.
Routledge, 1995.

McCoy, Kimeko. "'We Can't Cry About the Milk That's Spilled': As DE&I Fallout Con-
tinues, Multicultural Agencies Grapple with Changes." *Digiday*, November 4,
2024. https://digiday.com/marketing/we-cant-cry-about-the-milk-thats
-spilled-as-dei-fallout-continues-multicultural-agencies-grapple-with
-changes.

McDonald's Corporation. "Black and Golden: McDonald's Commitment to the
Black Community." Press release, 2019.

McDonald's Corporation. *McDonald's 2021–2022 Global Diversity, Equity and Inclusion
Report*. McDonalds.com, accessed June 7, 2024. https://web.archive
.org/web/20240928091212/https://corporate.mcdonalds.com/content
/dam/sites/corp/nfl/pdf/McDonalds_Corporation_Diversity_Equity_and
_Inclusion-2021-20221.pdf.

McGovern, Charles F. *Sold American: Consumption and Citizenship, 1890–1945*. University of North Carolina Press, 2006.

McGuigan, Lee. *Selling the American People: Advertising, Optimization, and the Origins
of Adtech*. MIT Press, 2023.

McGuigan, Lee, and Marcel Rosa-Salas. "Model Consumers: Numerical and Normative Constructions of Hispanic Consumers." In *The Routledge Companion
to Advertising and Promotional Culture*, edited by Emily West and Matthew P.
McAllister, 2nd ed. Routledge, 2023.

McKinley, Scott. "Why Removing Ethnicity from Consumer Data Sets Could Do

More Harm Than Good." *Broadcasting and Cable* (blog), May 26, 2023. https://www.nexttv.com/blogs/why-removing-ethnicity-from-consumer-data-sets-could-do-more-harm-than-good-guest-blog.

McMillan Cottom, Tressie. "Where Platform Capitalism and Racial Capitalism Meet: The Sociology of Race and Racism in the Digital Society." *Sociology of Race and Ethnicity* 6, no. 4 (2020): 441–49. https://www.doi.org/10.1177/2332649220949473.

MediaMath. "MediaMath Expands Purpose Driven Advertising Initiative; Champions Multicultural Media via Curated Marketplace." MediaMath, February 25, 2021. https://www.mediamath.com/2021/02/25/mediamath-champions-multicultural-media-with-expansion-of-curated-marketplace.

Mehaffy, Marilyn Maness. "Advertising Race/Raceing Advertising: The Feminine Consumer(-Nation), 1876–1900." *Signs: Journal of Women in Culture and Society* 23, no. 1 (1997): 131–74. https://www.doi.org/10.1086/495238.

Melamed, Jodi. "Racial Capitalism." *Critical Ethnic Studies* 1, no. 1 (2015): 76–85. https://www.doi.org/10.5749/jcritethnstud.1.1.0076.

Melamed, Jodi. *Represent and Destroy: Rationalizing Violence in the New Racial Capitalism*. University of Minnesota Press, 2011.

Meyerend, Daniel. "The Algorithm Knows I'm Black: From Users to Subjects." *Media, Culture & Society* 45, no. 3 (2022): 629–45. https://www.doi.org/10.1177/01634437221140539.

Miller, Daniel. *Capitalism: An Ethnographic Approach*. Berg, 1997.

Miller, Pepper. "'Total Market' Gets Lots of Buzz, but Multicultural Agencies Will Suffer Badly." AdAge, December 13, 2013. https://adage.com/article/the-big-tent/total-market-shoves-multicultural-agencies/245657.

Miller, Sean J. "Data Privacy Laws Are Restricting Marketers' Ability to Target by Ethnicity as the U.S. Electorate Is Diversifying." Campaigns and Elections, September 25, 2023. https://campaignsandelections.com/industry-news/data-privacy-laws-are-restricting-marketers-ability-to-target-by-ethnicity-as-the-u-s-electorate-is-diversifying.

Miller, Shannon. "Adweek Interviews the 3 Women Who Founded Black Lives Matter—And Started a Global Movement." Adweek, August 30, 2020. https://www.adweek.com/brand-marketing/co-founders-of-black-lives-matter-on-starting-a-global-movement.

Mills, Charles W. *The Racial Contract*. Cornell University Press, 2014.

Mills, Charles W. "White Ignorance." In *Race and Epistemologies of Ignorance*, edited by Shannon Sullivan and Nancy Tuana. State University of New York Press, 2007.

Mizrahi, Isaac. "7 CMOs Myths About Hispanic Marketing." HispanicAd, January 9, 2018. https://hispanicad.com/news/7-cmos-myths-about-hispanic-marketing/.

Mora, G. Cristina. *Making Hispanics: How Activists, Bureaucrats, and Media Constructed a New American*. University of Chicago Press, 2014.

Mora, G. Cristina, and Michael Rodríguez-Muñiz. "Latinos, Race, and the American Future: A Response to Richard Alba's 'The Likely Persistence of a White Majority.'" *New Labor Forum* 26, no. 2 (2017): 40–46. https://www.doi.org/10.1177/1095796017700124.

Morales, Ed. *Latinx: The New Force in American Politics and Culture*. London: Verso, 2018.

Morris, Michael. "Standard White: Dismantling White Normativity." *California Law Review* 104, no. 4 (2016): 949–78. https://www.doi.org/10.15779/Z38F55G.

Morton, Samuel G., and George Combe. *Crania Americana; or, a Comparative View of the Skulls of Various Aboriginal Nations of North and South America: To Which Is Prefixed an Essay on the Varieties of the Human Species*. J. Dobson, 1839.

"Most Americans Expect Brands to Take Stand on Racism." Consulting.us, June 11, 2020. https://www.consulting.us/news/4350/most-americans-expect-brands-to-take-stand-on-racism.

MRI-Simmons. "Hispanic Acculturation Segmentation." Sell sheet. Accessed July 16, 2024. https://cdn2.hubspot.net/hubfs/2405078/MRI-Simmons/Segmentations%20Sellsheets/Hispanic%20Acculturation%20Segmentation.pdf.

Muhammad, Khalil Gibran. *The Condemnation of Blackness: Race, Crime, and the Making of Modern Urban America*. Harvard University Press, 2010.

Mukherjee, Roopali, and Sarah Banet-Weiser, eds. *Commodity Activism: Cultural Resistance in Neoliberal Times*. New York University Press, 2012.

Nakamura, Lisa. *Cybertypes: Race, Ethnicity, and Identity on the Internet*. Routledge, 2002.

Nakamura, Lisa. *Digitizing Race: Visual Cultures of the Internet*. University of Minnesota Press, 2008.

Napoli, Philip M. *Audience Evolution: New Technologies and the Transformation of Media Audiences*. Columbia University Press, 2010.

NBC Universal Telemundo. *200%ers: The Power of Bi-Cultural/Bi-Lingual Hispanics; Qualitative Research Executive Summary*. Accessed July 16, 2024. https://together.nbcuni.com/wp-content/uploads/sites/3/2020/06/Telemundo_200ers_2020.pdf.

N'Duka, Amanda. "Sony Pictures Hires Ellene V. Miles as SVP Intersectional Marketing." Deadline, July 18, 2018. https://deadline.com/2018/07/sony-ellene-v-miles-as-senior-vp-intersectional-marketing-1202428169.

Neff, Jack. "9 Companies and Agencies Doing Multicultural Measurement Right." AdAge, August 8, 2022. https://adage.com/article/media/multicultural-measurement-leaders-include-pg-wpp-ibm-televisaunivision-videoamp-and-truthset/2425536.

Neumann, Nico, Catherine E. Tucker, and Timothy Whitfield. "How Effective Is Third-Party Consumer Profiling? Evidence from Field Studies." *Marketing Science* 38, no. 6 (2019): 918–26.

Newkirk, Pamela. *Diversity, Inc.: The Failed Promise of a Billion-Dollar Business*. Bold Type Books, 2019.

Nielsen. *La Oportunidad Latinx: Cultural Currency and the Consumer Journey*. Nielsen .com, 2019. https://www.nielsen.com/insights/2019/la-oportunidad-latinx/.

Nielsen. "The Making of a Multicultural Super Consumer." Nielsen.com, March 18, 2015. https://www.nielsen.com/insights/2015/the-making-of-a -multicultural-super-consumer/.

Noble, Safiya Umoja. *Algorithms of Oppression: How Search Engines Reinforce Racism*. New York University Press, 2018.

Nobles, Melissa. *Shades of Citizenship: Race and the Census in Modern Politics*. Stanford University Press, 2000.

"Nothing to Shout About: Things Are Still Getting Worse for the Advertising Industry." *Economist*, July 30, 2009. https://www.economist.com/business /2009/07/30/nothing-to-shout-about.

O'Barr, William M. *Culture and the Ad: Exploring Otherness in the World of Advertising*. Westview, 1994.

Odell, Patty. "Wells Fargo's Total Market Approach Journey." *Chief Marketer*, February 6, 2015. https://chiefmarketer.com/wells-fargos-total-marketing -journey/.

Ohmer, Susan. *George Gallup in Hollywood*. Columbia University Press, 2006.

OpenMIC. "Surveillance Capitalism." OpenMIC, accessed September 13, 2024. https://www.openmic.org/surveillance-capitalism.

Oza, Anil. "Trump's Talk of 'Bad Genes' Is Rooted in Eugenics: Experts Explain Why It's Making a Comeback." *STAT*, November 8, 2024, www.statnews .com/2024/10/28/eugenics-in-political-rhetoric-open-science-movement -expert-analysis.

Packard, Vance. *The Hidden Persuaders*. D. McKay, 1957.

Painter, Nell Irvin. *The History of White People*. W. W. Norton, 2011.

Patton, Erin O. *Under the Influence: Tracing the Hip-Hop Generation's Impact on Brands, Sports, and Pop Culture*. Paramount Market, 2009.

PBS NewsHour. "Watch Live: Biden Honors Victims of Tulsa Race Massacre on 100th Anniversary." YouTube, June 2, 2021. https://www.youtube.com /watch?v=TPPDoMhG3h4&ab_channel=PBSNewsHour.

Pegg, David, Tom Burgis, Hannah Devlin, and Jason Wilson. "Revealed: International 'Race Science' Network Secretly Funded by US Tech Boss." *Guardian*, October 16, 2024. https://www.theguardian.com/world/2024/oct/16/revealed- international-race-science-network-secretly-funded-by-us-tech-boss.

Pepviz. *The Circle of Joy: How Hispanic Families Are Shaping the Future Food and Beverage Landscape*. PepsiCo, Pepviz, April 23, 2024. https://pepviz.com /thought-leadership/hispanic-shoppers-and-familismo.

Petri, Alexandra E. "At the W.N.B.A., the Fight for Racial Justice Goes Way Back." *New York Times*, August 31, 2020. https://www.nytimes.com/2020/08/31/us /WNBA-say-her-name-racism-sexism.html.

Phan, Thao, and Scott Wark. "What Personalisation Can Do for You! Or: How to Do Racial Discrimination Without 'Race.'" Culture Machine, accessed August 15, 2024. https://culturemachine.net/vol-20-machine-intelligences /what-personalisation-can-do-for-you-or-how-to-do-racial-discrimination -without-race-thao-phan-scott-wark.

Phillips, Kristine. "Wells Fargo Targeted Undocumented Immigrants, Stalked Street Corners, Lawsuit Claims." *Washington Post*, May 4, 2017. https://www .washingtonpost.com/news/business/wp/2017/05/04/wells-fargo-targeted -undocumented-immigrants-stalked-street-corners-lawsuit-claims.

Phillips, Steve. *Brown Is the New White: How the Demographic Revolution Has Created a New American Majority*. New Press, 2016.

Portada. "Do DSPs Have Racist Behavior?" Portada Online, April 4, 2024. https:// www.portada-online.com/feature/dsp-programmatic-do-dsps-have -a-racist-behavior/.

Portada. "Leaders at PHD, UM and D'exposito Urge for Solutions to Improve Multicultural Audience Data Collection." Portada Online, January 6, 2025. https:// www.portada-online.com/latest-news/leaders-aum-and-dexposito -urge-for-solutions-to-improve-multicultural-audience-data-collection/.

Portada. "Minority Media Buys: Despite Plans of Leading Media Agencies, Publishers See Little Change for Now." Portada Online, November 1, 2021. https://www.portada-online.com/feature/minority-media-buys-despite -plans-of-leading-media-agencies-publishers-see-little-change-for-now/.

Precourt, Geoffrey. "GroupM Offers a Response to Industry's Cultural Isolation." WARC.com, accessed September 22, 2024. With subscription: https://www .warc.com/content/paywall/article/groupm-offers-a-response-to-industrys -cultural-isolation/en-gb/en-GB/126181.

Precourt, Geoffrey. "Toyota Makes 'Total Market' a Primary Marketing Driver." WARC.com, accessed September 22, 2024. With subscription: https://www .warc.com/content/paywall/article/event-reports/toyota-makes-total -market-primary-marketing-driver/en-GB/103297?.

Precourt, Geoffrey. "Walmart's Multicultural Strategy: Blow Up the Budget." WARC.com, accessed August 19, 2024. With subscription: https://www.warc .com/content/paywall/article/event-reports/walmarts-multicultura l-strategy-blow-up-the-budget/en-gb/95758?.

Precourt, Geoffrey. "Wells Fargo Builds Total-Market Insights." WARC.com, accessed September 22, 2024. With subscription: https://www.warc.com /content/paywall/article/event-reports/wells-fargo-builds-total-market -insights/en-gb/103985?.

Prewitt, Kenneth. *What Is "Your" Race? The Census and Our Flawed Efforts to Classify Americans*. Princeton University Press, 2013.

Pritchard, Marc S. "New Habits for Multicultural Growth." LinkedIn, October 27, 2021. https://www.linkedin.com/pulse/new-habits-multicultural-growth -marc-s-pritchard.

Puar, Jasbir K. "'I Would Rather Be a Cyborg Than a Goddess': Becoming-Intersectional in Assemblage Theory." *philoSOPHIA* 2, no. 1 (2012): 49–66. https://doi.org/10.1353/phi.2012.a486621.

Pulido, Adrienne. "Creating Marketing Impact with the Hispanic Community." Kantar, November 10, 2023. https://www.kantar.com/north-america/inspiration/sustainability/creating-marketing-impact-with-the-hispanic-community.

Purpose Brand. "Black Lives Matter Sparks Marketing Response." Purpose_Brand, October 21, 2020. https:// purposebrand.com/blog/business-tracker-marketing-response/.

Quick Facts About Selling the Negro Market: Where the Most Changes Are Taking Place; A Handy Guide for National Advertisers and Advertising Agencies. Associated Publishers, 1952.

Quinn, Patrick, and Leo Kivijarv. *U.S. Multicultural Media Forecast 2023–2027: Advertising & Marketing by Demographic, Platform, and Media Buying Strategies.* 2nd ed. PQ Media, 2023. https://www.pqmedia.com/wp-content/uploads/2023/12/PQ-Media-U.S.-Multicultural-Media-Forecast-2023-MASTER-EXEC-SUMM-v.F.pdf.

"Reimagining 'Multicultural' with UWG CEO Monique Nelson." *HuffPost*, September 12, 2017. https://www.huffpost.com/entry/reimagining-multicultural-with-uwg-ceo-monique-nelson_b_59b881cee4b06b71800c3565.

Reisdorf, Paula. "The Significance of Race in Neoclassical Economic's Concept of Homo Economicus." Academia, accessed November 23, 2024. https://www.academia.edu/40652449/The_Significance_of_Race_in_Neoclassical_Economics_Concept_of_Homo_Economicus.

Resonate. "Understanding the Nuances of Hispanic Audiences." Resonate, 2021. https://www.resonate.com/wp-content/uploads/2021/11/Resonate_Multicultural-Report_Hispanic-Audiences_2021.pdf.

Richardson, Rashida, Jason M. Schultz, and Kate Crawford. "Dirty Data, Bad Predictions: How Civil Rights Violations Impact Police Data, Predictive Policing Systems, and Justice." *New York University Law Review* 94 (2019): 15–55. https://nyulawreview.org/wp-content/uploads/2019/04/NYULawReview-94-Richardson_etal-FIN.pdf.

Rittenhouse, Lindsay. "Agencies Owned or Run by White Execs Jump to 90%, 4A's Diversity Report Finds." AdAge, July 20, 2023. https://adage.com/article/agency-news/agencies-owned-or-run-white-execs-jump-90-4as-diversity-report-finds/2504951.

Rittenhouse, Lindsay. "More Agency Consolidation May Be Coming as Creative and Media Converge Again." Adweek, February 4, 2019. https://www.adweek.com/agencies/more-agency-consolidation-may-be-coming-as-creative-and-media-converge-again.

Rittenhouse, Lindsay. "UM Promotes Deidre Smalls-Landau to U.S. Chief Marketing Officer." AdAge, August 6, 2019. https://adage.com/article/agency-news/um-promotes-deidre-smalls-landau-us-chief-marketing-officer/2189866.

Roberts, Dorothy E. "Digitizing the Carceral State." *Harvard Law Review* 132, no. 6 (2019): 1695–1728. https://harvardlawreview.org/print/vol-132/digitizing -the-carceral-state.

Roberts, Dorothy E. *Fatal Invention: How Science, Politics, and Big Business Re-Create Race in the Twenty-First Century*. New Press, 2011.

Robinson, Cedric J. *Black Marxism: The Making of the Black Radical Tradition*. University of North Carolina Press, 1983.

Robinson, Mark S. "Sharecropping on Madison Avenue." Fast Company, July 1, 2023. https://www.fastcompany.com/90913706/black-madison-avenue -mark-robinson-book-sharecropping.

Rodríguez, Clara E. *Changing Race: Latinos, the Census, and the History of Ethnicity in the United States*. New York University Press, 2000.

Rodríguez-Muñiz, Michael. *Figures of the Future: Latino Civil Rights and the Politics of Demographic Change*. Princeton University Press, 2021.

Rosa, Jonathan. *Looking Like a Language, Sounding Like a Race: Raciolinguistic Ideologies and the Learning of Latinidad*. Oxford University Press, 2019.

Rothstein, Richard. *The Color of Law*. W. W. Norton, 2017.

Rusert, Britt, and Whitney Battle-Baptiste, eds. *W. E. B. Du Bois's Data Portraits: Visualizing Black America*. Princeton Architectural Press, 2018.

Rutherford, Adam. *How to Argue with a Racist: What Our Genes Do (and Don't) Say About Human Difference*. Experiment, 2020.

Saha, Anamik. *Race and the Cultural Industries*. Polity Press, 2018.

Saunders, Doris E., ed. *The Negro Handbook, Compiled by the Editors of "Ebony."* Johnson Publishing, 1966.

Schiff, Allison. "P&G's Programmatic Strategy to Become the Top Spender on Black-Owned Media." Ad Exchanger, May 26, 2022. https://www .adexchanger.com/advertiser/pgs-programmatic-strategy-to-become -the-top-spender-on-black-owned-media.

Schultz, Jaime. "Racialized Osteology and Athletic Aptitude, or 'Black' Bones as Red Herrings." *Journal of Sport History* 46, no. 3 (2019): 325–46. https://www .doi.org/10.5406/jsporthistory.46.3.0325.

Sender, Katherine. *Business, Not Politics: The Making of the Gay Market*. Columbia University Press, 2005.

Shankar, Shalini. *Advertising Diversity: Ad Agencies and the Creation of Asian American Consumers*. Duke University Press, 2015.

Shankar, Shalini. "Nothing Sells like Whiteness: Race, Ontology, and American Advertising." *American Anthropologist* 122, no. 1 (2020): 112–19. https://www .doi.org/10.1111/aman.13354.

"SheaMoisture: Break the Walls #BREAKTHEWALLS." Advertisement, posted by SheaMoisture, April 5, 2016, YouTube. https://www.youtube.com/watch?v =uZwaWA5tOhg.

Siu, Antoinette. "Media Agencies Develop New Multicultural Marketing Strategies as Client Needs and Targeting Challenges Arise." *Digiday*, October 13,

2023. https://digiday.com/media-buying/media-agencies-develop-new
-multicultural-marketing-strategies-as-client-needs-and-targeting
-challenges-arise.

Sivanandan, Sajith. "Demographics Are Dead: Welcome to the Age of Intent."
Think with Google, March 1, 2018. https://www.thinkwithgoogle.com/intl
/en-apac/marketing-strategies/search/demographics-dead-welcome
-age-of-intent.

Sluis, Sarah. "Penguin Random House Amplifies Black Stories with MediaMath's
Multicultural Marketplace." Ad Exchanger, February 25, 2021. https://www
.adexchanger.com/platforms/penguin-random-house-amplifies-black
-stories-with-mediamaths-multicultural-marketplace.

Smedley, Audrey, and Brian D. Smedley. "Race as Biology Is Fiction, Racism as a
Social Problem Is Real: Anthropological and Historical Perspectives on the
Social Construction of Race." *American Psychologist* 60, no. 1 (2005): 16–26.

Smedley, Audrey. *Race in North America: Origin and Evolution of a Worldview*. 3rd ed.
Westview, 2007.

Snyder, Robert W. "European Americans and Advertising." Race & Ethnicity in
Advertising: America in the 20th Century, accessed July 14, 2024. https://
raceandethnicity.org/exhibits/show/european-americans-and-adverti
/european-americans-and-adverti.

Sobande, Francesca. *Big Brands Are Watching You: Marketing Social Justice and Digital
Culture*. University of California Press, 2024.

Sobande, Francesca. "Woke-Washing: 'Intersectional' Femvertising and Branding 'Woke' Bravery." *European Journal of Marketing* 54, no. 11 (2019): 2723–45.
https://www.doi.org/10.1108/EJM-02-2019-0134.

Soto, Terry J. *The 3.5 Trillion Advantage: A Marketer's Guide to Revenue Growth in Today's
America*. Xlibris, 2018.

"Statement on New SPD 15 Standards." AfroLatino Coalition, accessed December
6, 2024. https://www.afrolatinocoalition.org/statement-on-new-spd-15
-standards.

St. Félix, Doreen. "The National Geographic Twins and the Falsehood of Our Post-
Racial Future." *New Yorker*, March 14, 2018. https://www.newyorker
.com/culture/culture-desk/the-national-geographic-twins-and-the
-falsehood-of-our-post-racial-future.

Steel, Jon. *Truth, Lies, and Advertising: The Art of Account Planning*. Wiley, 1998.

Stoute, Steve. *The Tanning of America: How Hip-Hop Created a Culture That Rewrote the
Rules of the New Economy*. Penguin, 2012.

Sweeney, Latanya. "Discrimination in Online Ad Delivery: Google Ads, Black
Names and White Names, Racial Discrimination, and Click Advertising."
Queue 11, no. 3 (2013): 10–29. https://www.doi.org/10.1145/2460276.2460278.

Sylvester, Alice K., Carlos Santiago, and Jim Spaeth. "Addressing Biases in
Multicultural and Inclusive Identity Data: Best Practices in Data Transparency and Validation." Association of National Advertisers, February 2021.

https://www.anaaimm.net/ebooks/addressing-biases-in-multicultural
-inclusive-identity-data.

System1. *Feeling Seen USA: How Diverse Advertising Unites Us*. System1, May 27, 2022.
https://s3.amazonaws.com/media.mediapost.com/uploads/System1
_Feeling_Seen_USA.pdf.

Target. "Belonging at the Bullseye." Target.com, 2025. https://corporate.target
.com/sustainability-governance/our-team/belonging.

Tau, Byron, and Michelle Hackman. "Federal Agencies Use Cellphone Location
Data for Immigration Enforcement." *Wall Street Journal*, February 7, 2020.
https://www.wsj.com/articles/federal-agencies-use-cellphone-location
-data-for-immigration-enforcement-11581078600.

Taylor, Kate. "Leaked Memo Reveals McDonald's Is Collaborating with Rapper Tra-
vis Scott, as the Fast-Food Giant Chases 'Youthful Multicultural Customers.'" *Business Insider*, August 21, 2020. https://www.businessinsider.in
/retail/news/leaked-memo-reveals-mcdonalds-is-collaborating-with
-rapper-travis-scott-as-the-fast-food-giant-chases-youthful-multicultural
-customers/articleshow/77664926.cms.

Taylor, Keeanga-Yamahtta. *Race for Profit: How Banks and the Real Estate Industry Undermined Black Homeownership*. University of North Carolina Press, 2019.

Teslow, Tracy. *Constructing Race: The Science of Bodies and Cultures in American Anthropology*. Cambridge University Press, 2014.

Todd, Knox H., Christi Deaton, Anne P. D'Adamo, and Leon Goe. "Ethnicity and
Analgesic Practice." *Annals of Emergency Medicine* 35, no. 1 (2000): 11–16.
https://www.doi.org/10.1016/S0196-0644(00)70099-0.

Todd, Knox H., Nigel Samaroo, and Jerome R. Hoffman. "Ethnicity as a Risk Factor for Inadequate Emergency Department Analgesia." *JAMA* 269, no. 12
(1993): 1537–39. https://www.doi.org/10.1001/jama.1993.03500120075029.

Toyota. "All-New Toyota Camry Ignites the Senses." Toyota Newsroom, September
1, 2017. https://pressroom.toyota.com/all-new-toyota-camry-ignites-senses/.

Trouillot, Michel-Rolph. "Adieu, Culture: A New Duty Arises." In *Global Transforma-
tions: Anthropology and the Modern World*. Palgrave Macmillan, 2003. https://
www.doi.org/10.1007/978-1-137-04144-9_6.

Turow, Joseph. *Breaking Up America: Advertisers and the New Media World*. University
of Chicago Press, 1997.

Turow, Joseph. *Niche Envy: Marketing Discrimination in the Digital Age*. MIT Press,
2006.

US Census Bureau. "Hispanic Heritage Month: 2023." Census.gov, Newsroom, August 17, 2023. https://www.census.gov/newsroom/facts-for-features/2023
/hispanic-heritage-month.html.

US Census Bureau. "U.S. Census Bureau Projections Show a Slower Growing,
Older, More Diverse Nation a Half Century from Now." Census.gov,
December 12, 2012. https://www.census.gov/newsroom/releases/archives
/population/cb12-243.html.

US Census Office. *History and Statistics of the State of Maryland: According to the Returns of the Seventh Census of the United States, 1850*. Gideon, 1852.

US Department of Justice. "Wells Fargo Agrees to Pay $3 Billion to Resolve Criminal and Civil Investigations into Sales Practices Involving the Opening of Millions of Accounts Without Customer Authorization." US Department of Justice, Archives, February 21, 2020. https://www.justice.gov/opa/pr/wells -fargo-agrees-pay-3-billion-resolve-criminal-and-civil-investigations -sales-practices.

"US Multicultural Media Spend to Grow at Accelerated 8.3% to 45.8B in 2024, as Hispanic, African & Asian American Markets Benefit from Influx of Political & Sports Dollars." PQ Media, December 19, 2023. https://www.prweb .com/releases/us-multicultural-media-spend-to-grow-at-accelerated-8-3 -to-45-8b-in-2024--as-hispanic-african--asian-american-markets-benefit -from-influx-of-political--sports-dollars-302017473.html.

Vespa, Jonathan, Lauren Medina, and David M. Armstrong. *Demographic Turning Points for the United Sates: Population Projections for 2020 to 2060*. US Census Bureau, Report no. P25–1144, February 2020. https://www.census.gov /library/publications/2020/demo/p25-1144.html.

VICE Media Group. "VICE Media Group Announces at Newfronts: Global Expansion with *VICE World News*; Introduces New Iheart Media Audio Partnership; and Calls on Industry to Reform Brand Safety Practices." VICE Media Group, June 24, 2020. https://www.vicemediagroup.com/wp-content/uploads/2020/06 /NewFront-2020-Press-Release.pdf.

Vidal, Sylvia. "Inclusion as Personalization: The Key to Effective Marketing." HispanicAd, September 10, 2024. https://hispanicad.com/news /inclusion-as-personalization-the-key-to-effective-marketing.

Wailoo, Keith. *Pain: A Political History*. Johns Hopkins University Press, 2014.

Wailoo, Keith. *Pushing Cool: Big Tobacco, Racial Marketing, and the Untold Story of the Menthol Cigarette*. University of Chicago Press, 2021.

Walton, Aaron. "Opinion: The Total Market Approach Isn't Just Offensive, It's Dangerous." ANA AIM, June 17, 2020. https://www.anaaimm.net/news /opinion-the-total-market-approach-isnt-just-offensive-its-dangerous.

WARC. "McDonald's Eyes Ethnic Consumers." WARC.com, December 4, 2013. https://www.warc.com/newsandopinion/news/mcdonalds-eyes-ethnic -consumers/en-gb/32289.

WARC. "Wells Fargo Boosted by Multicultural Strength." WARC.com, November 15, 2018. https://www.warc.com/newsandopinion/news/wells-fargo-boosted -by-multicultural-strength/41329.

Ward, Douglas. "Capitalism, Early Market Research, and the Creation of the American Consumer." *Journal of Historical Research in Marketing* 1, no. 2 (2009): 200–223. https://www.doi.org/10.1108/17557500910974587.

Wayland-Smith, Ellen. *The Angel in the Marketplace: Adwoman Jean Wade Rindlaub and the Selling of America*. University of Chicago Press, 2020.

Weems, Robert E., Jr. *Desegregating the Dollar: African American Consumerism in the Twentieth Century*. New York University Press, 1998.

Wentz, Laurel. "Walmart's Tony Rogers: 100% of Growth Is Multicultural." AdAge, October 31, 2012. https://adage.com/article/hispanic-marketing/walmart-s -tony-rogers-100-growth-multicultural/238051.

White, William. "A Different Kind of Ad Campaign for a Different Kind of Membership." Walmart, September 10, 2020. https://corporate.walmart.com /news/2020/09/10/a-different-kind-of-ad-campaign-for-a-different-kind -of-membership.

Williams, Raymond. "Advertising: The Magic System." In *Media Studies: A Reader*, edited by Sue Thornham, Caroline Bassett, and Paul Marris. 3rd ed. Edinburgh University Press, 2009.

Wilson, Bobby M. "Race in Commodity Exchange and Consumption: Separate but Equal." *Annals of the Association of American Geographers* 95, no. 3 (2005): 587–606. https://www.doi.org/10.1111/j.1467-8306.2005.00476.x.

Wynter, Sylvia. "Unsettling the Coloniality of Being/Power/Truth/Freedom: Towards the Human, After Man, Its Overrepresentation—an Argument." *CR: The New Centennial Review* 3, no. 3 (2003): 257–337. https://www.doi.org /10.1353/ncr.2004.0015.

York, Emily Bryson. "Ethnic Insights Form Foundations of McDonald's Marketing." AdAge, November 6, 2009. https://adage.com/article/special-report-ana -2009/mcdonald-s-marketing-foundation-formed-ethnic-insights/140373.

Zalis, Shelley. "The Inclusion Imperative: Why Media Matters." *Forbes*, January 14, 2020. https://www.forbes.com/sites/shelleyzalis/2020/01/14/the-inclusion -imperative-why-media-matters/#7f307e3c2943.

Zuberi, Tukufu. *Thicker Than Blood: How Racial Statistics Lie*. University of Minnesota Press, 2001.

Zuboff, Shoshana. *The Age of Surveillance Capitalism: The Fight for a Human Future at the New Frontier of Power*. Profile Books, 2018.

Zunz, Olivier. *Why the American Century?* University of Chicago Press, 1998.

INDEX

Page numbers in italics refer to figures.

corporate racial expertise, 61–62; as "tastemakers," 57, 98; Toyota advertising to, 93, 95. *See also* verification

Hispanic creative and media agencies, 22–24, 36. *See also* multicultural marketing

Hispanic Marketing Council, 42, 43, 61, 109

Hispanic Market Overview, 109–11, *110*

Hispanic population: "acculturated" and "unacculturated," 65, 80–81; "bicultural," 65; compared with other official US racial populations, 25, 36; contradictory views of, 132; "Hispanic" Census category, 25, 61, 101, 151n27; as largest non-white US population, 24–25; as marketable data commodity, 79; shifting definitions of, 83

"Hit the Streets Thursday" (Wells Fargo), 104

Hoffman, Ann, 90

Holte, Clarence L., 58–59

Homo economicus model, 37

homogeneity, assumption of, 63–64

hooks, bell, 15

housing segregation, 34

humanity, racialized understandings of, 13, 28–29, 37–38, 48, 114

"identity entrepreneurship," 54, 147n10

identity politics, white American, 45–46, 99–100

immigration: El Paso as target of government initiatives, 132; policies, 18, 35, 100; from Southern and Eastern Europe, 31–32, *32*; undocumented workers exploited by banks, 104

inclusion, 13, 14; downsides to, 77, 89–90, 105; as personalization, 76; "predatory," 105. *See also* diversity

Indigenous American consumers, 18

InfoScout (market research software), 46

internet, 20, 24, 85, 149n29; social media influencers, 46. *See also* digital advertising; surveillance; verification

intersectionality: "femvertising," 131; indi-

vidualization of, 122–23; as marketing strategy, 21, 118–28; misappropriated in academic settings, 119–20; as term, 118–19. *See also* diversity

Intertrend (ad agency), 93, *94*

Ioanide, Paula, 21, 118

Jackson, John L., 82

Jacobson, Matthew Frye, 31

Jet magazine, 36, 60

Jewish Americans, 31–32, *32*

Johnson, John H., 36, 60

Johnson & Johnson, 33–34

Juárez (Mexico), 128, 132

J. Walter Thompson (JWT) advertising agency, 15, 55

Kantar (market research firm), 13, *14*, 130

knowledge production. *See* racial knowledge production

labor, division of, 26–27

"Latin Look," 22

Laukes, Edward, 93, 96, 97

lead agency, 38, 97, 106

"Leading with Ethnic Insights" (McDonald's), 7

#LikeAGirl campaign (Dove), 131

Linnaeus, Carl, 11

location data, 89

Lopez, Alex, 129

Lopez Negrete Communications (advertising agency), 128–29, *129*

Lynd, Helen, 32–33, 46

Lynd, Robert, 32–33, 46

"mainstream": and "acculturation," 80; "new," 98–105, 117; "transcultural," 93–96, *95*, *97*, 121; validated by "other," 37; "white ignorance," 44. *See also* national identity, American

"Man," Western bourgeois notions of, 37–38

Marchand, Roland, 33

"market democracy," 30–31

www.ingramcontent.com/pod-product-compliance
Lightning Source LLC
Chambersburg PA
CBHW030841270326
41928CB00007B/1164